Praise for
Elizabeth Gregory's *Ready*

"A positive portrayal of waiting, which Gregory says reflects a historic shift: One of every 12 babies born to first-time mothers in 2006 was born to a woman 35 or older. In 1970, the figure was one in 100."

—*The Houston Chronicle*

"According to Gregory, who interviewed over 100 women for her book and incorporated related research, older mothers have higher marriage rates (85 percent), and those who do remain single enjoy more stable support systems. With more established careers, they tend to make more money, enjoy more financial security and exhibit greater self-confidence. Their advanced careers often mean they've developed managerial skills that transfer well to the complexities of running a household. What's more, older mothers tend to live longer than younger ones. Best of all, mature mothers are generally emotionally ready to become parents."

—Salon.com

"In her conversational and crisp tone, Gregory provides a compelling look beyond the U.S. statistics, which show that in 2005, one in seven babies was born to a woman 35 or older."

—*Austin American Statesman*

"As a 30-year-old, I have worries similar to those of other women. Am I ever going to be a mother? Will I be too old for parenthood by the time I am established enough in my career to comfortably take time off? Should I jump in the fast lane and try to get pregnant as soon as possible, so that the chance doesn't pass me by? . . . Anyone who relates to these worries will want to read *Ready*. Author Elizabeth Gregory shares intriguing demographic information, illustrating the fact that later motherhood has become more and more common over the course of the past thirty years . . . This book is chock full of powerful profiles of real women who articulate why they have made particular choices."

—*Feminist Review*

"Helpfully, Gregory debunks a lot of the hysterical statistics surrounding infertility and dispenses the wealth of pregnancy and adoption offerings with equanimity and good cheer."

—*Publishers Weekly*

"A book that focuses on the positive effects of women's decisions about their working and family lives deserves a rousing welcome . . . lively, accessible and lucid."
—Mommytrackd.com

"Necessary and wonderful! Elizabeth Gregory normalizes late motherhood for the mobs of us becoming moms when we are finally 'ready.'"
—Deborah Siegel, *Girl w/ Pen*

"In this beautifully written and well researched book, Elizabeth Gregory explores contemporary transformations in what it means to be a mother, chronicling the exponential growth in the number of women over 35 seeking to conceive or adopt children. Without ignoring the risks, Gregory reviews the advantages to mothers of living on their own terms and the benefits to children of being reared by more experienced, settled and committed individuals, as well as the various options open to women who postpone child-rearing."
—Sarah Blaffer Hrdy, author of
*Mother Nature: Maternal Instincts and
How They Shape the Human Species*

"With clarity, compassion, and common sense, Elizabeth Gregory takes us on a captivating tour of the changing landscape of 21st-century motherhood. She offers a forceful and compelling challenge to those who view contemporary motherhood in ferociously negative terms, as an unholy blend of smother love, over-parenting, and unremitting anxiety and guilt. An insightful and extraordinarily informative look at how today's highly accomplished women balance the conflicting demands of prolonged professional training, high-pressure careers, and the yearning to raise children."
—Steven Mintz, author of
Huck's Raft: A History of American Childhood

"Elizabeth Gregory sheds light on an aspect of the contemporary family experience that has not been examined in great detail until now: the new later motherhood phenomenon. Many of the families Elizabeth Gregory examines are formed the old-fashioned way, but a growing number are the result of adoption and reproductive technologies. Finally, we have a wonderful book that provides us with a thoughtful and thorough examination of motherhood and family life in the 21st century."
—Adam Pertman, author of *Adoption Nation*

Ready

Why Women Are Embracing
the New Later Motherhood

ELIZABETH GREGORY

BASIC BOOKS
A Member of the Perseus Books Group
New York

The Library of Congress has cataloged the hardcover edition as follows:
Gregory, Elizabeth.
    Ready : why women are embracing the new later motherhood / Elizabeth Gregory.
        p.   cm.
    Includes bibliographical references and index.
    ISBN-13: 978-0-465-02785-9 (hardcover : alk. paper)
    ISBN-10: 0-465-02785-7 (hardcover : alk. paper)
    1. Middle-aged mothers.   2. Motherhood.   3. Working mothers.   I. Title.
    HQ759.43.G74 2007
    306.874'30844—dc22

                                                                    2007021050

ISBN 978-0-465-03158-0 (paperback)
ISBN 978-0-465-03304-1 (e-book)

10 9 8 7 6 5 4 3 2 1

To our ducklings,
who make their parents such lucky ducks

CONTENTS

PREFACE TO THE PAPERBACK EDITION

Welcome to the 2012 edition of *Ready*, a groundbreaking, in-depth look into the personal and social dynamics of the trend among U.S. women and their partners to start their families at or after 35, by birth or adoption. I call it "the new later motherhood" because later motherhood itself isn't new; women have been having kids in their late 30s and 40s for ages, but those kids used to be the younger siblings in big families. The difference now is that women are *starting* later, after finishing their educations and establishing at work first. It's an enormous change with big cultural and economic ripple effects, a topic of endless media fascination and of fierce political debate.

Ready gives the big picture behind the contemporary birth-timing shift. This preface updates you on how the scene has morphed since *Ready* first appeared in 2007.

Quick Context

The new later motherhood trend has grown steadily since the mid-1970s: Now one in twelve women starts her family later versus one in 100 in 1970. This trend shares basic dynamics with the global trend among women to start their families later than their mothers did. The shift was enabled by the introduction of hormonal birth control in a context of women's education, improved public health, and diminished need for big families to work farms—a set of changes that together constitute an evolutionary leap in the physical and social experience of human beings.

Such a big change has required much reweaving of the social fabric, designed for millennia around the expectation that women would spend most of their lives bearing and rearing children. Big change calls forth dispute, sometimes bitter. You can see evidence of that in the many issues of national debate that coalesce around fertility and, by implication, the size, skills, immigration status, and gender and racial makeup of the U.S. workforce of the future. Recent battles over abortion, birth control access, and gay families take on a new cast when viewed from an economic, gendered-work perspective rather than as discrete cultural or moral debates.

Within the relatively family-*un*friendly U.S. work system, women have discovered that delay of kids until age 35 or later provides a shadow benefits system, enabling them (aka, us!) to climb work ladders and to command salaries they would not otherwise have won, since having kids earlier results in big salary cuts that last across a woman's career.[1] Once established at work, with experience their employers value as well as a track record that creates employer trust, new later mothers can also command flexibility around family schedules that others cannot.

Apart from economics, delay of motherhood provides many women with time to establish themselves as individuals so that they then feel more prepared to guide the young lives of their children when they do have them.

Starting families later also intersects with our expanded longevity—thirty years have been added to the average U.S. life span in the past century. This offers people today opportunities to sequence their life events in new ways. In addition, finding the right partner for the long term and seeing a bit of the world before settling down are important factors for many.

Though delay begins with individual choices around birth timing, all those choices taken together are adding up to radical transformations of family life, the business world, and the polity. For the first time in history, women are accruing both education and financial power comparable with that of men. Increasingly, women are getting seats at the policy tables. Think Hillary Clinton, Elena Kagan, and Sonia Sotomayor in law and government, and in business Sheryl Sandberg, COO of Facebook; Ursula Burns, chair and CEO at Xerox; and Michelle Obama, hospital administrator; as well as hordes of lower-level, less famous folk. Many of these women acted "like men" within the business world, by either having no kids (and so never having to leave work early to tend a sick one) or delaying kids to the point where they could both afford a reliable babysitter and trade in flexibility chits they'd won through many long hours in the office in years past.

Questions abound about what comes next. Will women's presence at the table change policy? What percentage of women constitutes the critical mass that allows questioning of the business status quo to be heard and acted on? We've already redefined the *discourse* and in some cases the reality of work by introducing the concepts of flexibility and family friendliness. Will increasing numbers of women in policy roles make it substantially easier for women to combine kids and well-paid work without extensive delay, by enforcing fair pay laws and widening access to good, affordable childcare, as well as to parental leave, paid sick days, and fertility coverage? Or will even more women delay or eschew kids in exchange for access to better jobs, as has happened in low-birth-rate countries like Japan and Italy? Will the trend be reversed or altered if increasing numbers of women are denied access to birth control and abortion by legislatures, as per the 2012 rush of bills at the state and federal levels (in Virginia, Texas, Wisconsin, and Arizona, for example, as well as efforts like the [failed] Blunt Amendment in Congress)? Or will we continue to muddle along with the status quo? What will be the long-term effects on the workforce of any of those scenarios? Will unpredictable events transform the issues in unexpected ways? To some degree, that's already happened.

The Recessionary Later Mom Surge

Who knew back in December 2007, when *Ready* first came out, that an economic downturn was commencing? Or that that mire would intensify the trend to starting families later that this book tracks? The birth rate fell 7 percent overall between 2007 and 2010, but the bulk of that decline occurred among younger women—rates declined 17 percent among teens and 16 percent among women ages 20–24.[2] Recessions are contraceptive, but in selective ways. Most of the teens were putting off a first birth, as were a smaller proportion of the 20-somethings (some put a second child on hold). Some of those younger women will remain childless, but most of those refraining from kids now will have kids later—some a little later, some closer to 30, and others substantially later than that.

You can't *see* that effect quite yet because delay necessarily involves a time lag (just as it did when the trend began in the mid-1970s, fifteen years after the introduction of birth control in 1960). Although some may have delayed for only a year or two, those teens and 20-somethings who under recessionary pressure decided to invest their time in college and a career rather than family right now, as they otherwise might have done, have joined a process that puts many of them on track for longer delays.[3] The scene is set for a flood of older moms down the line. They may not be changing the number of kids they'll have overall by much, but they are changing the circumstances into which those kids will arrive.

Which is not to say there aren't a lot of new later mothers with babies in strollers right now. In fact, proportionately speaking, there are more such moms than there used to be,[4] and not only because the proportion of younger moms declined. At the same time that birth rates among other age groups declined to various degrees between 2007 and 2010,[5] rates among women ages 40–44 *rose* 8 percent (see Figure P.1). Women in that fertility-fragile age range are less likely to risk delaying further, *and* they tend to have more money than younger women, so as a group they didn't feel the same pressure to refrain.

Documenting the Benefits

That 8 percent rise is substantial, but it's not a recession effect. The 40–44-year-olds having kids in 2008, 2009, and 2010 had already de-

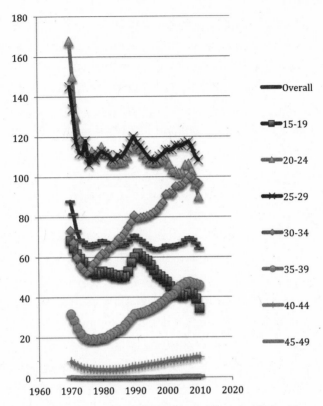

FIGURE P.1   U.S. Fertility Rates by Age of Mother, 1970–2010. Rates are live births per 1,000 women in specified age group. CDC Natality Statistics, 1970–2010.

layed motherhood and were part of the trend toward later families that started back in the 1970s, which *Ready* documents.[6] Economics has been a big part of that trend all along, but of a less immediate and concerted kind than that driving the recent recessionary declines.

Of late, we've had a surge in scholarship documenting the positive effects of delay. One recent study by Amalia Miller on compensation (based on a pool of women who first gave birth between ages 20 and 34) indicates that women who delay and get a college degree (or more) go on to gain 5 percent in wages per year of delay, and 12 percent or more in earnings per year of delay. (The difference between wages and earnings comes from expanded hours on the job—delayers can work full time before kids and maintain that schedule once kids arrive because they can afford good childcare.) Per this study, if you are 18 and childless, go to college, graduate at 22, go to work, then have a child at 25, you will make about 36 percent more per year from there on than you would have made if you had had that child upon graduation. If you delay till age 30, the average age when female college grads have their first child (for male college grads, it's 32), you will make roughly 96 percent more across your career than your younger-mom, college-grad self. And so on, increasing with each year of delay.[7]

Miller's research resonates with my salary analyses in Chapter 3, indicating that women who delay first birth beyond age 35 also make substantial long-term salary gains, with potentially even higher rates of annual increase. But even more telling is the evidence of the growing numbers of new later mothers. Though economists can now demonstrate that delay links to higher earnings and other benefits, for decades prior steadily increasing numbers of working women have been figuring that out without benefit of experts, through deduction, happenstance, and attention to one another's examples, as they've negotiated the still-shifting world of work in our post–birth control world. They've been making common sense, literally.

Along with the economic benefits, researchers are now documenting other gains from delaying motherhood as well. Further research by Miller finds that each year of motherhood delay leads to improved test scores for first-born children (the group studied), with indications of similar results for later-order children as well, due to the rise in the mother's own human capital.[8] This finding, she notes, will be of interest both to individual women as they plan their families and to policy makers insofar as various policies encourage first births at specific ages. The age at which women give birth today affects the human capital of the workforce of tomorrow—both that of the children and of the mothers themselves.

From a less bottom-line perspective, work by Rachel Margolis and Mikko Myrskylä based on long-term British and German panel data indicates a strong correlation between postponed motherhood and increased long-term happiness and life satisfaction. Where all new mothers have a spike in happiness around the birth of a child, it is particularly strong for moms who start their families after 35 and is not followed by the steep and sustained decline in happiness and satisfaction that occurs among younger mothers. The happiness effect breaks down by age similarly for fathers. This research, the authors note, gives "new insights into [the motives behind] fertility postponement."[9]

An expanding body of scholarly work explores the dynamics of the gendered division of work (family work being quite labor-intensive) and the many ways in which policy affects the interaction of women's paid work and fertility. Peter McDonald finds direct connection between lack of family-friendly work policies (around wages, childcare, flextime, and so on) and steep declines in fertility rates around the globe, and vice versa. McDonald advocates that government and other institutions recognize the social and personal significance of family life and prioritize its support because even if individuals would prefer to have more children, when family-unfriendly work policy brings a society to a stage of sustained low fertility, the culture changes to the point that reversal of low fertility becomes problematic.[10] (The rise in "brat bans" in various venues is one example of such change.)

Looking at fertility-affecting policy from another direction, Torben Iversen and Frances Rosenbluth document that increased female labor force participation sets the stage for growth in women's representation in government.[11] Once there, women can affect policy in ways that may make both home work and paid work more gender-neutral. For instance, analyzing workforce and fertility/child-rearing dynamics in Sweden and Germany, Rosenbluth et al. extrapolate that the effective way to ensure employment equity is to divide childcare equally between male and female workers so that employers cannot reasonably assume that men will work more consistently over their careers than will women, and so employers will not discriminate against women as a group in anticipation of inconsistency.[12] Research by the Families and Work Institute indicates that such equity is already the desire of most young workers, male and female, who both want to combine active family lives with satisfying work.[13] It turns out that "gender" has historically been as much a work-stratification system as anything else. Changing the dynamics around the work of production of children (aka, workers, citizens, and consumers) leads to changes in the function of gender in society.

A century ago, Sigmund Freud famously wondered what women want. At least one answer to that question, true for women around the globe, turns out to be *time*—in which to grow into and establish themselves, over varying numbers of years, before they start their families. The narratives of *Ready*'s 113 thoughtful and articulate later moms affirm these scholarly insights. Their voices personalize the statistics, explain the dynamics the experts are still working to document and understand, and actively counter what is still a steady stream of media warnings against delay.

Infertility

But wait, you say. Don't we need warnings? Isn't infertility a real problem for many women? Won't the recessionary birth rate decline only increase the numbers experiencing infertility in the coming years? And don't we owe it to women to give them the facts so that they can make informed choices that give them their best chance for happiness, including the chance to have the children that most of them do hope and expect to bear and raise?

I say, "Totally!" Both women and men need the facts about the functioning of fertility and the risks of infertility that both sexes face. *Ready* provides those.

But, strangely, the many media stories warning us about infertility still rarely give a full picture on these issues. Instead, perhaps in order to get our attention, they exaggerate or misrepresent the risks in ways that can undercut that aim. The audience loses faith when we hear yet another instance of fertility scaremongering, set to the sound of a ticking clock, that directly counters our experience not just with celebrities in tabloids but with people we see every day. Though perhaps well intentioned, their skewed versions of infertility facts often add up to active disinformation, even on otherwise reliable "news" sites. To give a sense of how the skew works, here are a few examples I've encountered recently.

Fertility Scaremongering

A 2012 article on egg freezing in a major news magazine asserted that 40 percent of women with college degrees over age 40 had no children. However, data from the Census Bureau's 2010 Current Population Survey Fertility Supplement indicate that 76 percent of college-educated women ages 35–44 have children, and quite a few of the remainder will yet have them.[14] This brings the number childless closer to the 18 percent rate reported for all women 40–44 in 2008,[15] with some of those childless by choice or default (due to lack of desired partner or other option-limiting circumstance), others having encountered infertility, and still others in the 40–44 set expecting to have children in the future. These numbers report on women who have given birth, so they do not include adoptive parents, most of whom would not consider themselves "childless." Might inflated numbers like 40 percent push some suddenly anxious readers toward egg freezing, a potentially helpful but also largely untested and quite expensive procedure?

A 2011 major news outlet story on women's underestimation of the pace of fertility decline based on a poll conducted by a fertility drug company offered as its key facts about the rate of infertility that 30 percent of women at age 30 and 10 percent of women at 40 can get pregnant in one month. That was it for fertility statistics. The takeaway for my suddenly stressed 34-year-old colleague was that the possibility of pregnancy at her age was similarly low. Though the stats in the story may be true, they are also irrelevant because infertility is defined not by who can or can't get pregnant in one month but who can or cannot do so in one year, and the number of women at 30 who *can* get pregnant in one year is more than 90 percent. Roughly 65 percent of women can do so at 40. The reporter cited the one-month stat because that was what the poll asked about—*but why was that the question in the first place?* Is it a coincidence that the drug company benefits when anxious 30-something women choose not to wait a few months longer? (See Chapter 6 for more discussion.) Or is the aim to make women in their early 30s anxious so they will get busy in the next few years rather than waiting into their 40s to start trying? Or a mixture of both?

A major news network reporting on a 2010 study warned: "For Women Who Want Kids, 'the Sooner the Better': 90 Percent of Eggs Gone by Age 30." Though the story (and the report) implied that low egg reserve means a low fertility rate, a closer look at the data makes clear that *there is no link.* Clicking through to the full report shows that *all women* have a hugely diminished reserve when compared to the number of eggs in *a female fetus at 20 weeks!* (the point of reference). Twenty-five-year-olds, generally understood to be at the height of their fertility, have only 22 percent; 20-year-olds a mere 37 percent; 15-year-olds just 52 percent, 10-year-olds all of 70 percent; and 5-year-olds about 87 percent. The study finds it's 12 percent at age 30, not 10 percent, as suggested in the headline. Because few women are infertile at 30, *apparently 12 percent is all you need.* But there's no anxiety-provoking story in that. The study also reported a 3-percent-at-age-40 figure, which does rhyme with diminished fertility at that age, but that was not the "news" featured here.

A 2010 newswire story run by many media outlets told us: "Older Moms Risk Autism in Children." While the study, based on 4.9 million California births in the 1990s, documented that the risk of autism increases with maternal age by 51 percent and that paternal age is also a factor, few of the reports asked the key question "*51 percent of what?*" and certainly not in their headline. It turns out that less than one-quarter of one percent of the 25- to 29-year-olds in the study had an autistic child, and that even though the odds increased by 51 percent over that for women 40 and older, that meant that *less than one-half of one percent of older women had autistic kids.*

Individually, these stories might be harmless, but as a group they indicate a pattern of active misrepresentation. This kind of fertility discourse becomes not objective information but rather a manipulative form of *pro-natalism* (meaning it aims to promote more births). It largely ignores the concerns that push women to delay and focuses on alarming them into having kids now, whether or not they want them or feel ready. Such talk confuses the issues rather than clarifying them.

Stories about infertility that don't exaggerate are the exception, not the norm, because there are too many players with a stake in the game here, at both small- and big-picture levels. We can presume that all involved share a real wish to save women (and their mates) from potential sorrow. But along with that wish, media headline writers also know that anxiety sells; fertility providers need patients; and businesses and the government want to ensure that there is enough of a next generation—of citizens, workers, and customers—to ease the negative social and economic effects they fear will be incurred when a smaller younger generation has to support a large aging population within one nation, or when the developed world's population shrinks relative to that of the less developed. These factors influence the way infertility stories are told. There are also racial prejudices in play (fear of the demographic changes that the 2010 census indicates will give us a minority majority in the United States by 2050). Recent legislative efforts to deny women birth control, a radical form of pro-natalism, also suggest that some sector of the U.S. political machine fears increased participation by women in policy making (more on this below). That adds up to a lot of pressure coming down on the shoulders and wombs of American women in the 15–44 fertility zone!

The dynamics in play around population are complex and require much more than a knee-jerk "let's have more babies" response. Global warming and the limited capacities of the planet to sustain itself and us with the *current* population, let alone *more* people, require us to radically rethink our economic models. Simply promoting more growth will not get us to a good place even in the short term.

But back to the smaller picture for a moment. Scaring women into starting their families sooner sometimes works: One woman I spoke with cited the 90 percent egg-loss story as the direct cause of her getting pregnant at 31, right after it ran, though she and her new husband had not felt quite prepared to start their family at that point. And indeed, her job was not flexible, so once the baby arrived, she moved from a full-time to a freelance position (helpful in the short term but, studies indicate, a problem in terms of her lifetime wage). Given the story, she was amazed at how quickly they got pregnant!

For the most part, however, falling birth rates and rising delay trends suggest that this kind of distortive pressure tactic is not very persuasive. Because the research indicates long-term negative effects for the skills and earnings levels of both moms and their kids if women have children before they feel ready, and because the trends show that these warnings have not been very effective anyway and may even have opposite effects, there are good bases for requiring media to vet their discussion of fertility facts more rigorously.

It's important to inform the public that age-based infertility is real and that treatment can be a saddening, difficult, and expensive process, with no guarantees that it will resolve happily, and that basically none of the celebrities you read about who have children over age 44 are employing their own eggs. It's also important to provide real data on the trajectory of age-based fertility decline and the success rates of treatments so that women can consider the data seriously and weigh them in light of their concerns regarding career and partner issues. Not all women want kids at any cost, and some actually prefer nieces and nephews.

Though most women would like to have children, many do not feel ready to leave jobs with long full-immersion initial investment periods, or have yet to meet Mr. (or Ms.) Right-and-Ready in their early 30s.

The most efficient way to help women combine happy family lives with satisfying work would seem to be both by providing them with full, undistorted information about fertility and by addressing the causes of delay—through restructuring work dynamics to allow women and men to combine family and work without penalty. Though the second of these may seem daunting, concerted activism by women and their advocates could make change fast. Parents and would-be parents could fruitfully toss their metaphorical TVs out the window and refuse to take it anymore. Many of our infertility issues could be best addressed not at the medical center, but through an expanded system of good, affordable childcare and shared parental leaves.

Dealing with Age-Based Infertility

Apart from the exaggerations, infertility (difficulty getting pregnant but with reasonable hope that that difficulty might be overcome given adequate time or technology or both, as opposed to complete sterility, associated with loss or malformation of reproductive organs or materials) can be a real issue for women seeking to become pregnant, sometimes before 40 and particularly after 40. There are no firm statistics on how many women encounter infertility because it is not a freestanding ailment; it's a condition you can "have" only if you try and fail to get pregnant. One CDC survey found that one in eight women between ages 15 and 44 had encountered some difficulty getting pregnant, though more than half of those women already had at least one child.[16] Chapter 6 provides details on fertility decline and deals with these issues in depth. Since 2007, egg-freezing technology has become increasingly available in clinics and may be of help to younger women with cash to spare, but it cannot assist most women at current rates. There are no guarantees that in your case it will work, even if you do cough up the $15,000 or so involved, though it might. And you may not need them.

The costs associated with all forms of fertility technology can be lessened by mandating that insurance cover the cost, as is currently the case to various extents in fifteen states. This is an ongoing political issue within states, where it adds minimally to everyone's cost of insurance but substantially lowers the cost of treatments overall via economies of scale. It is not currently addressed by the incoming national health plan, though that could be changed if constituent pressure were brought to bear. Coverage equalizes access to treatment so that it's not just the wealthy who can have babies later, but it does not guarantee success. A little less than one-third of the women interviewed in *Ready* either encountered fertility issues and resolved them, or did not resolve them and went on to adopt. While adoption is not an adequate substitute for bearing one's own child for all,[17] for many would-be mothers the fundamental point is to nurture and love a child.

Having Babies When You're over 50

Within the context of increased recessionary delay, *New York Magazine* featured an article in the October 3, 2011, issue titled "Is She Just Too Old for This?: New Parents over 50—Child-Rearing's Final Frontier." The story, supported by a cover photo of a naked, older pregnant woman (à la Demi Moore's famous *Vanity Fair* photo from 1991), explored the dynamics of egg donation in light of rising numbers of births among postmenopausal women, with particular emphasis on the growing group of mothers in the 50–54 age band. In 2009, 569 women in that age band had babies, and 7,320 had kids between 45 and 49, the great majority of them via egg donation (in 1990, there were only 1,638 total births to women over age 45). The piece generated much comment and discussion; in fact, readers' comments were built into the narrative, which included a poll of the writer's friends on the "yuck factor" involved in seeing a 50-something lady with a baby. About midway through, the article changed gears, arguing against ageism and for the right of older women to bear kids if and when they feel ready.

But the debate was over much earlier. Even before readers opened the magazine, the cover—which featured the pregnant belly of a younger woman photoshopped onto the head and body of a 63-year-old fitness guru—already made clear that a 50-year-old would not have turned heads. There are just too many moms in or near that age range among the article's New York audience.

Race and Class

Among biological mothers who started their families at or after 35 in 2010, 63.14 percent were white, 9.12 percent black, 13.43 percent Hispanic, 13.08 percent Asian Pacific Islander, and 0.42 percent American Indian and Alaska Native (AIAN). Viewed comparatively, 9.05 percent of white first births were to later moms, 5.21 percent of black first births, 5.37 percent of Hispanic, 15.39 percent of Asian, and 3.27 percent AIAN.[18] (For demographics of the women interviewed in *Ready*, see "Appendix A: Who's in the Study.") Later motherhood is not exclusively a phenomenon of education, but education plays a big role. Women of all races who have at least a college degree have an average age at first birth of 30 (men, of 32). Thirty is five years above the overall average U.S. woman's age at first birth (25.2 in 2009 and rising[19]). The delay reflected in that higher average age connects directly to the time it takes to go to college and maybe grad school and then to establish at work.

In 2009, when 30 percent of all U.S. first babies were born to mothers with BAs or more, 65 percent of all first-time mothers 30 and over had at least a BA, and roughly 27 percent had an MA or more.[20] Mothers who start their families over 35 are not generally more educated than women in the 30–34 group, apart from an increase in the proportion with PhDs,[21] but they have put in more time at work before kids.

Race and class dynamics are inflected by both education and delay. In 2009 69 percent of whites, 52 percent of blacks, 68 percent of Asians, and 38 percent of Hispanic first-time mothers 40–44 had a BA or higher. The level for Hispanics is low compared to the others, but that rate is substantially higher than in 2000, when it was 32 percent.

That's an increase of 20 percent in moms 40–44 with BA or more (compared to a 12 percent rise among whites, a 17 percent rise among blacks and a 24 percent rise among Asians in the same period). Higher education plays a much smaller part in the delay stories among Hispanic women at this point in history due to language, class and immigration dynamics, and a somewhat smaller part in the delay stories of black women, and fewer women delay overall in both groups. But as *Ready*'s interviews and statistics document, it is also an important and increasing part.

As Kathryn Edin and Maria Kefalas showed in their study of poor, single moms (white, black and Hispanic), lack of good job prospects for women and their partners fuels the trend to many poor women's decisions to have children earlier, often without long-term partners.[22] But through the same process by which delay of motherhood allows women to climb work ladders, it may also help them board a class elevator. When women of all races are able to delay kids in order to go to college and complete their degrees, they improve their economic situations and their cultural capital.

Figures P.2 and P.3 on the next page offer a quick rundown of overall and first birth rates among all moms and later moms, by age and race.

The higher birth rates of Asian later mothers indicated in the figures are particularly intriguing. Though their total birth rate across all age groups is very close to that of whites (59.2 vs. 58.7), the Asian rate is more than half again as high as that of whites among 40–44-year olds (15.1/9.2), and nearing that among 35–39 year olds (62.8/44.1). Similarly, *first* birth rates among Asians are markedly higher than all others in all later age bands (and markedly lower in the younger age bands.)[23]

A recent article by Emily Greenman explores the income effects of Asian women's work/family patterns, finding that as a group, Asian women engineers and scientists (her data set) take less time off from work when their kids are born than women of other races in the same fields with equal education.[24]

	Women 15–44	Women 35–39	Women 40–44	Women 45–49
All Races	64.1	45.9	10.2	0.7
Non-Hispanic White	58.7	44.1	9.2	0.6
Non-Hispanic Black	66.6	36.4	9.2	0.7
AIAN	48.6	22.3	5.2	0.3
Asian/Pacific Islander	59.2	62.8	15.1	1.2
Hispanic	80.3	51.8	13.0	0.8

FIGURE P.2   Total & Later U.S. Birth Rates per 1,000 women in specified age groups by race/Hispanic origin, preliminary 2010. CDC NVSR 60, no. 2 (November 2011), Table 2: 22–23.

	Women 15–44	Women 35–39	Women 40–44	Women 45–49
All Races	25.9	10.5	2.3	0.2
Non-Hispanic White	25.0	11.2	2.3	0.2
Non-Hispanic Black	26.4	7.0	1.8	0.2
AIAN	17.5	3.1	0.7	*
Asian/Pacific Islander	26.9	18.5	4.2	0.4
Hispanic	28.0	7.7	1.8	0.1

FIGURE P.3   Total & Later U.S. First Birth Rates per 1,000 women in specified age groups by race/Hispanic origin, preliminary 2010. CDC NVSR 60, no. 2 (November 2011), Table 4: 25.

As a result of this greater time at work, they make more money over the long term than their female peers of other races, and there is less of a wage gap between Asian men and women than between white men and women. (Hispanic and black men and women also have smaller wage gaps because, due to difficult economic circumstances faced by these groups, women have not stepped out of the work stream as much as white women have.) The Asian model Greenman explores is relevant not just as a pattern true of one culture (or set of linked cultures) but also for the model or basis for analysis it provides of potential work dynamics in all cultures.

Greenman hypothesizes that Asian women also may be more likely to have grandparents living at home or nearby, to make it easier to return to work quickly, as well as a culture that doesn't expect women to stop working when they have kids. Such a model, I derive, suggests what women's work could look like in a culture that made good childcare easily accessible, without stigma.

The pattern of taking less time off from work also seems to lead to the delay pattern seen here, suggesting that greater work adhesion by all women would lead to more later births (at least in the current, unreformed work environment), and also making clear that higher birth rates are possible in this age range (there is currently no way to track what proportion of these later births involve fertility technology). The question of what birth rates are possible among women in their 40s, with or without egg donation, cannot be gauged based on current overall U.S. numbers because even with the new later motherhood trend, relatively few women delay their first child into their 40s.

Numbers Update

In Figures P.4 through P.7, updating Figures 6.1 and 6.2 and adding new data on first births, it's clear that later births and first births have much increased since 1971 among women of each age tracked, though numbers remain relatively low, especially among women above 43. The decline after 2007 among women ages 35–39 reflects the recession.

Whither Patriarchy? Alternative Pro-Natalisms

In the days before birth control, women were stuck having kids, and a lot of them, ensuring that they could be compensated unfairly for the work they did both inside and outside the home, without recourse. Those women who did work outside the home were hobbled by their lack of education (due to early childbearing) and by their need for flexible schedules to care for kids in the absence of a national care system. Women

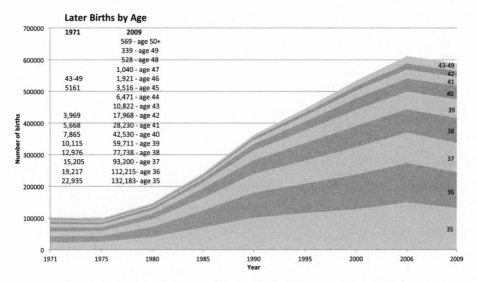

FIGURE P.4   Number of U.S. Women Giving Birth at 35 and Above, Cumulative by Age of Mother. CDC Natality Statistics, 1971 to 2009 (total number of births in 2009: 4,130,665; total later births: 588,981).

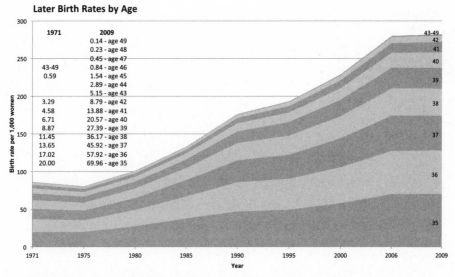

FIGURE P.5   Birth Rates for U.S. Women 35–49, Cumulative by Age of Mother. Birth rate per year per 1,000 women in each age band. CDC Natality Statistics, 1971 to 2009.

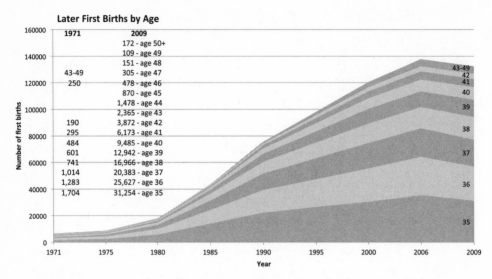

FIGURE P.6 Number of U.S. Women Giving First Birth at 35 and Above, Cumulative by Age of Mother. CDC Natality Statistics, 1971 to 2009 (total number of first births in 2009: 1,663,231; total later first births: 132,630).

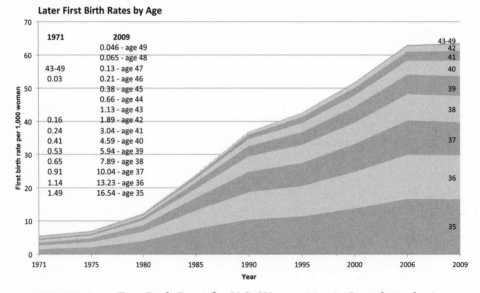

FIGURE P.7 First Birth Rates for U.S. Women 35–49, Cumulative by Age of Mother. First birth rate per year per 1,000 women in each age band. CDC Natality Statistics 1971 to 2009.

workers operated in a discriminatory, artificially constrained labor pool (all of the jobs open to them were linked to what they were doing at home for free—teacher, nurse, cook, cleaner, sex worker) and faced a lot of competition (all the other constrained women) within those few trades. So their wages were low. The fact that their jobs were done for free at home contributed to the general view that the work was not worth much.

But of course it was essential—not just to the survival of their families, but to the survival of industry and the nation. The fruit of their labor was people: citizens, workers, caregivers, and consumers. Child-rearing has historically been viewed as a personal choice, to be paid for by individual families, not least because it was not to business's advantage to acknowledge its dependence on women's childbearing and -rearing—to produce the bodies of the workers and then to teach them skills and a strong work ethic.

But women with access to birth control don't have to have *any* kids anymore, let alone several, which gives them new leverage. Though the ongoing media campaign for the pleasures of pregnancy and child-rearing continues, the deal may look less satisfactory and less necessary to increasing numbers of women in coming years. Discriminatory pay is a hidden tax on women and their families, averaging more than $10,000 annually. Add to that the additional costs that families bear of rearing and educating the next generation, and you've got a major disincentive. As we've seen, delay of childbearing supplies a work-around for many women, one that supplies individual benefits and leads to framework changes as women move up.

Already, female policy makers have intervened in the salary realm, aiding the passage of the Lilly Ledbetter Fair Pay Act in 2009 (not an advance in itself, but a corrective to a 2008 Supreme Court ruling that had set back women's access to compensation for discrimination). But those who feel they have a stake in maintaining the status quo of low pay for women and lack of support for families raising kids are not acceding to change without a fight. Though female legislators introduced the Paycheck Fairness Act to give teeth to the unenforceable Fair Pay

Act of 1963, it did not make it to a floor vote in December 2010. (Such legislation would not even have been considered if there hadn't been record numbers of women in Congress [at 17 percent].)

Although at first blush battles over pay equity may not look like part of the delayed fertility discussion, they very much are. Just as delay gives individual women the clout to demand flexible schedules for themselves, when large numbers of women delay motherhood for education and to establish in careers, the group as a whole commands new clout around family- and women-friendly policy changes. This is the case both by virtue of their human capital and experience, which their employers value and seek to retain, and because employers have at least some interest in making it manageable for them to have the kids who will be the workers and consumers of the next generation.

Conversely, battles over such fertility issues as birth control and abortion access have economic roots. Beyond debates over "morality," efforts to restrict family-planning access keep women in their familiar "place"— to which they were committed in days past by early and uncontrolled fertility and where they were policed by traditions of shame, violence, and penury. Such restrictions aim to limit women's access to power, specifically access to the power to change the operative economic model to one that acknowledges the efforts of mothers, provides them with a socially supported infrastructure to take over some of the basic time and financial burdens of childrearing, and pays them equitably. Instead, restrictions on birth control would keep the reins in the hands of the patriarchs (aka, the old-school fathers), who find it problematic that, along with women's relatively new access to the vote, the ability to control births allows women for the first time ever to participate in the shaping of national priorities as full, directly represented citizens.

But, you may note, it's been more than fifty years since hormonal birth control was introduced. Why has this change not already occurred? Though there has been progress, it has been slowed by the absence of a national childcare infrastructure. Circularly, because the support infrastructure hasn't changed, women haven't been able to move in sufficient numbers into positions where they could change it. Though many new-school fathers support women's progress, as a group our male leaders and representatives have failed to facilitate change on behalf of their female constituents, leaving the old and actively family-*un*friendly business model largely in place. Like John Adams, whose wife Abigail famously enjoined him to "remember the ladies" as he developed the constitution, most somehow forgot.

Gradually, however, women, many of them delayed childbearers or non-mothers, have been making inroads into legislatures, where they can vote on their own behalf and negotiate shared power deals with their male counterparts. The presence of many women in the workplace has likewise led to the introduction of some family-friendly policies, both at the national level (as with the Family and Medical Leave Act, which ensures that one may return to one's job after such a leave but does not supply pay) and within specific industries (some of which grant such benefits as extended parental leaves without wage penalty and sick-child care).

Bit by bit, the critical mass of women in policy-making roles necessary to change is coalescing. Paradoxically, in the current system a family-friendly world becomes possible on a major scale only when significant numbers of women delay kids, by a little or a lot, or don't have them at all.

As I write this, during the 2012 election cycle, the virulent politicization of contraception and abortion fills the newsfeeds. Though it might seem to signal a decline in women's political power, the long-term shifts in women's education, work, and fertility trends over the past few decades have already created a huge cohort of educated women with high expectations, who make a return to the old ways unlikely. In fact, the push-back against the gains that contraception has won for women seems likely to generate its own push-back and could speed up feminist change.

Business forces seem conflicted about their relation to women workers—with some embracing change that allows them to access the female half of the skilled labor pool (especially math-centric businesses with good wages and problems attracting workers, such as engineering and accounting), and others seeking to limit the costs that fair pay and family benefits involve. Can business resolve that conflict and develop a national system of good childcare, subsidized by a collaborative of taxpayers and employers? That would mean acknowledging that business has investments in both kinds of "women's work"—the labor done outside the home for pay, and the bearing and rearing of the citizenry, historically done at home for free. (Such a system would also be a good-jobs engine.) While there are some global positives to a falling fertility rate, a rate much below replacement also brings social and economic stresses. Though in the short term, childless working women can fill the jobs that previously would have been taken by their male children, *some* judicious investment in future generations seems crucial. The workforce of the future depends on convincing women to have children in sufficient numbers.

However "sufficient" may be defined in the fast-evolving global scene, the convincing may be done via *three basic forms of pro-natalist rhetoric and policy* (using the term "pro-natalist" objectively, without negative or positive valence): *persuasive, coercive, and optative*. The pro-baby media campaigns about the pleasures of family and the unhappiness of childless women (neither of them untrue per se, and neither true for all) represent a *persuasive* form of pro-natalism, which may fit with women's own desires or lead them to have kids they do not feel quite ready for, financially or personally.

Efforts to deny women access to contraception and abortion embody a *coercive* pro-natalism, which raises the rates of unplanned and often unwanted births and creates an underclass of cheap, unskilled workers, in the persons not only of many of those mothers and their babies but in the other members of their families, whose impoverishment and lack of access to resources are increased with each unplanned birth.

The third type, *optative* pro-natalism, creates the framework in which women and their partners are moved by the availability of good child-rearing options to decide for themselves that they want children and feel that they don't risk too much of their and their children's future security by having them. This would involve building a family-friendly infrastructure—including good, affordable childcare (can't say it too often!)—that removes financial and career barriers from the decision to have children for women or couples who would otherwise want them, while at the same time increasing the numbers of educated citizens.

Which form of pro-natalism serves us best? Though not all women want kids, many do. The world as a whole has a big stake in helping those women to bear and rear happy and well-educated children, the citizens and the workforce of tomorrow. There's much to work out in shaping the economies of the future. *Ready* looks forward to a world informed by women's policy insight, in which mothers of all ages and their children have access to a strong network of family support services. Until then, for many women in the United States and around the globe, the means of accessing such a network for themselves and their families and of shaping it for the group lie in establishing themselves first and starting their families later.

Introduction

Ready?

I never even thought about kids until my early thirties. But at that point, fresh out of grad school and starting the career I'd worked hard for, I could begin envisioning the future. Though there remained a few things I wanted to accomplish before taking the plunge, the attractions of children—of packing lunchboxes, telling jokes at the dinner table, and singing with my own kids the songs my mama sang to me—were exerting new influence.

A few years later, on a hospital visit to a good friend who had just delivered her second child, my husband and I admired the rather surprised-looking baby, listened to the heroic labor story, congratulated everyone involved, and got up to go. As we hugged good-bye, my friend looked at me and said, "Your turn!"

We knew she was right. Recently married and newly tenured, Patrick and I definitely felt ready to expand our family. A year later, our first daughter was born on a steamy August day in Houston. I was 39.

Fast forward to kindergarten: When we walked into the classroom with our daughter on her first day, she took off to connect with all the other 5-year-olds, and we met a collection of moms and dads. Unlike the kids, the parents varied in age—but I was particularly alert to the moms: some were 20-somethings, but most had passed 30 and six of us were over 40. At 44, I was not the oldest. As a group, our mix was pretty standard for urban schools these days, though in some urban neighborhoods you have to look hard to find a new mom under 30. As we worked on school projects together in the next few months, I learned what these women did for their livings; they were doctors, administrators, software managers, scientists, architects, bankers, and dentists. Most of them worked full time, but several had "retired" from long careers—for the time being, anyway.

What a different scene from the one my mother entered when she first took me to kindergarten. Though she started her family at 30, most of the other moms were in their twenties. And while most of them had worked and some kept on working, their career paths tended to be much less professionally oriented, much less well paid, and often much shorter than moms' careers today.

If you're a woman thinking about children these days—either because you have them already or because you're thinking about whether or when to have them—the link between job opportunities and age means something to you. Usually when you hear it mentioned in the media, it's presented as a problem—even a contradiction. You may remember how a few years back Sylvia Ann Hewlett's *Creating a Life* made a lot of us suddenly nervous about our fertility when she told us very firmly that, if women delayed their childbearing to focus on their careers, they were going to miss their opportunity to have kids. If you wait, you'll be too late, story after story since then warns us.

But what about all the 40-something moms dropping off kids at the grade school gates these days? How do they fit into the picture?

With that question in mind, I decided to explore. Aside from a few "how to get pregnant over 35" guides and some support-group books for later moms,[1] I found very little analysis of the trend and what it means for women, their families, and the wider community—though the day-to-day evidence suggests a revolution has occurred. Wouldn't such a big change have big effects?

I started by checking the statistics. It turns out that between 1970 and 2004 the average age at which U.S. women gave birth for the first time rose from 21.4 to 25.2—an enormous change. For college-educated women (as of 2003) the average age at first birth was 30.1. Pulling up this average are big rises in the upper age ranges. In 2005, one in every twelve *first* births was to a woman 35 or over. That's a lot more later families than in 1970, when one in every one hundred first children had a later mom. Add in the adoptive moms who start their families later, and you've got a substantial proportion of the population.

In fact, a vast number of women have had their first children after the age of 35 these days. In some places, it almost seems that *most* women begin having children after that age. The check-out line magazines are full of stories of celebrity moms on this timetable: Salma Hayek, Julia Roberts, Tina Fey, Geena Davis, Michelle Obama, Holly Hunter, Julianne Moore, Annie Leibovitz, and Susan Sarandon, to name just a few. Though lately we've had a spate of stories about fairly young celebrity moms, too, the impression that more and more women are starting their families later is confirmed by the statistics: over the past thirty years, the number of U.S. women who had their first child between the ages of 35 and 39 has *multiplied by ten*, increasing every year despite the predictions that women who wait will wind up living lonely, childless lives. And there are now *thirteen times* as many women giving birth to their first children in the 40 to 44 age range.[2] Or, taking into consideration that the population has increased since 1975, we can gauge the trend more accurately by noting that the first birth rate per thousand women starting their families at 35 or after has *quintupled* in the past thirty years.

If you're in this group, this statistic may not surprise you, but it does seem to be news to the media. If you tell your grandmother that women over 35 are having kids, it probably won't surprise her either. After all, women over 35 have been having kids forever—it just hasn't usually been their first child. My grandmother had her eighth child when she was 39, the same age at which I had my first. Hers was the old-fashioned kind of later motherhood. It's the late *onset* of motherhood that's new about later motherhood today.

After the first child, many new later moms go on to have more kids. Add all their kids together with the later kids of moms who started before 35 and then had more kids on the other side of that age line, and you've got an overall one in seven kids in the United States born to a mom 35 or more in 2005. That's almost 600,000 children.[3]

When I saw the statistics, I wanted to know more. I knew how good I felt about my own choice to have children later, but how did others feel about it? Did most later moms see the choice as a good one or a bad one in their lives? Did they feel they had waited too long, or was waiting the right thing for them? How did their choice affect their families, their jobs, and their relationships?

Pursuing these questions, I conducted a study of 113 "new later mothers"—women who had their first children by birth or adoption at or after 35. These are moms by both ordinary and extraordinary means: married moms, single moms, straight moms, gay moms, new moms at 35, and new moms at 56 and every age in between. They are biological and adoptive moms, mothers of one child, and mothers of several children. They are full-time working mothers, part-timers, and mothers who stay home full time. These are moms of many races and many professions—engineers, dancers, CEOs, doctors, teachers, lawyers, reporters, accountants, and on and on.

The results were fascinating. I went into this study expecting mixed responses and that the women would have conflicting feelings about their choice. But, while there was some complexity, the overwhelming majority of women viewed the choice to have children after 35 as *one of the most positive choices they had made in their entire lives*. That's the real story.

These new later mothers live in a very different world from the one the media portray. The women I've met enjoy motherhood immensely, and most combine it with satisfying work. Others have "retired" into motherhood, while still others have stepped out of the workforce but plan to step back in down the line. These women live in a world where most women succeed in starting their families later—usually in the standard way, sometimes by adoption (the route by which our second daughter joined our family), and sometimes with the help of fertility technology, but consistently with profound happiness. These women feel they've come to motherhood prepared and that their children, their marriages, their careers, and their sanity are by far the better for it.

These moms are *ready*. The word popped up time and again in my interviews. The precise definition of readiness differed with each woman, but commonalities emerged fast. Most consistently, I heard that waiting offered the women I spoke with the chance to establish themselves, as individuals and in their work, to find the right partner for the long term—or to determine that single parenthood made the most sense for them—and to achieve a measure of financial stability. They felt they'd sown their wild oats, tested their mettle, and established their senses of self, so that now they were ready to focus on their children's development rather than on their own. **Lena**, a journalist now in her mid-fifties and the mother of two teenagers, remarks that children care most of all about your being there for them—both literally and figuratively. She notes, "I could have never shown up [for them] in my twenties because I was busy trying to show up for myself."

By and large, the new later mothers I've met are having a very good time—a feeling helped by the fact that they've achieved good levels of financial security and personal growth. But what about the rest of the later moms out there? One hundred thirteen makes a lot of people to interview, but it doesn't in itself document a national experience. So I turned to some bigger databases to check whether the positives reported by the women I had met were mirrored on a wider scale. Not only did that data support what I had learned from the women I talked to, but they suggested that the effects of delay are very positive not just for individual women and their families but for their communities as well.

New later moms seem to be changing the world around them—for the better. This change comes not all at once, but bit by bit as they've climbed the ranks at work before having kids, achieved higher salaries and a new clout that allows them to negotiate more flexible schedules when children do arrive, and begun to work out the balance of business and family in a way that works for everybody. New later mothers gain a sense of competence from their work experience that they can then apply to advocacy for their kids and their communities. And starting families later raises moms' status in their relationships of all kinds. Communities benefit from having these educated, well employed, and actively invested moms as members. They're rocking the cradle and the world at once.

Although the results of my study were surprising because of the sustained portrait of happy later moms, it's not all ideal. Our culture often lacks the support some cultures have in place for families, so everybody struggles to some degree. Some women do end up having children by egg donation or adoption when that was not their original plan, and some end up without children when they wanted them. Fertility, we're reminded frequently, declines with age, especially after 40, and some women have encountered the effects of that decline. As more and more women wait to have kids and push at the limits, scientists have responded with a variety of new means to extend fertility. So far, none works perfectly. But when would-be parents meet difficulty starting their families by the usual means, many find alternate routes to a happy family.

The evolving life narrative of the new later mothers builds on the foundation of women's changed relation to their fertility. While the headlines have broadcast a tragedy about how *out* of control women's fertility has become for those who wait "too late," the real story is the happy tale of how much positive control women *do* now have over an aspect of their lives that ran roughshod over them for millennia.

It's time to explore this new world of motherhood. The rules have changed, so we must look clearly at the new scene to learn how to navigate. As the ranks of new later mothers steadily increase, these moms are creating new life stories—choosing to start families when they are *ready* to do so rather than sticking to a schedule set by narrow social expectations or lack of other options.

While most of the women I've talked to are the parents of their own biological children conceived in the standard way, a number employed in vitro fertilization (IVF), hormones like Gonal-F or Clomid, egg or sperm donation, or adoption to create their families. All report being quite happy with their families now, though sometimes the process involved work and emotional and financial cost. *Ready* explores some of the ways in which these pioneering families have handled these new roads to parenthood, looks at new technologies on the horizon, and shares insights and stories about what they mean for families long term.

Instead of dwelling on fears and negativity about later motherhood, *Ready* recognizes and celebrates this powerful new group of women who are changing the landscape of motherhood, one by one and collectively. At the same time, we'll look at the complexities, some that women are facing now and some that will become more apparent with advancing age, and we'll share solutions and ideas for dealing with problems at hand and upcoming.

My aim here is not to tell anyone when to have children—each of us determines the right choice for her family. So many factors play in, there can be no one "best" moment for starting a family. Instead I aim to consider the pros and cons of the decision to wait until 35 and later, a new option that makes sense for increasing numbers of women but the effects of which have yet to be explored.

Nor do I mean to claim that the trend toward postponing motherhood is necessarily here to stay. In the future, if working women decide they prefer not to wait as long for family, they are now moving into position to change the workplace to better accommodate the possibility of rearing a family and climbing the job ranks at once. But because so many of the women I talked to mentioned that part of their reason for waiting lay in their desire to explore the world and establish themselves as individuals, not just as workers, it seems unlikely that the trend will disappear any time soon.

Along with talking to what turned out to be an amazing group of wise and articulate women, I've spent a good deal of time analyzing statistics to get a sense of the wider effects of the new later motherhood trend. Many of these stats are hard to pin down since little research has been done in this area, and many of the bigger surveys just don't ask the relevant questions. The national census and the CDC national natality reports have provided the best data. The combination of data and interviews reveals a network of consequences, both positive and negative, when women start their families later. I'll summarize the key points here.

Among the benefits new later mothers offer their families:

- *Happy They Waited.* New later moms feel happy with their families and with the timing. They're proud of what they accomplished before they had kids, glad they could hold out to find the right partner, and happy that they can now move into motherhood with no second thoughts or resentments about opportunities lost.
- *Stronger Family Focus.* New later mothers feel *ready* to focus on family—they aren't trying to establish themselves at work and in life at the same time that they're raising young kids.
- *More Financial Power.*
  - New later moms make higher salaries than women of the same age who had their children earlier—comparing full-time workers with the same level of education.
  - Stay-at-home new later moms retire into motherhood with savings in the bank and a greater likelihood that a later dad's income will be sufficient to support the family well.
- *More Flexibility.* New later mothers have often advanced enough at work to have the clout that allows them to negotiate work schedules that accommodate family.
- *Higher Education.* Sixty percent of later moms having their first child in 2003 had a BA or higher, compared with just 26 percent of all moms giving birth in that year.

- *Rising Class.* Though many new later moms are middle class, not all of them started out there; when working-class women pursue education and establish themselves in jobs before they start their families, they may wind up rearing middle-class children.
- *High Marriage Rate and Singles Financially Stable.* In 2003, 85 percent, and in 2009, 81 percent of first-time moms 35 and over were married. Comparatively: 11 percent of first-time moms at 18 were wed in 2009, 30 percent at 21, 62 percent at 25, 83 percent at 30, 84 percent at 34 (the high), 78 percent at 40, and 77 percent at 45–55. Single moms who give birth or adopt later are generally more financially stable than their younger counterparts.
- *Greater Likelihood of Happiness in Marriage.* Higher salaries, job skills, and savings create a safety net so that women don't have to stay in unhappy marriages to avoid impoverishing their kids, and having assurance that you *can* leave is sometimes the best insurance that you won't want to.
- *Peer Marriages.* Peer marriages bring together "equal companions" who have similar education levels and job experience and who contribute similarly in all areas within the marriage.
- *Younger Husbands.* Close to 80 percent of married women who have their first child in their twenties have older husbands. But only about 60 percent of new later moms are married to older men. This change has many positive repercussions, including an increased chance that husbands will live to be their wives' companions in old age (since men die younger on average).
- *Greater Self-Confidence.* New later moms have generally had lots of work experience and have confidence as a result of their accomplishments. Self-confident women can be especially able advocates and models for kids.
- *Longer Life Expectancy.* A recent study shows that mothers who give birth at 34 live longer with fewer health issues than women who give birth at any other age. New mothers at 40 and older run

into more health risks with pregnancy, but their chances of a longer life are even higher.[4]

Of course, things are not entirely rosy; there *are* complications to starting later:

- *Greater Chance of Infertility*. The chances of infertility increase with age, especially after 40. But although infertility may block the usual road to family, many people find alternate routes to that happy ending.
- *Smaller Families*. While some couples choose to have only one child, others stop at one by default.
- *Less Grandparent Involvement*. The older a woman is when she has her first child, the older her mother and father are when they become grandparents.
- *Lower Energy*. Greater age can mean lower energy levels, but many new later parents respond by working harder at staying fit.

While different women experienced different combinations of these consequences, all of them expressed an enormous pleasure in their families ("best thing I ever did," said one happy entrepreneur). And many of the women I spoke with talked about how precious their children seemed to them as a result of their having waited so long. They felt they could appreciate their children more than they would have earlier because they had more life experience to compare motherhood to and could recognize, as one mom put it, that "there is nothing, *nothing* that will come close to this."

A nexus of factors grounds the "new later" trend. Women's new relation to work is perhaps the most obvious—climbing the ladder at work takes time and is often made easier when kids come after a woman has established herself in her field. Absent a social support network for parents, new later motherhood supplies the tools (like clout and higher pay) with which many moms build their own shadow benefits systems.

Other key factors behind the trend include the widespread use of reliable birth control, the huge rise in women's education, and the lengthening of the modern life span, which gives women new options for deciding how to sequence their life events. These are all enormous changes with big ripple effects. Though reliable birth control may seem like a normal feature of daily life, the world is still reeling from the interpersonal earthquake that its arrival wrought. If women aren't baby machines—what are they? How do they fit into the social fabric that was woven around the assumption that they were? What's their relation to the "women's" jobs their mothers filled at incredibly low pay rates—jobs that assumed they'd get a minimal education and that gave them flexibility to be at home with sick kids? Individuals may not raise these questions for themselves in exactly these terms, but we all live in their fault lines.

The choice by large numbers of women to have children later is a huge shift for our culture. If you make this choice it will affect every aspect of your life and the lives of those who love you. The choice to wait gives women the chance to get the education and the work experience that, in turn, give them a new perspective and status that allow them to encounter the world in a new way. It means they're more likely to have matured into their grown-up selves and to be with a partner they'll stay with for the long term. It means they'll have more funds with which to support their children, whether they remain at work or stay at home after kids arrive. It means if they stay at work that they'll be in a better position to negotiate family-friendly schedules because they've proven their skills and because their employers rely on their experience. It means they're more likely to be married to a peer who shares financial decisions as well as housework and childcare.

In addition, the change creates wider, positive ripple effects: for example, in the past ten years, the term "illegitimate child" has largely disappeared from use and, with it, much of the negative judgment that marked the lives of millions of children for centuries. I would argue that this change springs from women's new status, achieved because many women have been able to defer motherhood while they go to school and establish themselves in jobs. This new status allows women as a group to "legitimate" their own children, where before legitimacy required a man in the house. Now all kids are legitimate. The child of the single mom down the block lives a very different life today than he would have thirty years ago. Though being a single parent of any gender may involve difficulties, mostly because it means more of a time and money burden than when the job is shared, it's not the marital status of the parent that determines the way society views the child. That looks like progress to me.

Linked to this change is the new and expanding trend among lesbian couples to have kids—a trend based on evolving social attitudes as well as, in many cases, the fairly recent wide availability of sperm donation. Because this option is new, and because it often takes a while for women to move through the process of coming out, many gay moms are later moms.

The women whose stories you'll read here represent a wide range of experience. Each woman has her own story, but the stories have common themes, and the moms' responses to their children are consistently intense and joyous.

The key term here is "readiness," and different women in different circumstances feel ready at different times. Not every woman wants to go to graduate school, and many women yearn for and feel prepared for the pleasures of parenting earlier in their lives. Sometimes women find themselves pregnant when it isn't what they had planned, and they make something wonderful out of it. Readiness is not just a question of personal inclination; it matters what kind of support a woman has in the world around her. Partners matter, as do employment policies—both policies offered by employers and those mandated by law.

I undertook this study not to make the case for or against having your kids after 35 but to consider why so many women are doing just that and to respect their choice. Each woman I interviewed did what made sense for her and her partner. And pretty much to a woman, they reported themselves a happy group. Which is not to say they don't have complaints: some feel tired, and some wish they'd had a chance to have more kids. Some of the women I spoke with ran into infertility issues and then went on to find other solutions. But those solutions weren't available to all—either for financial reasons or for personal reasons that made taking extra steps too hard or undesirable.

By its nature, my study led me to talk to *mothers*—not to women who had no children (whether by choice or by default). And when a woman becomes a mother for the first time at a relatively advanced age, it's pretty much because she wanted to. So there is a built-in likelihood that she will be cheerful.

The news isn't that these mothers are happy, though you don't get much sense of that in the popular press. The real news is that they're happy not only with their families but with the path they took to arriving at those families. Some who married later would have liked to have found their love a little earlier, but given that they didn't, they're glad they waited. Those who are single parents feel pleased that they're in a position to support their children well. (Of the ten moms I spoke with who were single when their kids arrived, four have since married. One woman, whose husband didn't want kids, divorced in order to start her family.) The new later moms feel proud of what they accomplished before they had kids and are happy that they can now move into motherhood with no second thoughts.

Though some women feel ready earlier, increasing numbers of women today don't feel ready to start their families until they're 35 or more. Women's new option to decide to have children based on whether and when they feel ready—whether that's at 21, 25, 34, 40, or 57—rather than on a prefab schedule set by social convention, offers them the chance to sequence their lives in the ways that best allow them to fulfill their dreams for themselves and for their children. Each woman has to look at the big picture and decide for herself when all the elements best configure for her family. *Ready* offers a snapshot of the lives and families of new later moms—presenting their experience in their own words and exploring their role in the evolving scene of twenty-first-century motherhood, where changes already in place carry us toward a cascading set of changes on the horizon.

CHAPTER 1

Waiting

The Backstory

I n a contentious *Atlantic Monthly* article, a woman who calls herself an "ex-feminist" catalogs the shortcomings of middle-class women's options for combining work and family, while telling her own story. A would-be novelist with a snappy prose style, she dreamt big about a career, but the arrival of her children quashed those plans. She tried holding a job while a nanny watched her kids but eventually decided that she should stay home for the next ten years (with a housekeeper), writing the occasional essay. The article begins as something of a screed, but it closes on a more conciliatory note, suggesting that the initial claims meant to provoke more than to be taken seriously. While blaming feminists may grab notice, it doesn't solve problems.

We've heard this story recently, but this particular essay (in two installments) came out in December 1933 and January 1934.[1] Worth Tuttle, the author, feels ambivalent about staying home with her children, but sees no other choice for herself. She does have ideas, though, for how younger women starting out might manage better than she did: if you really want a full-out career, she advises, don't have kids! But if, like her, you really want both, she concludes with an argument for waiting:

> I believe that a woman who wants both a career and children should delay the children until she has achieved such permanence in her

art that she can lay it aside temporarily without injury, or until she has had such success that she can ensure her future by the employment of capable household assistants. To care for a young career and a young child at the same time is to run the risk of making a weakling of both.[2]

How much has changed since 1933?

Some important things *have* changed, including the fact that hundreds of thousands of women now follow Worth Tuttle's advice. As she predicted, postponing motherhood makes it possible for many women to have both family and career—though it certainly doesn't resolve all the issues. Tuttle's story reveals that women's struggle to harmonize home and office life has been going on for almost a century.

Progress has been complicated along the way by that aberration in family life that we've perversely come to regard as the norm—the 1950s. Although women were tapped to fill vacant jobs during World War II, after the war their skills on the home front got top billing. Although we romanticize the fifties as a time of calm order, the immense popularity of *I Love Lucy* (on air from 1951 to 1957 and then rebroadcast in reruns ever since) documents the tension that ruled that era. In episode after episode, Lucy tries to get a job but is thwarted and mocked for her ambitions by her husband and, to varying degrees, by her friends. But no matter how many times she is batted down, she keeps jumping back up. Clearly the status quo doesn't suit her. The paradox, as critic Patricia Mellencamp first pointed out, lay in the fact that it was, after all, Lucy's show (and its sixties incarnation, *The Lucy Show*, made that explicit)![3] While the character Lucy Ricardo was acting out the incompetence of women to do anything but keep house (housework didn't get much respect on the show, and even that she had problems with), the real-life Lucille Ball was demonstrating exactly the opposite. Here was a woman of great talent, who was exercising that talent, making big dollars, and raising a family all at the same time. For viewers from the fifties onward, this paradoxical message represented and continues to represent our confused national view of what a woman's role should be. The resonance of Tuttle's polemics from the thirties with the rhetoric of the present-day work/life debate reminds us that, despite progress, the issue continues unresolved.

Working Mom, Circa 1922

Worth Tuttle's tale gives a sense of history and suggests something about the gradual way big change unfolds. Though one hundred years seems an eternity in the contemporary world where so many things change by the moment, from the perspective of real historical transformation it's a mere twinkling. Except for the dates, Tuttle's bio mirrors those of many of our contemporaries—college, some graduate school, work, marriage, and big ambitions. Born in North Carolina in 1896, Tuttle earned her BA in 1916 at what is now Duke. She moved to New York where she attended the newly opened Columbia Journalism School, worked for pay part time as a home visitor for the Red Cross, and scribbled away in hopes of assuming the mantle of Modern Jane Austen. Though no anomaly—by 1920, 7.6 percent of all U.S. women graduated from college, up from just 2.2 percent in 1890—Tuttle was a progressive-minded woman, a trendsetter. In the big city, her forward-looking views fit in, where they hadn't at home.

In her New York boardinghouse, Tuttle met a younger college man named Walter Hedden, soon to join the Port Authority of New York and eventually to become its chief. In 1919 they united in what they viewed as a "companionate marriage"—a marriage of peers where both worked and had ambitions (though she still did the bulk of the cooking and cleaning). After Hedden graduated, they took a kind of working year abroad—traveling not to new countries but to different social strata. They went separately. Tuttle, a Southerner interested in improving race relations, taught for a year in New Orleans at Dillard University, a "Negro college" ("I wanted to learn to know the 'new Negro' as I had always known the old, and there was no other source of information"). Meanwhile, Hedden worked in New England in a textile mill. Back together in New York in 1922, they had a son (mom was 26, dad was 24), and by her account, the situation changed fast in ways she had not expected.

Quickly finding their apartment too small, they moved to Connecticut. Hedden commuted to the city and Tuttle stayed home with the baby. "By the end of six months I was suicidal," she writes, laid low by the combination of loss of intellectual focus and conversation and a feeling of incompetence at housewifery. A few months later, they hired a nanny, and Tuttle took a job working four afternoons a week for a novelist in the city and writing at home in the mornings. But not long into this routine, the nanny's rheumatism flared up and the novelist went to Europe; so Tuttle stayed home again for a while, writing less often. Gradually she adjusted to life at home with a toddler and found she could write while the baby slept. The couple wanted a second child, and since she was home anyway, it seemed like a good time for baby two. A few months after their daughter's birth, they hired a new nanny and Tuttle went back to work full time as a writer for *Encyclopedia Britannica*. She considered herself "the picture of a successful feminist, the wife and mother with a career."[4]

But that picture didn't hold for long. Tuttle's world apparently included some birth control, but her third pregnancy arrived unexpectedly and scotched her career hopes. Three young children felt like too many to leave with one nanny—plus she'd have to skip work whenever they got sick, which would have added up to a lot of personal days in an era before they were invented. She stayed home from then on, writing when she could. But the existence of the *Atlantic* pieces makes it clear that she didn't settle in quietly—and she kept pondering why things had turned out this way.

At the end of the first installment of her autobiography, Tuttle blames feminists for leading her to think she could have a career without accounting for her family life. By the end of the second installment, her tone softens; she stops looking to lay blame and tries to be practical. Since the world she and her readers inhabit falls short on good options for smoothly combining work and family rearing, Tuttle urges that women's education should include both intellectual *and* home-economical studies, as well as an expectation that mothers will use both skill sets. She aims to prepare young women to expect less in the way of career options than she expected—to save them some of the pain she felt and to remind them of the joys of being there for your family when they need you. The option of a husband's partnership in household management doesn't come up.

But though the article ends there, that wasn't the end of her story. Tuttle remained ambitious and tenacious. In 1944, ten years after the *Atlantic* essays, her first novel (a portrait of the Oneida colony and its free-love experiments as an old-people's sex paradise at the expense of the young) came out under her married name, Worth Tuttle Hedden. She was 48. She went on to publish two more novels (the *New York Times* favorably reviewed all three, and the second, an interracial romance set at a college modeled on Dillard, won a prize) as well as a memoir on family life, in which she speaks much less polemically than she had in 1933.[5] Despite her endorsement of compliance with the status quo, Tuttle continued to struggle to have both family life and career across the changing landscape of women's options in her lifetime. In the end she managed it—though not on the terms she wanted. Who's to say she wouldn't be better known today if she'd had a chance to start her novelist's career earlier?

Looking back, Tuttle's world in 1922 sounds almost contemporary. Among the biggest differences—she has no out-of-home childcare option (no handy Montessori down the road), though she had expected that would be available ("I had no idea where there was a day nursery, but in my Bible, *Essays on the Woman Question,* day nurseries were spoken of as a matter of course"). And though she'd like a salary for the independence it would signal, she feels no pressure to bring one in (most working women today don't have this option), and her husband does

MARGARET MEAD

Tuttle arrived at her views on deferring family at the same time that anthropologist Margaret Mead, born five years after Tuttle in 1901, wrote her landmark book on that very subject (though that's not the way it's usually characterized). Mead's bestseller, *Coming of Age in Samoa,* shocked America. She described a world in which young women deferred marriage and family until after a period of youthful freedom, when they lived on their own terms and engaged in sex at will (generally without pregnancy). Mead's subject was Samoa, but critics suggested that the dynamics Mead described were a projection of her own views on sexuality. Of course, nothing precludes the work from being both an accurate observation of another culture *and* an argument for fewer sexual restrictions and a later start at family-building for women at home.

However you understand it, Mead herself definitely followed an extended version of the pattern she described: she married three times and built a family with her third husband, Gregory Bateson. She had her first and only child with him in 1939, a week before she turned 38.

not do childcare (most dads these days do). She shares the modern sense that it's vital to get some worldly experience before starting a family, not just for establishing yourself at work but for establishing your *self* ("I believe," she says, "that for a girl a few years of self-dependence in the economic world are more valuable than any amount of travel").

Tuttle's story illustrates that, while the steady trend toward starting families later didn't begin until after the pill arrived, women had been ready for the option for a while—certainly since the twenties and arguably since long before. After all, humans have used birth control of some kind or another since the dawn of time. And it's women like Worth Tuttle and her peers (along with a few activists) who brought us to the point where reliable birth control and trustworthy childcare have become widely (though far from universally) available.

Many other things have changed as well. In Tuttle's day, fewer women *sought* to combine work and family, and even fewer succeeded,

LUCY LEADS THE WAY

In a neat twist, Lucille Ball, leading lady of the women-and-work debate on fifties TV, led the way in "contemporary" work/family balance
methods in her real life as well, because these methods made sense for
her, too. Born in 1911 (fourteen years after Tuttle), she began her acting career in New York in the thirties. It's possible she read Tuttle's *Atlantic* essays. Even if she didn't, she clearly learned the same sort of
lessons from the world around her that Tuttle did. Having married at
29 in 1940, Lucy and Desi Arnaz didn't have their first child until
Lucy was one week short of her 40th birthday (and Desi, six years her
junior, was 34). Their second child, Desi Jr., was born into the plot of
their show when she was 41, giving us a new later mom as one of the
most public mother figures on the world stage at the time. *TV Guide*
celebrated little Desi's birth on its very first cover.[6]

Lucy wasn't totally anomalous in the fifties. Although most new
moms then were in their twenties, there was also a fair share of
women who'd waited to start their families until their men came home
from the war. But the war didn't play a part in Lucy's delay. She waited
for her marriage to get to a stable point where she knew it would last
a while. For his living, her bandleader husband toured the country, and
he ran into his share of trouble while away from home. So when a
chance to make a TV show arose in 1950, Lucy wrote into her contract
that Desi would co-star, guaranteeing that he'd be home. For their
family, shared work ensured stability. Their first baby, Lucie, was born
two months before the show's debut in 1951. And the lines between
work and family blurred even further when her pregnancy with Desi Jr.
became a plot element. Like many later moms after her, Lucy used the
clout she'd established through her long career to structure her work
life to fit with and support her family life.

The DesiLu marriage ended in 1960, but the two remained in fond
daily contact until he died in 1986. And Lucille Ball, formerly "the
Queen of the Bs" (that's B movies) and the CEO of DesiLu Produc-
tions after buying out Desi, remained the queen of her own ongoing
TV empire and one of the richest women in Hollywood.

where today millions of women do succeed. But barriers to balance remain, and, as individuals and as a group, women continue—ambitiously and tenaciously—to work at managing that balance better. It's an extended learning process. And for many, Tuttle's advice that we delay kids until we're established in our work turns out to be a key factor in achieving balance in the contemporary world.

The Nexus of Change

"It's interesting the confluence of the arrival of this technology and of the social attitudes that make it usable," notes **Vera**, an engineer who, finding herself in a disappointing dating scene, took matters into her own hands and became a single mom at 37 via sperm donation. Interesting, but not accidental. Vera is talking about in vitro fertilization (IVF) technology (which allowed for the fertilization of her egg using donated sperm) and the social acceptance of single motherhood, but she might just as well be talking about birth control and the acceptance of women in the work world. In both cases, technology and attitudes shifted together in mutually informing ways.

In the past, social restrictions *were* the birth control for the unmarried, or an important part of it. "Hold out or suffer the consequences" girls in many cultures have been warned for ages. In the nineteenth century, unwed moms (especially the poorer ones) risked being sent to workhouses or prisons, and their children were labeled bastards and had only limited legal rights. Many starved or committed suicide. But as more reliable means of fertility control arrived (most notably, the pill in 1960), social restrictions eased. The birth rate fell in all age ranges as millions of women (married and unmarried) could choose for themselves how many children they wanted and when.

Though it wasn't the only factor bringing a halt to the baby boom (economics and a changing cultural scene also played roles), the pill's FDA approval and release in 1960 to immediate widespread use greatly influenced a swift downward trend in the birth rate: from 118 births per thousand among women 15 to 44 in 1960 (the same as in 1955) to 108.3 in 1963, 96.3 in 1965, 85.2 in 1968, 73.1 in 1972, and a low of 65.0 in 1976, the point at which it has roughly remained ever since (66.1 in 2003). That's a direct 45 percent drop in sixteen years, with 20 percent of it within the first six! As a result, many more women moved through their twenties without children. Then, starting in the mid-seventies, many of these women surprised the demographers and began having children much later than their mothers had done.

Of course, the pill didn't just emerge from the neutral womb of science back in 1960—it was developed because educated women with a vote and sometimes with careers (changes long in the making) funded the research. And post-pill, women who could reliably time their children then had further options in terms of education and jobs. Changes in one realm of life set off changes in the others, which bring us to the present moment.

The trend to new later motherhood springs from a nexus of changes in quite a few dimensions of women's experience, including education, birth control, careers, social expectations, marriage dynamics, politics, fertility technology, adoption opportunities, health, and life expectancy. Many of these changes affect all women, no matter at what age they first give birth, or whether they give birth at all. But they have special effects in together creating the environment that allows so many women today to become new later mothers.

Birth Control—"The Rich Get Richer and the Poor Get Children"?

"Thank god for birth control!" laughs **Letty**, now a happy new later mother (at 34, 36, and 40). "Without the pill, who knows what would have happened to me. . . . I didn't come from a family where anybody had a long history of not having children as teenagers." Letty's grandmother had her first child at 16, and her mother, who never finished high school, had Letty, *her* first, at 21. Angry at her situation, Letty's mom took it out on her kids. "For my mother, she would take those opportunities to really squelch any desires, any attempt to reach out beyond where she saw the boundaries. By god, her life was only this big, yours will be that big too, or you won't exist." So Letty turned to her grandmother, who had experienced her own troubles ("You can't start having babies at 16 and be a fully actualized person"), but who, by the time Letty arrived, was in her late thirties. "What I suppose in my mind is that by the time I came along, my grandmother was just getting ready to be a mother. She had just gathered those resources, so at least she was there for me."

As Letty sees it, the pill allowed her to break the family pattern, giving her a chance to grow up and see the world before starting a family. She went to college and then to work, got married and then divorced, clear that she and husband-number-one should not have kids together. A few years later, she married again with a refined sense of what she wanted in a marriage partner. When she and her new husband began their family, Letty was nearly 35, and they really felt ready—professionally, emotionally, and financially.

Of course the pill wasn't the *first* birth control—historians have cataloged quite a few earlier methods, most in use in some form since prehistoric times. These include vaginal sponges, coitus interruptus (a clear sign that the ancients did understand the basics of reproduction),[7] infanticide (not exactly birth control but long a method of last resort), abortion (considered a woman's decision in most cultures and recommended by Aristotle as a means by which a family could avoid having more children than it could well support), sterilization, celibacy, pessaries (anything that caps the uterus—including one ancient favorite, crocodile dung! "Could it be the smell?" an incredulous friend asked when I described this method. "That would chase a man off!"), spermicides, IUDs, prolonged lactation, potions, amulets and other magic, douching, condoms, and the rhythm method (not reliably understood until 1924).

Over the ages, different cultures have held different views on birth control: nomadic people, needing to pack and go quickly, encouraged birth control, as did many city dwellers. Farmers, however, needed (and could feed) more workers and so, especially given high mortality rates, often discouraged birth control. Fifth-century Athenian families thought two kids were ideal, as did medieval Italians. And they met their goals.

How did they do it? When needed, some women aborted, generally before quickening (the point when the child can be felt moving in the womb). But contraceptives seem to have been the means of first resort. Exactly what *kinds* of contraceptives were used has recently come into dispute. Just as in some circles today contraceptives breed controversy, there's controversy among contraceptive historians, too: while some think physical barriers and techniques provided the only successful contraceptives of yore, historian John M. Riddle believes that herbal recipes worked in ways akin to modern birth control pills—by influencing hormone levels—and nearly as effectively.

Apparently the world is full of plants that prevent pregnancy, and some people have known about them for ages. The invention of the modern pill drew on the knowledge of Mexican women, who ate a wild yam (the Barbasco root) as a contraceptive—that yam became the source for the progestin employed in the pill.[8] Demeter's daughter, Persephone, ate pomegranate seeds, which suggests an understanding of their potency as birth control since, in the myth, they caused the infertility of winter. Pomegranate seeds have been used as contraceptives in Europe and India, East Africa and the Pacific. And many other herbs have similar effects, like papaya, celery seed, and Queen Anne's lace.

Contraception information flowed freely for ages, but the flow slowed to a trickle during the Inquisition. Riddle argues that the purging of "witches" in the sixteenth and seventeenth centuries led to the disappearance of much of the old knowledge about birth control. Pope Innocent VIII began the witch hunt with a papal bull condemning their arts at "caus[ing] to perish the offspring of women . . . and hinder[ing] men from begetting and women from conceiving" (1484).[9] Was birth control the backstory at Salem? In any event, more than half a million "wise women" died by burning or other means as a result of the witch purges, and birth rates did rise between the fifteenth and the eighteenth centuries. But they started falling again at the start of the nineteenth century, and they've been heading down pretty much ever since, with the occasional reversal like the postwar baby boom.

In 1800, U.S. women had an average of 7.04 births across their life-times, but by 1900, the average had descended to 3.56, and in 2000 to 2.0. Improvements in health care (more children survived), the increasingly crowded city life, and the rising status of women raised interest in keeping families small. People managed the decrease with withdrawal, sponges, condoms, and abstinence within marriage. This last method called for self-restraint, but economics can be a big motivator. And before the women's movement taught us that women's pleasure mattered, many wives found their sex lives less than satisfactory anyway and didn't mind curtailing it. Neither did they mind escaping the burden of raising unwanted children. The nineteenth-century Voluntary Motherhood movement told women that they had the right to say no to their husbands if they didn't want more kids.

Then at the turn of the twentieth century, in combination with the women's rights struggles of the day, the birth control movement led by Maria Stopes in England and Margaret Sanger in the United States taught women that they had a reason to say yes. Along with fewer kids, the twentieth-century contraceptive movement brought a new focus on fun in bed (lose the risk of pregnancy each time, and women are suddenly interested), a new focus that husbands found exciting too (I leave it to you to picture the difference a willing partner makes). And the new level of frolicking allowed many to discover for the first time that women could orgasm—including Stopes, who made it part of her mission to share this revelation with the masses. And as awareness and demand grew, the contraceptive methods became more sophisticated, expanding to include diaphragms, cervical caps, and the rhythm method.

The biggest change came in 1960. Though the pill didn't inaugurate birth control, its almost complete reliability has revolutionized women's experience, especially in combination with the new acceptance of women's sexual autonomy. "It gave women my age sexual freedom without the fear of getting pregnant," explains **Olivia**, who became a mother at 39. Use of the pill (in tandem with more reliable versions of other forms of birth control) makes contemporary women different from all the generations of women before us.

Women today differ from their ancestresses in *when* they use birth control. In the past, birth control mostly meant women could decide when to *stop* having kids or to space kids out. Purposefully waiting to start your family until your late thirties and older is new. The women who waited in the past generally had to wait, either because the men were away at war or because economic hard times (like famine or depression) made them hold back.

Women began choosing to start families later when their options opened up. By that I mean options to do satisfying things that can't be done as well or as easily once children have entered the picture—like completing educations, working through the demanding early stages of challenging careers, or just generally being fancy-free. And those options coincided with the arrival of the pill.

Longer life expectancy introduces new *time* options too—opportunities to sequence the milestones in life in a new order. People used to have children early because they couldn't depend on living very long (the average U.S. life expectancy in 1900 was 47), and they hoped to last long enough to raise their children to adulthood. Plenty of moms didn't make it that far (roughly 1 in 130 died in childbirth in the United States in 1900—today it's about 1 in 13,000).

Though there's still a chance of dying of illness or accident at 60 or younger, the chances of living past that age have gone way up. And if you're likely to live to 90, what's the rush? If you have a child at 40, you can reasonably expect to be a healthy 70-year-old when your child reaches 30. And you've got good hopes of being a healthy 80-year-old when she or he hits 40. People who can reasonably hope to live long tend to work harder at getting there. Some predict that, just as life expectancy practically doubled in the twentieth century, it will again in the twenty-first.

CRYSTAL EASTMAN

Crystal Eastman's contributions to women's history were ignored for many years after her death, but her 1919 essay, "Now We Can Begin," written just after the passage of the Suffrage Amendment, sounds just as anachronistically of *our* moment as Tuttle's piece.[10] Like Mead and Lucy, Eastman started her family later—at 36 and 37—in a second marriage. Eastman, who graduated second in her class from New York University law school in 1907, wrote the first workman's compensation law, actively advocated for suffrage, published a leftist newspaper, was a founder of the National Women's Peace Party, as well as a founder of what is now the ACLU.

A feminist from her early life on, Eastman promoted birth control and free love and refused alimony as demeaning when she divorced her first husband. In "Now We Can Begin," she recommends two basic changes in society's structuring of women's work. They would be

> [first] to arrange the world so that women can be human beings, with a chance to exercise their infinitely varied gifts in infinitely varied ways, instead of being destined by the accident of their sex to one field of activity—housework and child-raising. And second, if and when they choose housework and child-raising, to have the occupation recognized by the world as work, requiring a definite economic reward and not merely entitling the performer to be dependent on some man.

The essay goes on to stress the importance of career men sharing the housework with their equally career-focused wives.

An amazingly active and public figure in her day, Eastman was blacklisted in the twenties and died at 47 in 1928.

Education: "The Neglected Education of My Fellow Creatures Is the Grand Source of the Misery I Deplore"

That's the view of **Mary** (single new mother at 34, married and dead of puerperal fever in her second childbirth at 38), back in 1792. Mary Wollstonecraft lived two hundred years before new later motherhood became a trend, but she foreshadowed the modern woman's life story in many respects (health care not being one). Her father's tyranny over her and her mother determined her to maintain her independence from men. Self-taught, she started a school to support herself and published *A Vindication of the Rights of Women*, condemning women's lack of educational and social freedoms. Despite her plans to remain uninvolved, she fell in love at 33 (with an American who said he'd marry her and then didn't) and bore their child at 34. Comforted in her abandoned state by the philosopher William Godwin, she fell in love again and turned up pregnant once more soon after. For respectability's sake, Godwin did marry her, though they lived apart, and when she died in childbed, he raised both her daughters. Their child, Mary, ran off with Percy Shelley at 16, and went on to write *Frankenstein,* a novel full of awareness of the physical and emotional complexities of childbearing and of parent/child relationships, and of the risks and attractions of knowledge.

Though radical in its day, Wollstonecraft's situation rhymes with those of quite a few of the women I interviewed, who spent their twenties in school and in establishing themselves at work. As one woman put it, "for me in my twenties, a lot of my emotional survival depended on proving myself through work." You could say that Mary Wollstonecraft had a lot riding on that, too. And it makes sense that she would wait until she was established as her own woman before having children (she looked forward to educating them according to her new systems). Even her single mother status, though not her choice, fit her independent philosophy.

In the eighteenth century and for most of the centuries prior (there were exceptional moments for the well-to-do here and there in the middle ages), girls didn't get much schooling. The kinds of knowledge that led to a wider worldview or a better-paying job were available only to boys. The circular logic had long run that, since girls hadn't been educated, they couldn't think very well, so there was no point in educating them: sex, childbearing, and housework suited them best. But a new day dawned (slowly) with the Enlightenment—Locke's concept of the mind as a *tabula rasa* didn't distinguish by sex. In the United States, the emerging democracy implicitly recognized the value of all citizens (though the logic didn't fully unroll until 1920). And, to cut to the chase, after years of gradual increase, women today comprise about 52 percent of all college students (just our proportion in the general populace) and a growing proportion of students in all graduate schools.

With few exceptions (4.5 percent), all the women I've interviewed graduated from college (the exceptions had some college, were missing just a credit or two, or had an associate's and/or a vocational degree). More than half have a graduate degree of some sort. Proportionately, my interview group was more educated than the group of new later moms overall,[11] but waiting to start your family until you've completed your education (since for many, starting a family means a de facto end to schooling) is a key factor in the readiness effect. Indeed, education is a factor that affects most women today. The rise in women's schooling plays a big role in the rising age-at-first-birth worldwide—in the United States, the average age is now 25.2 overall and 30.14 among college graduates (2003 CDC figures). Millions of women who used to go straight from high school to marriage and kids now take the college route, and they often spend several years at work before eventually starting their families.

Women who have their first child at or after 35 have a high rate of education. While 60 percent of new later moms giving birth for the first time in 2003 had a BA or more, that was true of just 26 percent of all first-time moms; 80 percent of new later moms had at least some college; and 95 percent of new later moms had a high school diploma in 2003.[12] The increased education rate happens partly because new later moms are older and have had more time to finish their degrees. But a big part of the new later mom phenomenon has to do with many women's choice to get the degree in hand before going on to devote themselves to their families. For many, it's a preparatory step that puts them in position to get the working life they want and the salary they need to contribute to the support of a twenty-first-century brood. As one later mom put it, "a lot of my history was, first, search for self and work that would be meaningful, and some of it was driven by fear that I had to take care of myself, financially." Education underpins all those searches.

Educated women become eligible for jobs that used to be just for men. These jobs offer higher salaries and more cultural cachet. And education provides the tools for deciphering the cultural codes, as one science-savvy later mom explains:

> Of course through the education I know vastly more than I would without it. I don't think it's really altered my kind of intelligence, if it does for anybody. But what it has given me more than anything else is the tools for thinking through a different kind of problem. And also knowing how it is that other people are beginning to operate. When I hear a certain kind of argument being formulated, I can put it in a framework that makes it manageable. I don't feel at all powerless in the world.

While lack of education reduced women to "ignorance and dependency" and made *them* miserable, Wollstonecraft argued that it also badly served the children they raised. Women needed to know more in order to be good models and teachers. In my interviews more than two centuries later, I heard the same argument quite a few times, from the side of experience. As a result of her own education, **Amy**, a lawyer and mother at 36 and 38, feels she's better able to guide her kids: "I value education and learning for its own sake. I think that I tend to model for my children learning new things, encouraging them to learn, to grow—encouraging them to get the most out of their education." **Marcy**, a professor who had her boy at 39, says,

> I do have a sense of myself as being someone who's going to be informed and not just park them in front of the television or not let them eat junk food. I mean, I think all mothers probably feel that

way, but hopefully I'll have some tools for helping them avoid some of the many pitfalls that seem to be surrounding them in modern culture.

Claudia, an adoptive mother at 45, now 53 and the owner of a small firm, has seen a lot of the world since finishing her education and counts that in what she can offer her daughter: "My [formal] education has given me the opportunity to have some pretty high-level jobs, I've traveled all over the world. And I can bring different perspectives from different cultures to the table." It's not just the mothers who benefit from their own education, children do too.

Ann Crittenden (motherhood scholar and new later mom) points out that, for the past two centuries, the expanding education of mothers has supported the expanding need of capitalism for more highly educated citizens. As the work world demanded more from its workers, she notes,

> the mounting demands of child-rearing . . . provided the rationale for the education of women. . . . Literate mothers devoured magazines offering "how-to" advice on child health and discipline and reminding them that they were shaping "the character of the whole of society." Again and again the message of the educational reformers of the Enlightenment was repeated: Successful child-rearing requires a kinder, gentler, more patient hand, and an enormous amount of care and vigilance. Cold, rigid authoritarianism could not do the job of instilling in children the desirable qualities of self-reliance, honesty, industry, and thrift. Thus women were recruited to the crucial task of producing the kind of human capital that the modern industrial economy needed.[13]

As women's education spread, so did the family-planning movement, and the birth rate fell. Nowadays, highly educated mothers spend intense amounts of time stimulating creativity in small numbers of children, preparing those kids to be the innovative workers the market now demands. But they're not always with those kids full time. These same moms also contribute directly to the climate of innovation since many of them work, or have in the past and will again.

For the women I spoke to, education was a key first step on the road to readiness. It can lead to satisfying work, provides a scene for social growth, and offers a chance to see a bit of the world. And it means the first big step on the road to more money. This last point got lots of mention—women want a good salary both because it allows them to be a contributing partner in a twenty-first-century marriage and because it allows them to support themselves if the marriage fails (or if they're going it alone in the first place). **Ellen**, a teacher who became a mother in her late thirties and early forties, remembers that her husband started talking about kids before she had a good job.

> He'd say, "Why aren't we having kids?" "We should get serious and have kids." I didn't want to have kids, if I could not support them by myself. . . . I'd watched my mother, who had five kids. And from my perspective as her child, I always felt that she was trapped by her lack of ability to—I mean she couldn't leave my father because her terminal degree was just an undergraduate degree and she'd never worked really. I don't know when actually that formed in my mind, but that was there somehow.

Avis, a businesswoman and mother at 35 and 37, harbored the same concern:

> [My parents] married straight out of college. . . . And they had me 10 months after they got married. So I *knew* I didn't want that, cause my parents' marriage wasn't great—my dad was an alcoholic . . . and my mom stayed in the marriage; he always had managed to keep pretty good jobs, but she stayed in the marriage purely because she felt she couldn't raise us on her own. So I knew I never wanted

that—that was another reason I always knew that I wanted to work, just so that if anything ever turned horrible in my marriage I wouldn't be in it just for the money.

Olivia, a mother at 39, had a successful career that paid her very well, but after her baby arrived, the heavy time commitment became too much, and she's now at home. Her husband Jim has done well, too. From an early age, her own mother's situation warned her against financial dependence:

> I think she found herself with a very—a bad partner, a crummy partner. After the first or the second child, the realization of who my dad was as a human being dawned on her. I have said to her, "You know, why didn't you leave?" and she says, "Well you kids would have had nothing, and we would have been in an apartment, and I couldn't have gone back to my father. I would have been a single woman being a teacher with three children. You guys would have had nothing, nothing, nothing." So she stayed for economic reasons, feeling like we wouldn't have a washing machine if she left my father.

Taking that history to heart, Olivia waited "until I felt that I could afford to have my daughter separately even from Jim, and that together we could afford to have her many times over, and that I wasn't scared. And to this day I have my own nest egg. I'm not going to leave now, but it was very frightening to me to hear my mother say, 'I am trapped.'" Education and the good job it can lead to means that a marriage gone bad doesn't have to be a source of endless misery. Many of the women I spoke with mentioned that similar anxieties kept them from leaving work, even if they could afford to. Having the assurance that you *can* leave is sometimes the best insurance that you won't want to.

In the early days, women who attended college, and especially women who got advanced degrees, were less likely than the general population to marry and even less likely to have children. But in the intervening one hundred or so years, much has changed. Now women with a college degree are more likely to be married than are women without the degree and equally likely to be moms, and women with advanced degrees are edging toward equality in marriage numbers with women without them (less than a 5 percent difference and descending). These women often do put marriage or children on hold while they get their degrees, but where before they were exceptional and hard to marry off, now they're part of the mainstream and attractive to their peers. They just start their families later.[14]

The nature of both work and marriage has changed. Where before the work that followed advanced degrees was a male province, defined by the assumption that the workers had a wife at home, that world is shifting to accommodate a big influx of women. And marriage, opines researcher Elaina Rose, author of a 2004 University of Washington study on the subject, "has become less about what economists refer to as 'specialization and exchange'—the wife taking responsibility for the home while the husband brings home the bacon—and more about shared roles and commonality of backgrounds." More like a fuller version of the "companionate marriage" that Worth Tuttle expected when she started out.

CHAPTER 2

Ready

Willing and Able

There was no way I was ready to have children in my twenties. I knew I wanted to work . . . to be the best at what [I] do. . . . [Now my husband and I] have been to-gether forever, so we're in such a good place to have kids, and we were so ready for it. And I think . . . your kids are happy if you're happy, and we're both really happy.

—DORCAS,
TV commentator, mom at 38 and 39

The word "ready" came up over and over in my talks with new later moms. And if they didn't mention the word itself, the concept shimmered in the margins of the conversation, as they explained how they felt either more *willing* or more *able* to parent than they would have ten years earlier.

It turns out that "ready" for kids generally means some special combination of "willing" and "able" particular to each woman. Quite a few felt *willing* now, where they didn't before, because they'd succeeded in getting some important life experience under their belts, whether it was something they'd dreamed of doing or considered a necessary first step, like traveling the world, establishing themselves in the work they love, finishing their education, or having the freedom to party until dawn as often as they liked. Others didn't feel willing until they had met the right guy (or, sometimes, the right gal). Unlike their mothers' generation for whom pressure to marry and bear children by a certain age often felt irresistible (whether or not Mr. Right had shown up yet), these women felt free to hold out for a real match. Or, if they married and then found out the hard way that they'd picked wrong, they held off on kids and divorced quickly, moving on to apply the knowledge gained from their mistakes to the process of choosing husband-number-two, the man who *would* be the father of their children.

Feeling *able*, for these new later moms, often meant feeling financially prepared. For many women, waiting can have a big positive effect on salary. Waiting also meant becoming *emotionally able* for quite a few—a condition helped in many cases by several years of therapy, either on the actual couch or through the life therapy that is the process of maturing and distancing yourself from whatever was dysfunctional about the family you grew up in.

❖ PROFILE: Melanie, New Mother at 35 and 38

Melanie, a dentist and the mother of two teenagers, joined the new later motherhood trend in its early days; she had her son at 35 in the mid-eighties and her daughter three years later at 38. Now 54, Melanie exudes a calm self-confidence. She can speak from experience to later moms with younger kids. Trim and attractive from years as a weekend runner, Melanie looks like a friendly and efficient suburban mom, but one with a life of her own as well as a life lived for her kids. She is the kind of person you can trust to be thoughtful and honest with you if you come to her with a question, but who won't waste a lot of time on small talk.

Back in the eighties, significantly fewer women had their first baby at 35 plus than do today, and Melanie didn't particularly plan to wait. Like many of her friends, she got married when she graduated from college. The newlyweds moved to the big city, and she worked as a journalist while putting him through school. Melanie soon found that her BA didn't get her the job she wanted, so, aiming for better credentials and a pay raise, she enrolled in a degree program that would help her move up the ranks as a health reporter. Once there, all her plans started shifting. She explains:

> About midway through that program, I'm still working full time, and I decided I don't want to do this for the rest of my life. I had always been interested in health-care, but stumbled in high school with math and science, so I didn't pursue that, and pursued the journalism thing instead. Long story short, I decided to look into going to medical or dental school and [went to the local university] at night and on the weekends and did all my math and science.
>
> And then I started looking at what to do. . . . I found that dentists were happier people, felt like they were in more control of their lives than physicians were. So I got accepted to dental school, and he wanted a divorce. You know how it goes. But that turned out to be, as they frequently do, the best thing that ever happened to me. We had no children. He went on and got married, and I went to dental school and I met my current husband [a lawyer] when I was a junior. I graduated from dental school when I was 31, and [we] got married in June. And we waited about four years before we had children. So there were lots of reasons not to be having kids earlier, most of it having to do with financial considerations, and *I* just wasn't ready. I must have known that [the first husband] wasn't the one.

With a new degree under her belt, Melanie gets married again. But this time there's a difference—she's had time to get her bearings. After looking around a bit, she's figured out what she wants, both in terms of her work and her love life. This time she *is* ready. Whereas career-number-one had been a default, her ultimate career choice fit her strongest interest and reflected her grown-up sense of what would make her happiest in the long run. And whereas husband-number-one had been something of a brat, husband-number-two was prepared to be a partner, and that's what she now knew she needed. They spent a few years getting to know each other as a couple, and after four years of marriage, they had their first child. ❖

❖ PROFILE: **Rita, New Mom at 45 via Egg Donation**

Rita, who married for the first time at 40, has a different story, but one with many of the same underlying themes. At 45, she's the exuberant mother of a happy 9-month-old, but for a long time she didn't think she'd ever want kids. She knew from high school that she wanted a career, so she got a graduate degree, then found work in an international corporation. She loved her fast-paced work and loved seeing the world.

> I was just having such a great time. One of the wonderful things about my business is that when you get successful, it's just like finding the pot of gold at the end of the rainbow. . . . It's hard, but it's so much fun. You're constantly getting information, and you're at the top. . . . People respect you and they appreciate what you do. So you get this kind of gratification, which makes it fun, and then you're well compensated. You get to travel, you meet a lot of people, and you're entertaining, and you're eating at all of the best restaurants, and you're just having a great time.
>
> My mom was really funny, she was like, "Are you ever going to get married?" And I'm like, "Of course not, why would I want to do that? Look at what I'm doing here. I mean I've stayed at the finest hotels. I travel. . . ." I mean, I would just do whatever I wanted. . . . And I never had any desire or thought that I wanted to get married or have a family. It just wasn't there. Not even in college. I was going to have

a career. . . . I was that generation that came out of high school [in the early seventies], and the women before us, they're out there burning their bras and doing all of this stuff. They're struggling with their families, and they're getting divorced, and you're seeing all that. And you're hearing about all of these horrible stories of women getting divorced and penniless and struggling. You know that's what we're hearing, that's my generation. . . . It just made me clear I was never going to have that problem.

But over time, things changed. The fast pace eventually took a toll. Though she kept working, Rita started looking for other sources of satisfaction. She broke off with the boyfriend she'd been dating for years, but who had never inspired the next step. A few months later, at 38, she met Frank, the man she'd marry.

Though they knew they wanted a child, they took a while to get started. When they did, Rita had turned 42—a point at which many women cannot get pregnant. Fertility is *the* key area in which women do not naturally become more able with age. In fact, between 40 and 43, most women (except for a small percentage) quickly become much less able or definitely *un*able to conceive by standard means. So Rita and Frank moved on from discussion of IVF to egg donation, a solution with which they are very happy. At 45, she gave birth to a beautiful baby boy. "I could not have done it better if I had done it myself," says Rita. "I just could not have, he's fabulous." Rita now spends her time enjoying combining motherhood with well-paid part-time work.

There are times when I look at all of those young mothers out there, and I go, "God I wish I was younger." But I am so much happier having had the career and had the success and made the choices that I've made that I truly appreciate my son in a way I know I could not have appreciated when I was younger. I would have worried, because I know when I was younger, I was worried about what I was missing. If I was not out every night, I wanted to know what I was missing. I burned that candle at both ends *for years*. . . . I mean, we joke about it all the time, cause I couldn't burn that candle the way I did at all anymore.

Both the pleasures of work and the demanding process of establishing themselves in their jobs lead many women to wait. ❖

❖ PROFILE: Sylvia, Mother at 34 and 42

Sylvia, now 50, went to law school right after college and started with a firm in the early 1980s. In her late twenties, she met and married Hugh. As young black professionals in a gradually integrating corporate world, they both had a firm sense of purpose. Sylvia's situation was further complicated by gender:

I was not ready from a career perspective to allow anybody to make me have to change focus [when I married]. . . . I wanted to be able to work late hours and take business trips and compete. . . . There was only one female partner at [my firm] at the time, and she had no children, and she wasn't married, and it was clear for many of us who were married and trying to climb that ladder that you couldn't have children and successfully do it. . . .

And part of that, in all honesty, was that when I entered the profession it was a new profession for minorities and women. . . . So if you look around at that group of women that I entered with, the common element is that all of our kids tend to be around the same age. Which means all of us deferred, because we all knew [that was the best move] from a career perspective—you know, the firm didn't have a maternity policy, so that sent a message to you that there was nothing inherently built in the system to support women if they did have children. . . . I needed to explore. I needed to push as far as I could career-wise just to see how far it would go. So I put off having children.

For the first few years of their marriage, both Hugh and Sylvia focused on their careers.

And so I said, you know, we're climbing together, and it was perfectly fine. And then, I think what happened was, I started thinking, you know, we can't do this forever. I mean, work 12 hours a day and travel. We used to pass in the halls. And I think the first time for him [was when] we both became god parents; I do believe that had a huge influence on our lives. . . . And he said to me one day, . . . "You know, I really think this is something I want to do." And he was close to the partnership . . . but at that point in time, I was still growing a law practice, and I said, "I don't know if it's the right time." And then finally, we both agreed when the time had come, and we said, "Okay, we think we need to do this," and we did.

Their daughter Carolyn arrived seven years into their marriage, when Sylvia was 34 and Hugh was 33. They planned for one child, but they found parenthood more exciting and satisfying than they'd expected. They decided they wanted another child when Carolyn was 4.

This kind of change of plan happens not infrequently. Not only does parenting introduce moms and dads to a new set of relationship pleasures, especially if they're in a good situation for all concerned, but it gives them a new kind of competence that also satisfies. A first child requires that parents build many new skill sets. And once those skills develop, lots of people want to use them again—both because they're fun and because in the process of developing them parents are bound to make a few mistakes. Additional children give parents the chance to get it right—or at least righter.

But at 38, Sylvia's body did not cooperate. They tried for a while, and then, rather than press on down the fertility road, they decided adoption made the most sense.

> Hugh and I sat down, and we saw no reason that we couldn't parent [an adopted] child—it didn't *have* to be biological, we just wanted to have another child. And so the adoption made more sense. And so we did it. I mean, like he said, there are children in the world already. And so there was no compelling reason why we had to physically or biologically have this child. So, you know, we did it.

Sylvia had just passed her 42nd birthday at the time they adopted James, and today they are a very happy family. ❖

❖ PROFILE: Amanda, New Mom at 45 by Adoption

Amanda, now 49, a techie, had been married and widowed before she adopted a child as a single mom at 45. Shortly thereafter, she met, fell in love with, and married a man she met at her church—a man who felt ready to become a husband and a father at once. Amanda feels that the years she spent without children helped her develop healthy ideas that her parents weren't able to transmit about parenting and relationships:

> I am a much better mother than I would have been as a younger woman—after a *lot* of therapy, okay! [laughing] I would not have been a very good parent. I think I would have been a very—I learned a lot about myself [in therapy], and I learned how, you know, when you go through that you kind of re-parent yourself? I got a little practice on how to do it right, as opposed to what I saw at home. . . . Stuff comes up when you parent. You deal with a lot of stuff that happened to you when you were a child. How you deal with it is the

whole crux of the situation, and after years of looking inside, you find you look differently. You handle it differently.

Having lost a husband to illness, Amanda knows firsthand that life is brief, and you do well to make the most of every minute. Though she wanted children in her first marriage, her husband did not. And now she feels it was for the best.

> I think what I did was perfect; you know, I was sad that I could not have given birth to my daughter, but it would have been her. It wouldn't have been another child. It would have been her—you know, from a spiritual perspective. And so I just know that this was the time. This was how it had to be. I think that the way that you become a family is totally unimportant. It's just a different story. ❖

❖ PROFILE: Allison, New Mom at 37 via Sperm Donation

Allison (businesswoman, now 39) had been in a committed gay partnership with Nell for eight years before becoming a mom via sperm donation at 37. She also found maturity an important benefit of waiting for kids:

> [Motherhood] has been wonderful. And frustrating and terrific and trying. And I know that if I was any younger, I wouldn't have been able to do it. . . . I was too selfish, too busy, too impatient—yeah, all those things. . . . I don't know if there was any one thing that occurred [to change that]. I think it was just the build up of experience with people, getting me to the point where, I mean, I had a lot of work to do on myself, and I think just being in business and . . . having relationships every day with many people, who are so different

and so varied, taught me about myself and moved me along in my emotional maturity. I think that got me there. . . .

I think there should be a law against marriage and having children until you're 30! Because I just don't think you get it. I mean, your twenties are all about you and finding out who *you* are. And I just think at 30 things turn, they turn.

And there are other kinds of maturity benefits as well. Because Allison had an established reputation and a senior position, she could shape her working hours to fit her new family dynamic—one of several benefits of being the boss. ❖

❖ PROFILE: Veronica, New Mom at 35

The new later moms I spoke with were educated, middle to upper income, and urban, but that's not always where they started out. Veronica, a lawyer whose mother was 15 when Veronica was born, had her daughter last year at 35. She explains:

I'm Hispanic, and my family tends to have their kids very young. [But] we're transitioning into where, I'm like the first wave of the family to actually get an education, but now my cousins, who are much younger than me, they're all going to college. But prior to that, it was more working class—I knew I always wanted to have kids, having lots of cousins and all that. But I didn't want to do it the way I'd seen my aunts do it, and my mom do it. I wanted to wait till I was more established and able to fully care for a child. I did go to college; I wanted to be able to support myself. I knew I always wanted to have kids. I was waiting for that opportunity.

Education has long been the principal means to class mobility in America, but historically, men have been the ones who've gotten the degrees and climbed the social ladder. Although often it is not an option, nowadays when women born to working-class parents defer having children to pursue schooling and job advancement they may end up rearing middle-class children. ❖

❖ PROFILE: **Delia, New Mom at 37**

About half the women I spoke with spent several years married before trying for kids (in one case almost fifteen years, and in another case almost twenty), while others married late (sometimes for the second time) and had their kids very quickly thereafter. Delia, a marketer now almost 40, married at 34, had a daughter at 37, and plans to start trying for baby-number-two in a few months. She had a clear sense of how she wanted to spend her twenties, and it didn't include children:

> I did not think that I would get married and start a family until I was 30. And I knew this when I was in college. It was just, my reasoning is, I felt that, number one, once you get your degree, you're going to want to get out there and get to work, and you're not just going to go out there and be at the top. You're going to have to roll up your sleeves, and you're going to have to work. And in order to do that, you're going to be very selfish with your time. Your job could take you to another city; you may relocate a couple of times. And so, I felt in all honesty, in order to put—I like to put 100 percent to 150 percent into everything that I do. And so, I felt that if I were to devote that kind of time to my family, I would have to go through that selfish phase and then come back out of it to where, okay, I've got this under my belt, and now I'm ready to give. I'm ready to have a partner that I can compromise with, that it's not my way or the highway; it's a true relationship, partnership. And then from that solid foundation, grow a family. So I didn't think that was something that I'd be mature enough or ready for until I was at least 30.

But when she turned age 31, she suddenly felt *very* ready. And in a move that several of the women I've talked to have described, Delia became very efficient about finding a life partner:

> I know the exact moment. A client on an out-of-town business trip took me to a professional football game. So I'm sitting there, with a guy on the right side, [another] man on the other side, and I'm sitting there thinking, this is great; however, I'd rather be at home right now with a family, hanging out. So I came back from the trip, and I was dating someone; we had been dating a couple of years at the time. And I said, "You know what, I'm ready for a family." . . . And he wasn't ready for a family, because he looked at me, and he goes, "I think you're—no, I think it's all in your head." And I said, "No, . . . I've just reached this point, I'm ready." And we ended up breaking things off because he wasn't ready to get married and have a family, and I was very appreciative that he was honest with me.

Over the course of the next year, Delia went out with four men in quick succession, rejecting the first three out of hand. She knew within a few weeks of meeting the last guy in that series that he was the one. ❖

❖ PROFILE: Diana, New Mom at 38 and 40

Diana, a software manager who married for the second time at 37 and had her children at 38 and 40, describes the later dating dynamic:

> I don't think there's as much angst about it. And I don't want to deglamorize it or deromanticize [it], but there's almost a process. I mean, by the time you're 35, you date somebody, you say, "Can I be

married to this person, or not?" And if the answer's *not*, then you don't go out with him again. And then you go find the next person— or maybe you don't, if you're not looking to be married. But I did want to get married; I did want to have kids. I mean, I wasn't speed dating or anything. . . . I wasn't wasting my time on people who were just taking up my time. You know, if I was dating somebody, it was because I thought he had potential.

There's a certain efficiency born of deadline pressure. ❖

❖ PROFILE: Margaret, New Mom at 37, 39, and 42

Margaret took a more leisurely approach. She invested time in law school, because she'd learned something from her mom's example. "Education was always very important in my family," she notes.

I think it's probably even more so because I'm Hispanic. My dad went to college. He went on the GI Bill, which he's very proud of. He got an accounting degree. But my mother's the brains. She finished high school in the States, but came over when she was about 14. She's just a really, really smart woman, always wished she had gone to college. But got married young. So education was very important.

Margaret and both her siblings got advanced degrees.

Her mother managed to work her way up the corporate ladder even without a degree, but the conflict between early marriage and work success resonated for Margaret. After law school, she entered the corporate world and met Stephen, the man who would become her husband. They married when she was 32 and he was 28. They knew they wanted kids, but they didn't want to rush into that stage of life.

We always knew that we wanted to wait to make sure that we knew each other before we had children. So we spent about five years married, traveling, and just relaxing, happy hours with friends. And when I turned 35, we knew that it was time that we should think about it. I actually had some issues getting pregnant at the beginning [with endometriosis—a problem that can occur at any age], which were pretty much taken care of with two laparoscopies and some hormone treatments. And as soon as the doctor said that it was time, that we could start trying, I got pregnant within the first couple of months.

But along with wanting to spend time as a couple, Margaret and Stephen wanted to be financially set.

I would not say it was career so much that influenced our decision around kids. It was more economically where we thought we'd be. Regardless of where I was in my career, we knew we needed a house; we wanted the cars to be in good shape. So we wouldn't have major outlays of money after—it goes hand in hand. It was that we needed to be in this position, economically or financially.

They managed that, and they are now the parents of two boys and a girl. ❖

❖ PROFILE: Colleen, New Mom at 34

Colleen saw my flier and insisted on being part of this study—even though she didn't quite make the age cutoff—because she felt that she was part of the trend to delay and had lots to say (it's true the cutoff at 35 is a statistical convenience, based on the categories in which the government collects data on births). Like Margaret, Colleen also had several reasons for waiting, including her husband's own sense of un-readiness: "he thought it would require a lot of giving up of himself, which he didn't know if he was up to the task." She had her baby after being in a committed relationship with her husband for nine years and married for seven of those—they waited on purpose to establish themselves both personally and professionally. Her own mother was 19 when Colleen was born—she got married because she was pregnant—and divorced when she was 22. Colleen remembers her mother "living in the backyard of her mother-in-law's house in a trailer with a man she didn't love. Pretty bad." She wanted to do things differently:

I thought that we should own a home. And I thought that we should have stable jobs, ones we'd held for two years or more. And I thought that we should be relatively sure that we were going to stay married. Well, at least for a while. Because my parents got married because they got pregnant with me—I didn't think that was a good way to enter into parenthood, less than ideal let's say. So I thought definitely we should enjoy being around each other. We should do a few things that we thought were important. . . . We took some trips together, we went to Europe a couple of times, which was important to both of us. So I felt like I was at a place in my career where I could relax a little bit. Because I kind of had a sharp ascent, in terms of after grad-uate school, I worked for [a company] and founded a division, and I felt like I had enough money and staff under me that I could breathe a little bit. And it wasn't necessarily intentional, but it all worked out really well.

Colleen could relax because her job was secure (and her husband's situation had firmed up, too). She didn't have to worry about her boss's view on pumping milk in the office—she was the boss. She gets her work done, but she can set her own schedule when needed without fearing that her job will disappear. ❖

Quite a few women told me that the difference between their own experience and their mothers' revolved around choice. For millennia, women have had motherhood thrust upon them whether or not they felt prepared for it. Although sometimes this has worked out well both for the children and the parents, more than a few mothers have felt ill-situated to tend their children as well as they would have liked, either for financial reasons, for reasons of personal maturity or education level, or for lack of the right partner.

For **Susan** (writer and new mother at 40), a woman with a very responsible full-time job, her experience of motherhood seems very different from her own mother's experience. She explains her take on it:

> I'm not at all ambivalent about the responsibility that [my daughter] creates in my life. I was so ready for it. And I remember saying out loud to [my husband] and to my friends, "I want more responsibility in my life. I'm sick of having nothing to do. Nobody beholden to me. It's time." My mother was resentful of the responsibility; . . . she just didn't feel like it. She just didn't feel like driving me [around]. And you know, I get bone tired, but I don't resent the baby for waking me up, or whatever it is. So I think that's different.

Susan had come to a point where her job felt under control, and she felt prepared to move into a new phase of life, one that combined work with reveling in the home life, including diapers, endless baseball games or gymnastics classes, homework, and responsibility. A big part of the new later motherhood story is plain, old-fashioned family happiness.

CHAPTER 3

Moms in the Workplace

The Benefits of Age

*I actually think a woman working nine to two
can probably do a full day of a man's work.*

—AMY,
mother at 36 and 38 and
flextime lawyer

Somewhere in the recesses of childhood, I remember being in the backseat of our family car, my dad at the wheel, and he was bragging about my mom. A nursery school teacher in the Philadelphia public school system, my mom had taken a skills test that all the teachers had to take. When she'd gone to pick up the results, the person at the desk looked down and protested, "No, that can't be right—it's too high!" Of course it *was* right, and we all felt proud to have a high scorer right there in our car. Nobody wondered why she was teaching nursery school.

Not that it's not fine to be a nursery school teacher, and if you'd asked my mom, she might have chosen that out of all fields. We all hope that smart people who love their work are teaching our children. But students who choose to earn a degree in early childhood education today do so in a very different world than our mothers did—it's not their only option, while back then, it very nearly was.

The relation of gender to work has changed a lot over the past fifty years. Though most of my mother's peers worked before they had children, and some, like her, kept on working, their career paths tended to be much less professional than middle-class women's careers today. Back then, women (of all classes) worked for pay mostly in areas that looked a lot like what they were already doing at home: domestic work, educating children, nursing, and helping men stay organized (often in clerical or secretarial jobs). People called these jobs "women's work," and they tended to involve low wages, partly because they so strongly resembled what women at home did for free. We still fill more of those service jobs than men, but many women have other choices now as well, which means some hold jobs that pay high salaries, and some of the low salaries have begun to rise to stay competitive. Women still make less, but nowadays it's less less.

In bragging on my mom, I want to brag on your mom, too. All our moms and grandmas had talents they couldn't develop in the limited employment field women faced in the past. Or if they did get to exercise their talents, it was generally at the low end of the status and pay pole. Now women have many exciting options, though lots of logistical problems remain to be worked out. In appreciating the new world we operate in today, we must acknowledge the work our mothers (and sometimes our fathers) did to bring us here—it's been a long process in which each generation has learned from and built on the efforts of the one before.

One big lesson that increasing numbers of women have been learning from the women just ahead of them over the past few decades is that delaying motherhood makes work *work* better. In the course of my research, I've discovered that the new later motherhood correlates to *higher long-term salaries*—the differential is sometimes staggering. New later moms' work experience and credentials give them more clout with the boss than their younger colleagues have, putting them in a better position to negotiate a work schedule that meets their family needs. And more often now, they *are* the boss, which definitely gives them influence with HR.

There's an enormous amount to say about our changing relation to work (not less work but different), and the women I've talked to have quite a few opinions on the matter. But first, let's cut to the bottom line.

Higher Wages

New later moms work in many fields and make a wide range of salaries—some quite low. Nonetheless, many new later mothers do have higher salaries and more advanced positions in their fields not only than they did when they were younger (which might seem obvious), but also, and significantly, than women who are now their same age, with the same level of education, but who had their kids earlier. As a result, many new later moms are better off overall in terms of salary and savings than their peers who started families sooner.

My analysis of census 2000 data, correlating salary to a mother's age at first birth, indicates that, when you compare women who have the same university degrees, a mother's age at first birth links to long-term salary differences.[1] In 2000 for instance (see Figure 3.1), of the full-time working women between 40 and 45 with professional degrees (like JDs and MDs), those who'd had a first birth at 20 made an average of about $27,000, whereas their peers who were also between 40 and 45 in 2000 with professional degrees, but who'd had a first birth at 35, made $79,000. That's more than a $50,000 difference in annual salary.

Once again, that was $50,000. Per year. Would that make you pay attention? Not that every new later mom lawyer makes that much more than every earlier mom lawyer. In fact, there weren't that many women with professional degrees who'd *had* their first kid at 20—so that affects the stats. But clearly, delay has a positive relationship to wage. You can see it as you progress upward on the age scale: those women with a professional degree who'd had a first birth at 25 averaged

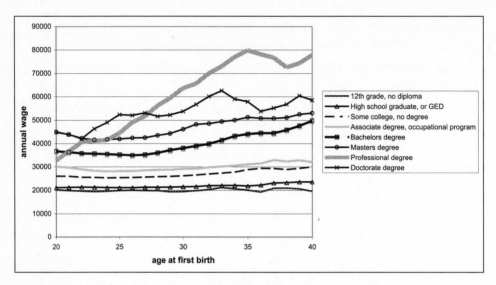

FIGURE 3.1   Women Aged 40–45 in 2000 (Average Wage in 2000 by Age At First Birth and Highest Degree)

Data derived from U.S. Census, 2000.

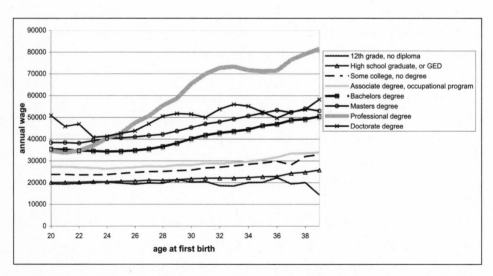

FIGURE 3.2   Women Aged 35–39 in 2000 (Average Wage in 2000 by Age at First Birth and Highest Degree)

Data derived from U.S. Census, 2000.

about $46,000 when they reached 40 to 45, while those with a first birth at 30 averaged $63,000 when they reached the 40 to 45 age range. The particular salary numbers are less the issue here than the overall upward trend linked to delay.

Why such big differences? The census doesn't tell us cause, but we can extrapolate that it wasn't the delay itself that caused the rise, but what the women involved were doing with that extra time. We can postulate that, on average, those who gave birth later got their degrees earlier than those with earlier births and spent more total time in the workforce, moving up the ladders of experience and position. These women were more likely to have not taken time out of the workforce at the time of their children's births (see Chapter 4). They were also more likely to have been in a position with some clout (or an established client base) before they had kids, so that they were less likely to lose ground when kids arrived, whether or not they took time off or reduced their work schedule for a while.

While the curve is not as steep for women with undergraduate degrees, it is notable. Among full-time working women whose highest degree was a BA and who were between 35 and 39 in 2000 (Figure 3.2), those with a first birth at 20 averaged $36,600, while those with a first birth at 35 averaged $45,300. The difference for women with BAs who were 40 to 45 in 2000 (Figure 3.1) was very similar. In the age ranges in both charts, there was a small but still visible wage difference linked to age at first birth for women without a college degree—who make up about 40 percent of the group of new later moms. (The dip in the wages of women with no diploma giving birth after 35 is due to there being very few in that category.)

My reading of the wage effect linked to delay through age 40 is supported by recent research on the effect of delay among women 16 to 36 years old. That research documents a 3 percent annual return to delay among these women (meaning women's average long-term salaries increase by 3 percent for each year they delay children)—90 percent of which return the author attributes to education and job experience gained during the delay period.[2] The women I spoke with said the same.

Women who delay motherhood often use the extra time before kids to get the schooling that gives them a leg up in the workforce, and then to establish themselves there. Contrary to old economic views that women who behaved this way were a small group essentially different from other women (less interested in kids and more work focused), this trend has been increasing steadily and significantly for thirty years. Clearly many women see positives to this way of sequencing their lives, either for personal or financial reasons or for some combination of the two, and more and more are choosing this path.[3]

Whether the delay phenomenon involves women who *purposefully* wait to have children until they've attained higher salaries to better provide for their young (to use the terminology of strategic animal behavior), whether it involves women who defer children for other reasons and, as a consequence, are rewarded with higher salaries, or whether it involves women who already earn higher salaries and, therefore, defer children because they are involved in their work, we can't tell. It may be the result of all of these causes and more. But we *can* see the effect, and you can be sure that women observing those around them can and do make these same observations. Though salary options will not be the sole criterion, they are part of the process of deciding when to start a family, and they have contributed to the growth of the trend to starting families later.

The Clout Effect

Because our work system offers few reliable options for balancing job and life for young women starting out, women have been building their own *shadow benefits system*—taking the well-being of their families into their own hands when they can't rely on employers or the government to look out for them. For many, a key component to that shadow system turns out to be delaying motherhood until they've got the clout to make their own deals. It's the standard American boot-strap story redux—only now it's the strap on a pair of Jimmy Choos or plain Mary Janes.

In order to guarantee a good wage and viable career growth, many women find it best to wait. "If I had had a baby at 30, I wouldn't have written all those front-page stories," notes **Susan**, a 40-year-old East Coast journalist and new mom who is a few rungs higher up the ladder in a job all those good stories earned her. She still works very hard but has a flexibility and an income she wouldn't have had earlier. "That's one thing I like about being an older mom," says **Fiona**, now 44, a Midwest-ern mother of two at 35 and 37, who'd been at her job twelve years when she had her first child. "You've earned the extra vacation and earned goodwill at your job, where I don't feel like 'Oh my gosh, I can't go to the kids' Fall Festival,' or whatever. I like being an older mom for many rea-sons—I didn't do it on purpose, but it's ended up much better."

Jill, now 47, a new mom for the first time at 46 (without fertility help!), has worked in her nonprofit field for more than twenty years in the Southwest. Her group of about eight friends, who also had their first kids in their forties ("but I'm kind of the latest of the group"), have similar job histories. From her own experience and from watching theirs, she's found that "the higher your position, the easier it is to have the flexibility to work from home. I don't see that on the lower end—some of the employees like administrative assistant or a lab assistant, you don't have the option of being able to work at home, which you do at a higher level." Because of her responsibility, she doesn't have the flexibility to work three-quarter time ("it's a full-time job"), but she can "hook up at home, and work from home if my child, say, has a doctor's appointment."

Moms who've established themselves in their jobs, moms with work experience who've achieved a higher post in the office hierarchy, can use their experience as a negotiating chip and swing personal deals that piggyback on the (so far only semi-successful) efforts of HR ac-tivists to change the available work/life options.[4]

Work/life options vary a lot by industry (pharmaceutical reps have much more flexibility than, say, lawyers on a partner track). Because many businesses haven't yet figured out how to meld effective business practice with family friendliness, women in those fields have had to forge their own tools. New later motherhood has become such a tool for women building their own flexible systems. It provides the *clout effect*. **Leslie**, a highly skilled professional and new later mom, explains:

> The irony is I'm one of maybe two [people] in the world actively employed [in what I do]. . . . So these guys aren't going to tell me that the door's closed, to come back later. Nobody else in the world has done all the projects that I've done, and it's an emerging field at a really interesting point in time. And of course, I realize if I had not waited I wouldn't be in the position to be here.

As a result of her position, Leslie doesn't have to worry when she carves out time to be with her child, whereas at an earlier stage in her career she might have: "I'm not giving anything up when I spend time with her, and that was, I know, a big problem for my mother—she really felt that her life was being sacrificed to spend time with me, to be a mom."

Not all new later moms are the leading experts in their fields, but they often have experience and credentials that make them extremely valuable to their employers, who are willing to negotiate special deals that they are not yet prepared to make for all their workers. Because their skills are known and valued, many new later moms are in a position to negotiate for what they want—for the flexibility to set their own hours, for results-based work as opposed to specific hours on the job, for job shares, for salaried part-time work, for highly paid hourly work without the time commitment of partnership, or some other arrangement that best suits their situation. Because work/life integration has not been achieved across the board, and even within individual companies may be only spottily available, the ability to set their own schedule and create their own terms can make an enormous difference. **Carey**, a financial services manager who married in her late thirties and adopted at 43, finds that, in general, "the older, more successful you are, the more flexibility is just built into your career. Although it's flexibility *you* have to take, not the right somebody gives to you."

In a move taken by several of the lawyers I've talked to, **Amy** left a partner-track position in a firm for an in-house corporate job that paid better overall but that didn't have the bonus potential or the long hours. A few years later she moved again, as she explains with a beautiful drawl: "In my [corporate] position there really wasn't any room for career growth. While I think as a working mother sometimes the growth has to be lower, it shouldn't be *no* growth. And I felt like I'd learned all I could learn in that position, and I was doing the same things over and over."

In addition, the new job offered her more money. "It's always been my philosophy not to take a pay cut," she observes. "I know people who have taken pay cuts in order to get a deal that's more suitable to them, but I've always tried not to. In fact, I've always felt like, well, I should be making more, progressively."

The new position in a firm, not on the partner track but very well paid, had a ceiling on hours—about the same amount of time as being in-house. "They wanted me over there because I could mentor young associates and also because I had substantial trial experience. And whereas they may have some associates who can do the work, they didn't have the experience I had or the client management and counseling skills that I had." The clout effect gives Amy a big salary. And she can take her kids to school, be home for dinner by six, and schedule in school plays in the middle of the day when they're on.

Of course many new later moms, like plenty of people in other categories, make nowhere near as much money as Amy, partly because most professions don't pay that much and partly, Amy observes, because many women don't have the skill or the nerve to negotiate a fair wage. Her job has given her a window on many hires and she reports

I['ve] got to say . . . that women don't negotiate well on the front end for what they want. They don't ask for more money. If they've been given an offer they say "Thank you, I accept. I will go to the dance, and aren't you cute." They don't say, to make a funny analogy, "Well I really want you to pick me up later, and I want a more expensive restaurant . . . a better corsage." They don't feel like they have bargaining power—they feel like they're lucky to be allowed to continue their careers at less than full time.

But Amy has learned this skill, and like Amy, new later moms as a group position themselves to break the self-effacing attitude she describes. Amy's goal, as she says, is to always make more. That's a goal that many women have yet to learn to be comfortable with.

Because new later moms have accrued lots of work experience before they begin bargaining about time, they know the value of asking for what they really want (if you don't ask, you don't get it). So like Amy, they can more often combine flexibility (whether on a full-time or part-time schedule) *and* higher wages (relative to the going rate in their line of work). That's an important difference from the usual pattern in which, if higher wages and flexibility are options at all, women have to choose one or the other.

And when women work part time, Amy notes (as did quite a few of the women I spoke with),

[they] tend to be very productive. . . . They're saying, "I don't have time to stand and talk at a coffee bar." In my case, . . . I want to get my work done so I can get out of here, even though I love my work. . . . I actually think a woman working nine to two can probably do a full day of a man's work.

That's the multitasking carryover from the motherhood drill—or perhaps more accurately, the parenting drill. Amy could have substituted the words "active parent" for "woman" and described the same effect. Someone with kids to pick up at three will be very efficient in organizing her or his time and effort between nine and two.

Job experience also underpins the ability to multitask well. If you've built up a work history, you've built up a knowledge base so you don't have to spend as much time figuring things out; you've established relationships that mean you don't have to prove yourself to fellow workers. You can go straight to dealing with the task at hand, working at maximum efficiency.

Though personal work/life deals often function well in individual cases, these deals might have a downside for women in the long run. They may create mommy-ghettoes, ensuring that, although they do well financially, the women who take these deals don't attain the upper reaches of management, don't get the biggest bucks, and don't shape company policy directly, at least not while they're actively mothering. Nonetheless, because they haven't stepped off the track in the short term, just eased up a bit, there's great likelihood that some of these moms will step up their involvement in management later.

The Benefits of Age

Starting families later gives women more time to establish themselves in the early stages of their careers—to get the extra degree if it's required, to learn the rules of the game, to develop the on-the-job skills, and to make the connections that will get them ahead and keep them there after the kids arrive. Or if they decide to stay at home, full time or part time, having worked a good span already means they don't regret not having tried that route. And it means they're much more likely to have savings and retirement accounts (and sometimes even a paid-off mortgage) that allow them to choose to stay at home, and/or a later spouse in a position to support the family well on one, well-established income.

This is a huge story, but while the media have been preoccupied with reporting on fertility declines for women over 35, they've missed it. Women's fertility does decline with age (and men have fertility issues, too), but the over-35 crowd is the only demographic with *steadily rising* first birth rates, though 30- to 34-year-olds also show rising birth rates overall. Why are more and more women choosing the new-later-motherhood route every year? And where does the rising later-parent adoption rate fit in the story? Somehow, without the press's guidance, many women have decided that later motherhood makes the most sense for them in today's world—providing job satisfaction and financial security. For years now, women have been acting upon that knowledge in greater and greater numbers.

"In my case," notes **Dara**, a banker, "I certainly wasn't in the upper echelon financially, and I wanted a certain amount of security before I had children." She had achieved that by the time she had her first child at 36. She and her husband, also a banker, waited a year past their engagement before marrying, and she became pregnant six months later. Dara and Bob, now in their mid-forties, were intentional about their delay: "We might have gotten married earlier, but we kind of waited until we got more established in our jobs," she explains. Dara had even checked in with her gynecologist in her late twenties to make sure that waiting into her mid- to late thirties would give her time for a family. He gave her the green light. Once she and Bob felt ready, they got busy, and they now have two healthy and happy children who are less than four years apart in age. And both parents earn good wages.

Employment benefits represent only one element in the nexus of reasons why women choose to delay having children, but it's a powerful element. And this element is evidence that women who wait often do it as part of a strategy to provide well for their children and themselves. In doing so, they demonstrate their resourcefulness, their concern for their families, and their awareness that society offers few other reliable means to women who are trying to maximize their income across a career.

If the world finds the new later motherhood solution problematic, then we, as a society, need to offer other good options for combining family and career. In the meantime, the move by women in all age brackets toward a later motherhood than they might have chosen in an earlier era signals women's responsible attention to their families' welfare.

Along with the financial benefits, new later motherhood leads to gains in work satisfaction. Most of those I've met love their work for its challenges and opportunities—and the experience of meeting those challenges builds self-image. As one new later mom (now working part time) describes, "It gives me more confidence. I feel like an accomplished person. I worked a long time before I had children, fifteen years, and felt proud of what I had accomplished at work. Felt very competent in my job." That kind of experience can strengthen a woman's confidence about her choices for her children. Another later mom emphasizes the view of the work world she wants to convey to her daughter: "Not only do mommies work, but mommy's work is awesome. It's a blast!"

This sense of excitement and pleasure in work depends in large part on having advanced to a level where you feel your work matters and you can see good results from your efforts. Often that comes with advancement to a level where you call the shots—achievement that happens more easily when you can give full attention to your career from the start.

The Trickle Up

The movement of moms up the ladders of power and influence in the workplace has happened gradually but steadily—I call it the *trickle up* effect. It's happening more slowly than many had hoped, but it *is* happening. Whereas 22 percent of women workers were in managerial and professional positions in 1983, in 2002, it was 34 percent.[5] Whereas 9.6 percent of Fortune 500 board seats were held by women in 1995, that number had risen to 14.7 percent in 2005.[6] Not big rises, but they are rises.

At the same time that it gives women the clout to carve out their own deals, the trickle up feeds a gradual transformation of the culture of work that can lead in the long run to more equitable HR policies for everybody. Though there's still far to go, it's women's movement into the upper levels of the work world, along with management's efforts (and of course management includes people of both sexes) to retain their good female employees, that have brought the work/life discussion as far as it has come. A range of new benefits and flex options are increasingly available to all people, regardless of gender or family status. Two questions remain: How long is the long run? and, When will we reach the critical mass that changes the playing field and allows cultural transformation to move faster?

The women trickling up the business ladder have not all had kids later. But many have. Some have found other ways to balance work and family; for example, a good number of the female CEOs of big U.S. companies have househusbands who stay home to take care of the kids and run the household.[7] This arrangement allows the mom to concentrate on work, knowing her kids have a loving parent at home and that the dry cleaning will be picked up on time. Some female managers have defied the odds and managed to build a career and a family at the same time. And some managers have no kids: some never wanted kids, some would have been happy to have them but found other satisfactions, and some may mourn the loss of family (though given the changing fertility and adoption scene, some of those may have children yet). There is no source of clear statistics on exactly how many women fit into any one of these categories (in fact, there's an amazing dearth of statistics on family in general, even in our heavily studied world). But we see the evidence of women delaying family all around us, and it's confirmed in the birth data.

All these women collectively affect the way America does business. Sometimes they affect it directly, once they're in positions of authority.

For instance, **Annette**, mother at 36 and 38 and co-founder and CEO of a successful investment firm, offers her employees twelve weeks of paid maternity leave, as well as adoption assistance, lactation facilities, flex and work-from-home options—"because I want them to be as happy as I am." (These kinds of policies also make employees loyal.) On a smaller scale, **Melanie** the dentist allows her hygienists and receptionists to flex around kid activities and even occasionally cancels office hours when the hygienist's baby has a fever and needs to see a doctor. Echoing Annette, Melanie says, "Because I could do it, I like for other people to be able to do the same thing."

But most companies, even those headed by women, aren't so generous—yet. Nonetheless, the environment around family issues has changed mightily in the past thirty years. A study by the Work and Family Institute in 2003 found that 43 percent of workers had some access to flexibility in their work schedule (as opposed to 29 percent ten years earlier), which allowed them to accommodate both their families' and their employers' needs. A study by the Society for Human Resource Management raised that number to 57 percent in 2006.[8] That change has occurred because, in that same thirty-year span, women have flooded the workplace. In 1975, 47.4 percent of the female population with children under 18 was in the labor force, and 46.3 percent of the total adult female population. In 2005 those statistics had grown to 70.5 percent of the female population with children under 18 (down from a high of 72.9 percent in 2000) and 59.3 percent of the total adult female population (15 percent part time, and 44.3 percent full time).[9]

Work/Life Balance and the Flextime Movement

The move toward accommodating the care of families within the working world—called "work/life integration" or "balance"—began in response to the demands of talented mothers. I asked **Evelyn**, a 51-year-old HR manager who had the first of her two boys at 35, whether women managers began the movement.

No [she answered], this was done before there were women in influential positions. I think one of the major drivers is when talented women, and they don't have to be in high positions yet, they can just be up and coming, begin asking for it. And when the alternative is that they're going to leave the workforce or go somewhere else where those benefits are offered, I think it's a very powerful case for businesses to get involved. You can't really talk about these issues theoretically very well. You need someone to stick their neck out the first time and say, "I need this, and I'm willing to go somewhere else if I can't get it."

Though she didn't instigate them, Evelyn developed the family-friendly policies in her corporation because "they wanted somebody with management experience who was sort of living the issues. And that was me to a T." After a BS and an MBA, she'd married at 32, had her children at 35 and 37, and has worked full time all the way through except for her maternity leaves. Evelyn always expected to hold a job and never doubted that she could. She wanted the financial security two salaries would give her family, along with a challenging and satisfying occupation: "I was determined to make career and family combine. . . . I've worked full time through my entire career, even though I work in an area that promotes all of this part time and all of these other options for other people. *Now*, I do use a lot of flexibility."

But formerly, that flexibility wasn't an option.

It was a challenge for me when my children were young. I was promoted into this new role, and my new boss wanted to have 7 a.m. meetings. And the [off-site] childcare center opened at 6:30 . . . and when it was that early, my husband wasn't the one taking them. . . . It was tough, and I became one of the strong advocates. That's why I was so excited about moving into this new role when they were 2 and 4, because there was just a screaming need.

Evelyn's first efforts included convincing existing childcare centers in the community to open earlier and close later to accommodate the schedules of working parents. Soon afterward, her office opened its own on-site childcare center. Her employer was looking for ways to make the lives of its employees work more smoothly, and her experience gave her special insight into how to make that happen.

Corporations like the one Evelyn works for often respond to demands for innovations more quickly than public sector businesses or small companies, to do whatever's needed to stay ahead of the competition. And once one corporation within an industry innovates successfully, others often follow suit in order to compete for employees.

Among the principal changes the work/life integration movement has introduced is the concept of flextime. Flextime offers the possibility of restructuring the workweek so that *when* employees do the work doesn't matter as long as they put in the hours. Place doesn't matter either; if it makes the most sense to spend the day tending a sick child, then work gets done at home while the child naps or in the evening after bedtime. Flextime allows this kind of scheduling because it is often based on a results model—the important thing is just that the job gets done, not that any set number of hours gets worked.

Clearly flextime works better in some jobs than in others—a factory worker has to be at the job when the conveyer is running, and clients need their lawyers to be available for consultation at predictable times, usually during regular work hours. But there are ways to flex within these constraints: workers needn't always work the same shift, and lawyers can carry BlackBerrys and cell phones and consult from the soccer field. And many do.

There's plenty of resistance to the move toward expanded flexibility, but women's new expectations are effecting change: not immediate or fully realized change, but the beginnings of a widespread rethinking of the way we integrate motherhood into society.

Though flextime might make life more manageable, it doesn't address the basic problem of the time-crunch experienced by many

American working people. Some advocate a move toward a thirty-five-hour workweek—as has been done with mixed success in France—to provide relief both for those who are overworked and for the large number of Americans who are underemployed and want more hours. And there are other issues. For instance, when part-time workers work on a project basis, who ensures that they won't end up doing as much work as before, for half the pay? And how do you make the top jobs flexible, when they've always gone to the few who were willing to work unstintingly?

Margaret, a 45-year-old mother of three kids 8 and younger and a corporate HR executive, wonders about the overall effect of work/life integration for ambitious employees: "I think that work/life integration is not driving toward working less, you're definitely driving toward working more, and that's been in the literature a lot, that this whole work/life integration thing is really ultimately a benefit to employers."

Some employees won't work more, they'll just move around their finite amount of work—and employers will benefit from their added loyalty and focus. Anybody can turn off a BlackBerry, close a computer, or not return a voicemail after 4:45. But those who don't stop, who really merge their work and personal time via the new portable technologies, will work even more in hopes of rising faster. The effect on their personal lives probably won't be much different than for workaholics past. Of course, there is a middle ground, which involves some extra work in exchange for more flexibility but not twenty-four-hour availability.

Margaret works at home on Fridays, and she likes that. When she really needs to be in the office on a Friday, she goes in without complaint because "I figure that I need to be as flexible as my employer is with me." Even though she's in the office pretty much standard hours the other four days, she doesn't feel guilty if she has to leave for a kid activity, but she tries to make as many of those commitments as she can on Fridays. As needed, she gets up earlier or just stays online later to make up the time and get the work done.

As a result, she feels very loyal: "I don't know where else I could do this. It absolutely makes me work harder. Because you don't want this to be taken away. And you want your boss to see that you're making it work." It's important to Margaret to prove to her bosses that flex works because

> the whole trust thing is huge in this field. . . . [Some employers] don't trust that the employees are either really going to work at home, or . . . that they're really working the hours that they say they're working. . . . [HR] argues that it doesn't matter what the hours are, that [pay] should totally be based on results and productivity. I'm not sure that that many people buy it yet. Some people do; not everybody. In HR they do.

So do many workers who can shop not just for jobs but for professions, according to what they see of work/life integration patterns in various industries. For the moment, the employees most likely to be trusted are those with a track record, who have proven themselves in the past. This situation creates an incentive for women to delay their families until they reach the point where they can ask for and receive more flexible schedules.

What Is Part Time?

Historically, many women with children have chosen part-time work. Once children are in school or daycare, part-time hours can coincide with school hours, which allows mothers to be home when their children are. When their children are not home, mothers can earn money the family needs and get the pleasures of adult contact and work satisfaction. But part-time work hasn't gotten much respect—from employers or from the general public. The principal sign of this low respect is the low wages part-time work pays. For a long time, part-time work was largely available only for tasks with low-skill requirements, and often workers were paid even lower wages than they might have been paid in the full-time version of a job. This disparity occurred because employers were seen to be accommodating the special needs of the worker (you could get flexibility *or* higher wages, not both) and because the workers were often women and women have, for ages, been seen to deserve lower wages than men.

In the world of economics, part-time work gets largely disregarded. In part, this is because it's hard to track, and it's hard to compare part-time workers (who work a wide range of hours per week) with full-time workers or even with other part-time workers, so their data gets scrapped when economists need to analyze comparables.

Prejudice appears in the public sphere as well: for example, a 2005 *New York Times* article generated a lot of irritated response when it announced on the front page that "many women at elite colleges set career path to motherhood."[10] The article provided plenty of grounds for complaint: it interviewed a small set of female undergrads at Yale about their plans for combining motherhood and career, and then declared a national trend on that basis. Sixty percent of those who responded to the survey, a total of eighty-five women, said they planned to step out of the workforce or work part time when they had families. The fact that they had different financial options than most women and that they hadn't yet started careers, let alone left them, made the trend claims dubious. But most egregious were the reflections on whether this "trend" meant that women shouldn't be given spots at elite colleges and grad schools (nationally, most women need and want jobs as well as families). The implication was that the education would be wasted on women who stayed home with kids. The article also implied that, if women were going to stay home, there was no point in changing work/life policies in business.

There are many issues percolating here. But the key underlying question for me, and one I'd pose both to those who wrote the article and to those who objected to it, is, Given that life spans are long, why is a plan to stay home with kids for a few years or to work part time viewed as a betrayal of the investment in women's education? Just because part-time work has been a career breaker for many women in the past, due to the way the work world has historically been structured, must we allow it to be a career breaker in the future? Rather than lecturing women either on the need to stay at full-time work without interruption or on the need to stay home with kids full time (both arguments have been much in the air of late), can we envision (and create) a different kind of work structure? This has been the effort of the work/life professionals over the past decade—to develop work options that acknowledge the importance of the contributions of both men and women to the work world *and* that recognize that people have families. After all, the work world depends on those families to produce the workers and customers of tomorrow. Not the loveliest way to look at the role of family, but true.

Part-time work makes sense for many, allowing parents to contribute to the well-being of their families by spending more time with kids as needed. Parents working part time thus contribute to society in two ways at once. The forty-hour workweek (or, worse, the fifty- or sixty-hour workweek) is not the only way to get things done. If a mom or a dad can afford to stay home or to work part time and finds that option attractive, why not? Sometimes this arrangement might be for a few years, sometimes for many. Why not allow workers more flexibility in the time they work and the way they organize that work to shape their schedules to their family's changing needs? And those needs do change, both from day to day and across the years as children grow.

If we consider raising children a valuable activity, we might find it reasonable that kids sometimes deserve a little padding in their lives. Though nine hours in daycare can work well in good circumstances, it doesn't leave a lot of room for dealing with difficulties when they come up. That's why so many moms have relied on the flexibility that part-time work can give. For example, **Mariam** (now 54) has a 10-year-old with several issues that she felt called for some expansion of her time at home: "Our son has had developmental issues, and some health issues, and so because of that I decided I should cut way, way back. I was going to quit, and my boss convinced me that they'd like to keep me on in a minor role for a while, in case I decided I wanted to come back."

You can note in her employer's solicitude a clear interest in retaining Mariam's services. And what is she doing at home?

Nothing—that's the thing. I told someone, "It's not that I have to do a lot, I want to know what's going on with him." . . . I probably could have a full-time physical therapist working with him, and then I could say, "Okay, that's fine," because I have my housekeeper at my house and she loves him and he loves her. So next year we'll see. . . . With my daughter I worked full time, and she rocked and rolled. My husband and I traveled, and she never missed a beat. But my son, I feel like he's had a struggle. . . . And I always say, when he's a little bit older and in middle school, and I see that he's rocking and rolling and he's in a groove, I probably will go back to work [more]. But I've got to see him in that groove first. Children are all so different.

Part of good parenting (what we still sometimes call "mothering") is watchfulness, being there to recognize when a problem arises so it doesn't have a chance to get out of hand. If Mariam has the flexibility to do that, why would the world not honor her choice and see it as a gift to her son's future employers and to the community he'll be a member of in years to come? And what about the parents who don't have that flexibility now? Can we envision a world where more parents would have the opportunity to follow their instincts about a child in need, either through cutting back on work hours themselves or through a reliable childcare network, or both?

Parents can be watchful of their children on their own, or they can share that job with trusted caregivers. But nothing substitutes for being able to give comfort and a reliable support system by some means when a child needs it. If the importance of child-rearing to the "village" was taken seriously (not just vice versa), then we wouldn't hear that workers who take time off aren't "serious" or that their skills will quickly atrophy so much that they can't climb back into the work world at anywhere near the same level as when they left. If they held the jobs in the first place, they're smart people; if employers allow time for returning employees to catch up rather than expecting them to step right in (a way to guarantee failure), it won't take long in most industries for workers to learn the new program or the new business approach, the same way they learned their first skill sets in school. But employer attitudes have to change to allow this to happen.

In some workplaces, part-time work is now getting a bit more respect—again, due to the credentials of the women demanding it. These women, coming from careers where they were treated well, don't see why they should be paid less per hour when they work part time if they're giving the company the same value per hour. And they don't see why they shouldn't still get the benefits that mothers, of all people, need access to most! It's due to their pressure that the work/life integration movement has introduced the concept of pro-rated salaries for part-time work. Amazing idea!

Part-time work done for a prorated salary and benefits is new and relatively rare. When it happens, it's often new later moms who find this option available, because their credentials make them valuable. Often their employers hope they will return to full-time work once their home work becomes less demanding. **Dominique**, an engineer employed by an international energy corporation and a mother at 37 and 40, found this to be the case:

> I think [flex options are] probably more easily available to people with more experience. I think a person who'd only worked a year or two might have a harder time finding a [supervisor] who would agree to part time than me—I had fifteen years or so of experience before I asked to work part time. And actually, when I asked to work part time, when I first presented it as something to consider to my boss

when I was pregnant with Elora, he was very open to it, but he also didn't feel 100 percent sure that I would be able to find [a project manager who would be willing to take me on] part time. But I was able to. And I've always, since I've worked part time, I've always done project work for small projects or portions of small projects. Which has seemed to work out very well.

Dominique works from 8:30 to 12:30 five days a week for a prorated salary and benefits, giving her two hours of wiggle room to run errands, go to the gym (an option not generally available to mothers after school hours), or stay late at work if a project runs over, before picking up her 7-year-old from first grade and her 3-year-old from preschool at 2:30. Dominique's work on alternative energy sources feels like a contribution to the greater good of the planet, and so does her ability to be available to her kids after school. She wonders why this option doesn't get more use, since

the stay-at-home moms I know say that, if they could find a part-time position that was challenging and well paid, they would happily take it. . . . I think society can benefit if part-time work is offered to more people—if it's an easy option to choose. My supervisors have always said they get two-thirds of a job out of my half-time work, because I'm so focused on work when I'm at work. And so, I think society is losing a lot by not presenting this opportunity to other women who have experience to contribute but don't want to do it full time. I think there's a lot of experience out there that's not being used.

Dominique's friends' desire for part-time options points up the underlying story in the recent media focus on women's desire to leave work to be with their children. Most women report a desire to find ways to combine work and family life. And new later moms are at the forefront of the effort to make that happen.

But it hasn't quite happened yet, at least not in a way that's accessible to most workers, including many later moms. Instead, the version on offer now can often be a trap that creates more resentment at the same time that it doesn't much ease the workload. **Fiona**, now 42, came to part-time work by accident. She asked for four months off when her first baby arrived, but once the child was in her arms, her thoughts changed. "Instead of full time, I wanted to come back part time, and I wanted to take six months." Her boss wasn't happy ("but I didn't *know* what I wanted before I had the child"), but he agreed to allow her to work four days a week at 80 percent pay. At her company, however, it was hard to do her job part time, so she ended up putting in extra hours. "And I ended up being resentful because I was working way more than full time, but only being paid for four days, and it was a disaster." And because her boss was also resentful about her request for a change, she didn't dare renegotiate.

Then a new boss arrived,

> and that gave me the motivation to say, "You know what, could I go back to being full time?" but with the acknowledgment that on our slow days, I wouldn't be, like, nonstop working in the office. It would be more flexible, and I could work from home. . . . So that happened, and weirdly, I've been more productive than in my entire career.

The focus switched from being in the office and doing make-work when there was no real work to getting recognized and paid for results. For Fiona, that change meant a change in attitude as well. "When I went back to full time, I didn't feel resentful. I felt like I could be a good mom *and* a good worker." So now, when she talks with new moms, she tells them, "Part time is a horrible thing! . . . Do not go part time, if you're at all hard-working, which most women I know are. If you're at all hard-working, you're going to give any job your full-time effort." She concludes, "I was so much happier and remain so much happier being a full-time worker."

The problem for people who do need or want to go part time lies in enforcing the limited time commitment. In the face of pressure to get a project done, what's to keep a supervisor or even (maybe more likely) the worker herself from feeling that the right thing to do is to finish the whole task now? The answer, says Evelyn the HR manager, comes in having regular, honest, and open discussions with supervisors about what works and what doesn't—and the grit to stand up for yourself when work slides consistently over the part-time line. And, clearly, it also requires supervisors dedicated to fairness and to making the part-time option real. This will take a major change in attitude from the top down. In the long run, the successful melding of motherhood and work is all about HR.

Job shares give employers a way to offer part-time work and get full-time coverage. Job sharing is described as a "dynamite" idea by **Vivian**, an engineer and a new later mom at 35 and 38 who hoped to utilize that alternative to full-time work. The term explains itself—one job is shared between two people who see the same clients and work the same projects. Both get benefits, and both work a short week at a prorated salary, which means they get paid at the same hourly rate they would for a full-time salaried post, but for part-time hours, rather than at the lower hourly rate that usually goes with part-time work. In a friend's case that Vivian observed, "two very compatible women managed a marketing department. They had the same mission, and each had three days of work with one day of overlap so they could coordinate efforts." This schedule allowed both women to maintain their job connection and to spend two days each week with their families. But when Vivian was offered a job share, it didn't work because, though "the other woman and I were very compatible, . . . we were given separate job responsibilities and were not covering for each other—we had separate jobs. It was a terrible model, and we both quit at the same time in frustration."

These options clearly need refining, and some employers recognize that progress on them will have to happen soon to avoid losing lots of current contributors to the workforce and discouraging many others from entering. Vivian (the engineer), a middle manager when she gave birth at 35, went from keeping her first child in daycare twelve hours a day to quitting entirely when the job share failed after the birth of her second child. Her husband, a doctor, worked similar long hours. For Vivian, the progress was not fast enough. She focused her considerable energy and insight on homeschooling her two boys when they were young and remains a very involved mother now that they've begun elementary school. But **Mariam** sees job shares as the wave of the future:

> Well, you have a job situation where two people have been hired, and you're going to be doing the same job on different days. [If you don't get along] it gets a little more complicated. But in the right scenario with the right two people, it works. Women just need to feel like a 'we're in this together' kind of thing. And the boat either floats or sinks.

And when dads board the boat, all the better.

While the kinks are getting worked out for part-time employment in highly skilled jobs, the next step will be to export the prorated, part-time work concept to low-skilled work so that part-time workers there can also command a decent wage relative to full-time workers employing the same skills. It may take a while to deal with the remaining prejudice against "mothers' work," but if the movement of the baby boomers into retirement leaves us with a shortage of workers (who's going to take care of all those aging boomers?), that may create the pressure needed for change. Employers will be competing to hire caregivers and service providers, many of whom may be women interested in working part time for a good prorated salary with benefits.

Though most of the women I spoke with had found a way to make it work, many had difficulty "balancing" job and family. As **Melissa**, now 43, a child psychologist and mother at 38 and 42 who works thirty hours a week, put it:

> I still think that this society hasn't made significant gains in the area [of motherhood and work]. And I don't think that there's a balance. . . .

I'm not miserable, but I don't always feel very comfortable. And I love doing both things, so I wouldn't be a stay-at-home mom. . . . But the aspect of society not making it easier for families to work and have quality care, whichever one they choose, I do think that's a serious problem.

It is a big problem, and one that will get increasing scrutiny. **Carey**, the financial services manager, oversees many employees and focuses on facilitating their family choices within the work world. She doesn't see not working as a long-term option for most women:

I think it is true that just about ending with our generation, not ending completely, but ending as an expectation, was the theory that you could *not* work, as a woman. . . . I knew so few people who reached 22 and didn't think that they were going to work. A lot of people I knew figured out some kind of working career, some of them married, some of them had children a little bit later, but everybody developed an expectancy that they were going to work.

Judging by the patterns to date, most women will continue to choose to work, both when they have young kids and (especially) before and afterward. The change Carey describes has its roots in economic need as well as in a changed cultural expectation about women's role in society. How best to fit child-rearing into a successful career path is an issue we still wrestle with, however. This is a concern not just for individuals, but for employers and government policy makers as well, since such a significant percentage of the work population is female.

❖ PROFILE: **Karen, Finance Expert and New Mom at 39 and 41**

Part-time work can create an in-between status, since the part-time worker doesn't participate fully in either the at-home or the at-work world. Karen, who works twenty-five hours per week in the finance world, for a very good rate of pay, reflects on her situation:

> I am still working both shifts: the work shift while they're at school and the kids shift when they're out of school. . . . When I'm at work—I'm doing pretty high-caliber stuff, and I've made it very clear I don't want to manage projects—I'm kind of there, but I'm not as much a part of it; I'm not like the other managers and their career advancement, by design. And I'm very happy with that. I'm not a [regular] worker. And then when I'm picking up the kids from school with all the other stay-at-home moms, they know I just came from work, so I'm not really a stay-at-home mom either. So I'm not a worker, and I'm not a stay-at-home mom, so I'm in la-la land. Which is very fine with me, but if I had time to worry about, like, "where do I belong?" you know, I could make it an issue. . . . But having said that, I mean, it's not extreme, because there are plenty of older moms at the school that I connect well with, and even the younger moms. So I could see it being an issue, if I wanted to make it an issue. Do you know what I mean? I could say "Oh, I don't fit in anywhere." But in reality, I do fit in both places.

Karen recently transitioned from independent contract work to employee status, and that change has added to her sense of community, though she works the same number of part-time hours that she did as a contractor.

When her kids were young, Karen took six years off from a long and active career in finance, then returned to work part time because the family needed the income. When I first spoke with her, she was wishing she could be home full time still. When I talked to her two years later, she'd discovered that what she disliked was the job she was in, not working per se. By then she was in a new twenty-five-hour-a-week job and loving it. She finds the work fascinating, loves the community she gets there, *and* enjoys the flexibility to take occasional days off as her part-time status allows. And she's still making a wage most people would be happy with for full-time work. For Karen, new later motherhood has "just been such a positive experience—you know, you're wiser and financially more stable." ❖

The ideal work/life balance program might offer a palette of choices to meet the varying needs of employees at different points in their lives. The choices might include, at least: more good and reliable childcare options, flextime options, furlough options, and prorated part-time options like job shares or other reduced schedules. As we've seen, since neither the government nor the business community has made such options real for many workers, many women delay their families in order to provide those options for themselves.

But the new-later-motherhood route does not make sense for everybody. Policy makers at all levels have to find ways to accommodate workers with families—especially if they want them to keep on having families. The average U.S. woman in 2007 has 2.09 children in her lifetime—that's just at replacement level, and high for a developed country. In Japan the average woman in 2007 has 1.23 children, in Italy it's 1.29, in Turkey it's 1.89, in Mexico it's 2.39, in Canada it's 1.61, in Russia it's 1.39, in South Africa it's 2.16, in Afghanistan it's 6.64, in Denmark it's 1.74, in China it's 1.75, in the United Kingdom it's 1.66, in Saudi Arabia it's 3.94, in India it's 2.81, and in France it's 1.98.[11] Although personal choice, public policy, and work/family balance issues affect the numbers in all countries, it's clear that birth control has made an enormous difference across the globe.

Child-rearing undergirds all our assumptions about what our nation is and where it's going, for not only do we assume there will *be* a next generation, we expect them to be good citizens as well. That means we expect mothers to bring children into the world and to do a good job rearing them, too. But birth control has changed the economic playing field—in the past, women's production of the next generation could be taken for granted, and that is no longer the case. This de facto change in one part of the reality field requires thoughtful adjustments in all the others. Unless the government addresses the possibility of shrinking population by offering public policy solutions that make it attractive to women to continue to have families, we too may face a future as a much smaller country. As my colleague Janet Chafetz put it, "women are voting with their wombs." In this regard, as a nation (and as a world), we have much to discuss.

In business today, as the smaller Gen X steps up to replace the soon-to-be-retiring boomer generation, management is starting to think these issues through. And as it happens, a high proportion of the women in management doing this thinking are new later moms like Carey and Margaret and Evelyn. Government, too, is beginning to address these issues, as discussions of family-friendly policy initiatives proliferate in state and national legislatures. Will we fund the Family and Medical Leave Act (FMLA)? Will we view parenthood as a kind of national service in a few years? All these decisions are being closely watched by the younger generations coming up.

Small-Business Moms

While the transformation of the business culture takes time, many women (new later moms and not) find it much easier to effect instant change in the HR rules at their place of work by starting their own businesses. These women create their own clout. Owning their own companies means they can set their own schedules and their own work/life policies. **Allison** (now 39, mother at 37) and her partner **Nell** (now 42, adoptive mother at 40) run a small business in a big city. They brought their daughter to work for the first eighteen months of her life, before she started preschool. Allison sees small businesses as the route to sanity for moms:

I think the future of business and the future of motherhood is going in the direction of—you have to make your own way. Be an entrepreneur, start something on your own. That's the best way for you to have the life you want to have, I think. I mean there are a lot of people who make a whole lot more money [than I do] and can afford the nanny and whatever . . . [say] a lawyer in a large firm. But I have the time, and I have the flexibility that they may not have. That is more, means more to me . . . than going out there and making whatever.

Allison and Nell had so much flexibility that they could reorganize their business hours to fit their new life. Because they had a lot of experience and a well-established reputation (and are a bit older therefore), these moms could have more wiggle room to shape their new business to their new needs. Their clients would have accepted almost any schedule they chose.

Marie, 39, was an advertising executive before the birth of her daughter Meghan, now nearly 2 years old. Marie's maternity leave coincided with the offer of a severance package, when the company she worked for closed its operation in her town. She took the offer and didn't start back to work until her daughter was 8 months old. Her severance package and her husband's job gave her the luxury of choosing to return to work on her own terms. When she did return, she felt very ready and took an offer for a freelance, short-term assignment.

You know, I really hate to admit this; I think it really shows my ego is larger than I thought it was; I really don't feel good about myself unless I am working. . . . I don't think I am a very good mother [when I'm not working] because I become bored, and I think depression creeps in because I'm so used to being so busy and so challenged on a daily basis. . . . And while having a child is the biggest love affair I've ever had, it doesn't fulfill my need for, you know— Meghan can't say "Oh mommy, good job, good job—you're doing a great job," and so, I guess I need that praise as much as she needs that praise. And then the other side of it is, I don't want my daughter to grow up thinking that mommy doesn't work. I want Meghan to understand that her place in this planet is to contribute, and it's part of her responsibility here, so I can't see how I can require that of her if I wasn't doing the same.

Since it feels important to her that women contribute in the public arena, Marie is building up her client base and working on starting her own consultancy. When she has employees, she expects to offer them flexible schedules, as was the case in her former job where the CEO traveled extensively, did all his business by phone, and didn't care where his employees were as long as the work got done. Marie sees this scenario working for her business because, as she says, "I'm pretty flexible you know, I really just like to work with people who are hard workers. I don't care when they get it done or how they get it done; I just want to know someone's committed to a project, you know, and will help me get it completed."

❖ PROFILE: Julie, Businesswoman and New Mother at 39

Julie grew up with a divorced mother and four siblings and knew she didn't want that kind of hard time for herself. She went to college, got an MBA, and started work. At about 30, she met Gareth, her true love. They founded a company together that took off and made them a tidy sum.

You invest a lot in an education and obviously you want to pursue that. And having a child is kind of a daunting idea, especially if you take your role as a mother seriously. And I had a very excellent mother, so I knew what it would take to be a good mother. It was just something that I just couldn't . . . I was traveling around the world, I could go anytime I wanted to, and it was great—life was great. And I never thought that I would never have children, it was just not something that I thought about in my 20s at all.

When she hit 35 they began trying for kids, but nothing happened, "so I kind of resigned myself that it wasn't going to. We talked somewhat about adoption, but my husband was just not feeling very good about that, so we kind of dropped the whole subject, and all of a sudden, lo and behold, I got pregnant."

Their baby, Lily, arrived when Julie was 39. She took three months off, then hired a live-in nanny, so she could go back to working the twenty-four-hour-on-call life of an international business owner, while never having to worry that the baby wasn't well cared for. (That nanny is with them still, fourteen years later.)

As a business owner, she could flex her schedule and take her daughter to the park during the day, and then work in the evening after the baby had gone to bed. Her experience as a mom influenced her HR policies. Though she expected all her employees to perform consistently and well, she didn't care how they arranged their schedules—face time means nothing in her field. She provided extended paid parental leaves.

Julie describes herself as a hands-on mom—their family eats dinner together every night, they talk a lot about everything that interests them, and when Julie and Gareth travel, Lily comes, too. Julie would have liked to have a second child, but it didn't happen for them, and they felt no interest in pursuing IVF, which was then in its early days.

Julie remained at the head of the company for several years after Lily's birth, at which point the business morphed, and she retired, looking forward to spending more time with her child. But while she's enjoying their time together, kids in school are gone a lot, so after a few months of leisure, Julie, who felt a bit depressed and isolated at home, started another small business on the side. She now works about four hours a day. Once her daughter goes off to college, Julie expects that she and Gareth will start another larger-scale business together.

Though she dreams of having grandchildren, Julie advises her daughter and her daughter's friends to wait until they're at least 30 to have kids:

Get yourself an education, establish a career, and then get a family. I think you need it not just for financial and security reasons, but you need it to get to know yourself, and to appreciate yourself and know who you are and what you can do. So I think it's incredibly important, just for your own identity, to get to know yourself.

Julie feels that having established herself first makes her a better parent than she would have been earlier. ❖

Making Work Choices around Family

But not everybody can start her own business. Most women (like men) depend on existing businesses to supply them with the benefits their families need and, they hope, a good wage. Though some are activists within big companies, others find they do better by keeping their heads down and working out their own arrangements. The chances that your needs around family time will be heard, let alone accommodated, vary widely by industry—and that variety often depends on the level of machismo there. For instance, **Connie**, a new later mom who works for a company with a bad gender record, finds it easiest to get her work done and go home. By the time she had her kids, her client base was so established and loyal that she had no financial worries, but she does worry now and then that she's not doing much for younger women coming up. In another environment, it might seem more worthwhile to try.

The major work/life benefit offered to employees by the U.S. government is the FMLA grant of up to twelve weeks of maternity and paternity leave to new parents. The drawback, of course, is that those weeks are unpaid, unless you can cover the time with vacation leave or personal days. Younger employees have fewer of these paid days. And then there's the difficulty that taking time off can impose on colleagues. **Linda**, a new mom at 35, works in the oil and gas industry and notes that, even though you're out on leave, unfortunately your job still stays, and it's not like they have an extra person who's just going to move right in. So what happens when you're gone for a significant [time]—three months or so, is that they carve up your job to everybody, and so people who were already over-worked, and not spending time with their family, are now going to be spending less time.

Given the stereotypes, she notes, a woman can take the leave ("they don't want you to but they kind of expect it"), but if a man takes the leave, it can have negative repercussions. Linda recalls that "when I was in the Dallas office, there was a guy who took a family leave." The reaction he got wasn't positive. "You know, he was 'the guy who took the family leave.'" So you don't see many more men in her office doing that. A female engineer reported that, in her firm, the one man who took a paternity leave soon left the firm, after an evaluation in which he was rated "not serious enough" about his job. But it will only be when men start taking these leaves in numbers that they won't signify negatively for everybody else. Only when com-panies are committed to covering for employees on family leave (by cutting back on work or providing real temporary support) will work-ers feel comfortable taking the leave or not feel resentful when coworkers do the same. If workers without kids are always left hold-ing the bag for those who have kids, it doesn't promote a sense of fairness and collegiality. The most forward-looking work/family bal-ance plans allow all workers their own version of family leave time, for whatever purpose: eldercare, pet care, childcare, or even just per-sonal down time, as needed.

Audrey, who also works in oil and gas—on the HR side—became a later mom at 40. Some of her male colleagues do come to ask about paternity leaves. But

with men, so much of manhood, if you will, is tied to economics, and they want to be the provider and what not. And most men don't want to . . . take this unpaid leave. . . . I think for men to be more accepting of that and then society in turn, some portion, if not all of it, will have to be paid. Because right now, it's almost like a fantasy of, "Oh yes, you can take twelve weeks off." But that's twelve weeks of mortgage and insurance, and there's no money coming in to help with that.

There's lots of room for improvement here. And funding FMLA would publicly recognize the value of the work it allows—a move that would make it much more likely that men would want to do that work.

Because the workplace isn't providing as well as it could for employees at all levels, workers are left to negotiate their own benefits as best they can. Sometimes that means waiting for kids until you're well established in your job, as many new later moms have done. And sometimes that means changing jobs—as Amy the lawyer did. **Polly**, another lawyer and a new later mother (at 35, 36, and 40) of three children under 9, also moved from a law firm to a corporate legal department after her second child was born, as did her husband. She explains: "Our model is that we both have jobs that are pretty regular, in terms of the hours and the demands." They have a nanny who tends the younger kids during the day and runs errands.

> I try to farm out as much of the things that take away from the time I have with my family when I'm not working. And then, our jobs are not inflexible . . . so I can go to school, and read, and I can watch them or pick them up and take them home, and then I can go goofily back to work for an hour and then come back [home]. But you know, I do that so I can go and meet the moms. Those are the kind of things that I try to do. . . . I coach their sports teams.

Polly and her husband George both wanted to be active parts of their three children's day-to-day lives, so they both made conscious choices not to stay on the very fast track. This allows them to operate as equals in the household, making similar salaries and sharing chores, because neither one's job is more important than the other's to the family well-being.

> We don't have these big high-powered careers. . . . We each have careers that are certainly good careers, but they offer us more flexibility than, like, a partner in a law firm or some international job that would cause us to be flying around all the time. . . . I have lots of friends who don't have a job outside the home; their husbands travel and are gone constantly and their kids never see them, you know, or they work these crazy hours. So, I don't know what the perfect model is, but this is the model we picked, and I like what I do, and I derive a lot of pleasure from it, and I still feel like I'm a big part of the kids' lives. . . . My work doesn't define me, I think my motherhood, my role as a mother defines me. But my work is a big part of what makes me a happy camper.

Polly didn't start out with her current point of view—she started out at a downtown law firm and learned from experience that it wasn't going to work with her family.

> I saw it's not going to get any better, it's only going to get worse, so—it's awful. I saw their lives—horrible. . . . I left after I had finished six years there, and it would have been two more years before I made partner. That was close, and I knew I just had to get out of there, because if I'd stayed one more year, I'd have been sucked into a vortex you know, and I just had to leave. . . . Because that whole law firm thing, or consulting, it's all about how many hours you bill, and there are only so many hours in a day, and the metric by which you'll always be compared is how many hours did you bill. How many fees did you bring in. . . . I've seen partners, female partners with children—not a model that was at all appealing to me. I wasn't impressed. It didn't look like the kind of family life that I was looking

for. And the husbands didn't have time to pitch to their sons, so they hired someone to pitch to their sons. So you know, I'll farm out the grocery store and the cleaning any day of the week. But when it comes to playing catch with my child, those are the things I want to be doing. That's how we make it all work. . . . It was very conscious. It was like, I've got to get out of here, because if I don't, then it's really hard to leave, because you start making all this money, and you know, it's bad.

While some law partners may manage to avoid this pattern, it has to be a struggle. On the other hand, while Polly holds a very good job, it doesn't offer the influence or the money that a partnership would. Polly and George chose the best available option for their family now, but a better world would offer flexible schedules for caregiving law partners. Of late, even the law profession is beginning its own self-critique, and eventually, the rules may change in firms as well, moving toward a model less dependent on face time and billable hours and more focused on effective work done at any time of day or night from any location.[12]

These problems might seem rarified, but the reality is that to really change the culture in the work world for women means changing it at all levels, and it means that women have to play a role in shaping policy at all levels. So it matters even to those of us who aren't making big salaries whether or not *some* women are. When a 2003 *New York Times Magazine* article reported a trend among well-to-do female lawyers to "opt out" of their jobs when they had kids, the letters to the editor decried these women as undermining the work of the previous generation, those who strove to get women into position to get the jobs in the first place.[13] But though the article stressed that women were leaving their jobs, the key lay buried in a few lines at the end of the article, which concluded that most women left not because they didn't want to work, but because their employers offered no option for mothers who wanted to keep working *and* be available when their kids needed them. By the end, the article was already backtracking, noting that remedies were emerging for the lack of flextime options that had caused the women profiled to leave their jobs a few years back.

But in the finance and legal industries in particular, these changes come slowly. Another *New York Times* piece in 2006 suggested that Wall Street may finally be recognizing the business case for accommodating women workers and their newly family-centered male counterparts, since not doing so means losing half the talent pool. At the same time, female clients who want advisers who look like them, at least occasionally, may feel alienated when they steadily do not.[14] But old habits and attitudes linger, and the changes come gradually.

Clearly, the work world has faced, and still faces, a lot more thinking through of its policies, but the process *is* under way. Meanwhile, as the process unrolls, many women are taking their fate into their own hands, creating flextime systems by reshaping their work circumstances to fit their needs and by delaying motherhood until they have the clout to make their own terms. These women may choose full-time flex schedules, they may stay home for good or for a while, or they may go part time for a while or forever. Or they may start their own businesses. But most of them will not disappear from the work world, because they need the pay and their employers need them.[15] And they will be there in the workforce to carry the revolution on as their children grow up.

In circles where the work/life discussion has been heeded—in companies planning for the long term—the revolution may have already occurred. Several of the women I spoke with felt that younger women and men were already behaving differently than their immediate predecessors. These new workers have listened to the flexible workplace mantras their employers and the media have spouted, and they're now expecting those benefits. Margaret the HR executive notes:

The Gen Xers and Gen Yers . . . don't believe that they need to work as hard as their parents did. And by the way, look what happened to mom and dad, they worked there for thirty years and they still got laid off. They want more time with their families, and they come in asking for that from the very beginning. So the whole recruiting and retention issue is big, and it's really, really there. We hear from recruiters that the young kids out of college are really asking those questions, "What is work/life balance at this organization?" . . . [We invest in flextime] for our [current] employees, but we also know that that's the way that we're going to get the best and the brightest, . . . the young kids who are the leaders of tomorrow.

Though the Gen Yers I know work plenty hard, all of these younger workers will have the advantage of a relative scarcity of competition in the workplace. As the 76 million baby boomers move into retirement, they will be replaced in business by fewer post-boomers. That might seem like a natural downsizing process, but the businesses will still have all the retirees as clients, with limited employee resources. Although some of that slack will be taken up by overseas outsourcing, as well as by baby boomers who just don't quit, the scarce supply of younger workers here will give them more bargaining power—so they can insist on real flexibility and part-time options, not just the promises.

Sylvia's daughter Carolyn has suggested that she will not want to wait as long as her mother did to have kids and that she will want to stay at home with her children. This concerns Sylvia:

My biggest worry for my daughter is if she didn't spend the time to get a skill, so that if she got into a relationship that one day she needed to get out of, for whatever reason—husband didn't treat her right, abused her, or she was unhappy, or he just—you just never know what's going to happen. And she wouldn't be able to take care of herself.

The problem she sees is that many girls don't understand the full ramifications of their mothers' work:

> You have the two [partners in a marriage] and they're making a lot of money, or whatever, they have girls saying, "I don't want to do that, I'd rather just stay at home." They don't understand that [they might] have to go out and do that—cause they don't see a mom who's trapped. You see what I'm saying? So they don't know the other side of that equation. Whereas with my father, he was very insistent that my sister and I get an education and be independent, as he saw his mother and his sister trapped.

On the other hand, another new later mom sees younger women and men in her workplace taking advantage of family-friendly policies and having kids earlier than she did, while holding onto their jobs through an extended furlough program. The furloughs are unpaid, but they allow a parent to be at home with a baby for a considerable time without losing her connection to her employer. In many businesses that would still not be an option. The whole *language* of flexibility has been created over the last fifteen years, and many young women and men now speak it fluently. They can say, "we want job shares and prorated part time and job furloughs, and if you want us to stay, you need to give them to us." They're in a position to bargain, and their companies will have to work out a deal if they want to keep them. We're seeing a revolution in stages, with certain industries and certain segments of the work world leading the way while others lag. If the first stage of the revolution involved inventing the language for describing a flexible work world, maybe in the second stage we can devote our energies to writing the life stories of the inhabitants of this flex world.

But while options are opening up every day for people with family responsibilities, as employers recognize how much deeper and more talented their hiring pool becomes when they offer flextime (a no-cost way to boost retention as well), there remain miles to go before everybody has that option. As opportunities to combine family with challenging remunerative work expand, it may be that women who feel ready for kids sooner on other counts (like self-definition and finding their life partner) will start their families earlier than they might today. If so, that option will have developed in part because many of the women just before them chose to delay.

But if the trend to later motherhood slows in the next few years due to such changes, it isn't likely to disappear altogether, because women who wait do so for many reasons. The key to a better world for moms, kids, and families lies in providing women with many good options for education, jobs, and family, and then leaving it to each woman to define readiness for herself.

CHAPTER 4

Moms at Home

When Is a Job Not a Job?

> *Mothers are basically servants.*
>
> —PAMMY (age 5),
> on being handed a milk shake after
> water-play in the backyard

Anybody who's had one knows that mothers have always worked, hard and plenty. The woman whose work was "never done" in the adage definitely had kids—tending them would have been a big part of her energy expenditure. So did the iconic W-O-M-A-N in the song (written by men, but made famous by Maria Muldaur and Reba McEntire) that spells out the word while reeling off the housewife's multitude of tasks. Working the "second shift" is nothing new; we've always been busy. Back in the day, moms did a lot less one-on-one playing with kids and a lot more providing for their basic needs. Although we no longer have to weave cloth and sew our family's clothes while farming, baking, pumping water, mixing medicines, and scrubbing the laundry in the river, there's still lots of work to be done to keep the home running, and mothers still do most of it (though that's changing to some degree; there's more discussion of the dynamics of shared housework in the next chapter). Mothers in different financial positions have different access to help and machinery, and different individuals have different definitions of adequate care. But here follows a fairly basic job description for an attentive American mom.

First there's the physical work of bearing the young (*labor* being a key term there), and once they're born, there's doing their laundry and cooking for them and picking up after them for years (that's the *housework*). There's the shopping (for food, for clothes, for toys, for books). There's the childcare component—watching over them, feeding them, rocking them to sleep, taking them for walks, reading to them, talking to them, playing with them. There's all the emotional work of helping kids deal with sibling rivalry and schoolyard bullies, of guiding them through the minefields of infancy, childhood, and adolescence, and so forth and so on, times the number of people in the family. And there's worrying about them. And then there's what my friend Ann calls "stuff management"—planning weekend and after-school activities, remembering who needs new shoes and what kinds of birthday presents count as cool this year. On top of that, for the mothers with some time left, there's advocacy work for their kids—which can range from running a school fundraiser to becoming an expert on the learning issues their children turn out to have and then running the follow-through. Put it all together, it spells multitasking. That's a lot of work, sometimes satisfying, sometimes dull and wearing. In general, this job involves no cash payment, though it often means a share in the funds that other family members bring in.

Moms who also hold a wage-earning job either hire someone to help them with some part of the list (childcare and maybe a cleaning woman—telling phrase!), or they find a way to do both. And if finances permit, sometimes moms at home hire help too—even for those moms with "nothing else" to do, there's often enough workload to share.

So why do we do it? What makes us want to take all this on? Well, at least partly we do it because we like it. Even if we don't like every task, we like the fact that we're there for our kids. It's this aspect of our calling that gets thrown back at us when we complain about anything to do with the treatment of mothers—after all, it was "your choice," so it's your tough luck. Then, we've often been made to feel that rearing children is expected of us—something we're biologically and culturally prepped for (so our "liking" has a ventriloquistic dimension to it).

But though the common parlance tells us that moms rear *their own* kids, this view overlooks the essential contribution to society at large that moms make. Although our kids are also the world's kids, somehow it's the "mom's job" to train responsible citizens, to civilize the wild young barbarians we all start out as, and to ensure that the kid on the corner smiles politely rather than banging passersby over the head and stealing their groceries. As **Marcy** (mom at 39) tells her son when she's being firm with him, "mom and dad's job is to raise you so that you won't go to jail." She has to teach him the rules.

The adage that it takes a village to raise a child stresses the way that the social network helps the family, but there's a flip side to that, in which the village depends on the child when she or he grows up to become a citizen of the village and an essential contributor to its functioning, as well as a member of a family. Moms (and other primary caregivers) provide factories and corporations with the workers they need as well as with the customers they depend on. All without pay or even an occasional "thank you very much." To the extent that we don't question the assumption that all this is the natural order of things, moms appear to have been sold a bill of goods. But that particular bill of goods was written up before birth control.

Keeping the talk about motherhood focused on the personal makes it easier for the general public to evade a discussion about overall fairness and to ignore the degree to which society counts on mothers' work as its backbone. But as women have more choices about whether or not to have children, and as more and more women choose not to or to have fewer, the discussion has begun to change. How long before the government and big business see it as in their interests to make mothering more appealing to women? Mothering could be made more attractive by compensating caregivers for their work or by making it easier to combine caregiving with other kinds of work. Or those in power might try to scare us or discipline us (via changes in the tax law, lectures about infertility, or other such tactics) into accepting the old deal. If more and more women decide not to have kids, as has been happening in Europe, in Japan, and among some sectors of the U.S. population, then mothering may come to be recognized more directly as a job and a service to the public weal, as they used to say. In a basic way, the common wealth *is* our kids. And that wealth isn't calculated just in numbers of bodies: our investments in the education and in the innovative, ethical, and community-building capacities of children have value as well. So fewer but more resource-laden kids constitute part of the common wealth, too.

But as Ann Crittenden and others have pointed out, the work that creates the wealth that is our children has never been counted in the Gross Domestic Product (GDP). Given that omission, it might better be called the GIDP, since it's fundamentally Grossly Inaccurate. The labor of millions of women goes uncounted every day because, some will tell you, there isn't a good way of measuring it, since people aren't paid for it (it's the value of the wages paid that adds up to the GDP). But another part of this equation is the risk that, if you set a value to this work, then you *might be asked to pay for it.* If housewives and househusbands commanded a salary and had clout in the divorce court, the dynamic around housework and childcare would change.

People have mocked seventies feminists who tried to develop contracts outlining the division of housework between spouses. But a contract that entitles a stay-at-home parent to put half of the household income into a bank account with her or his name on it, while the working spouse keeps the other half, and then the two divide up the household expenses, could have good effect. So could a contract that commits a substantial portion of the working spouse's ongoing income (even after a marriage ends in divorce) to the raising of any children through high school or college. Either of these options would highlight the contribution the home worker makes to the family and offset the cut that the move out of the workforce makes in her or his long-term wage-earning ability. Contracts like that might result in fewer stay-at-home moms, but they would also mean that those who were would be better provided for in the long term. When we're feeling romantic, home work and childcare are priceless, and they're tasks that can be done well by nobody but mom. When we're feeling like divorcing, home work and childcare often turn out to be worth the wage paid the cheapest of domestic workers.

Employment-wise, mothers have long been assigned perhaps the most essential job in the world, but they've been taught that mothering is not really a job and, therefore, doesn't require compensation, or at least not directly. So how does all this inequity intersect with the new later motherhood experience? As we saw in the last chapter, women who defer children can establish themselves at work in positions where the value of their "other job" does get acknowledged and ac-commodated—at least functionally (in the form of flexibility) if not outright. But not all new later moms stay in the workplace to enjoy those benefits. Why not? Before we look at some answers, let's define the terminology.

What Is a Stay-at-Home Mom?

What used to be called *housewifery* gets a low value in the market of general opinion of late: we've all heard the "just a housewife" comment—sometimes coming out of the mouth of the housewife herself. Housewife is such an objectionable term that we rarely even use it anymore. Though most mothers at home still do housework, now the term is "stay-at-home mom" or sometimes SAHM. But how often is it true that SAHMs really *stay* at home? Miriam Peskowitz points out that today most SAHMs have been working women at one stage, and may well plan to be again, and many "working women" have taken time away from work for family, or have wished they could. It's hard for mothers to line up so firmly against one another as the talk show tease lines suggest.[1] The lines blur even further when we talk about part-time working moms, some of whom call themselves working mothers, while others think of themselves as SAHMs who occasionally take a job here and there. And many "full-time moms" do loads of community service work in addition to covering the many tasks associated with mothering. At best, the SAHM moniker is blurry, and often it's outright wrong.

The Stay-at-Home New Later Mom: What's the Difference?

There are all sorts of moms—great, bad, and in between—in all age ranges, but experience can bear good fruit.

Skills and Education

When new later moms leave the work world to stay home, they take with them a boatload of skills and education. This movement homeward comes up regularly in the national debate over women and work: "Why educate them if they're just going to let the skills rust in short order?" goes the critique. But skills taken home can be put to new use in positive ways. Here's an example.

❖ PROFILE: **Kim, New Mom at 39**

When Kim, scientist and PhD, became a mom at 39, she found her time-intensive lab job didn't allow her the flexibility she felt she now needed. So she went back to school for an urban studies degree. Now she combines her two areas of expertise as a very active volunteer urban environmental activist. Her new work still takes lots of hours, but she can do it at home and set her own schedule. Her sense of the importance of her work for her daughter's future, as well as the future of her community and of the next generation, is extraordinary and quite moving. Her work has a direct effect on the world her daughter, Lois, will grow up in, and it offers Lois a great model of what's possible in her own future: "My education is definitely used," Kim says, "and gives me a perspective that a lot of people don't have. . . . I feel completely confident to go in either direction. And I think she's picked up on that. . . . I mean that kid is amazingly confident and unafraid."

Kim can choose to stay home now because her husband's income allows it—but she expects to move back into paying work in a few years. Meanwhile, she "doesn't work" more arduously than most full-time workers I know. ❖

The education issue often gets gendered, because women are more likely to take time away from paid work and more likely to change jobs over the years. But the midlife change of course is becoming more common among men as well (maybe because we're all living so much longer). I spoke with a stay-at-home dad with a PhD, who left his job to raise four kids while his doctor wife earns the family wage. With all his kids in school now, he's turned to working toward a degree in a new field. He sees education as a kind of venture capitalism for both men and women and opines that "we need to encourage people to invest in themselves and move up, wherever that takes them, not head for some nasty grey middle ground." Rather than questioning women's (and men's) decisions around staying at home or staying at a job, it would seem more useful to offer real alternatives for staying at work and raising a family well at the same time, and then trusting people to make the best decisions for their families.

Self-Confidence

Like her counterparts who work, the new later mom at home is likely to have more in the way of financial resources and thereby have more options in terms of her children's schooling and household assistance. Less materially, because she's tested her judgment over years, she may be less apt to be rattled by the kinds of hyper-mom anxieties that Judith Warner described in her recent book *Perfect Madness*, which drew largely on the experience of moms at home with time to ferry their kids to all the available "educational" activities (though I know many younger moms, both SAHMs and working moms, also questioned the relation of that madness to their lives).

Maureen, who had her first baby at 41 and is now staying home with two, emailed me on Warner's book:

> My perspective on [it], with respect to my age, is that I don't feel a need to be everything to everyone. I had 18 years to make the best out of my career, which turned out to be pretty decent. Now that I'm a mother, I want to *enjoy* this very brief time that I have with my children, and I don't want to spend it shoving pseudo developmental classes on a baby or shuttling them around to a different activity every afternoon. Besides, that much stimulation for a child is *too much*, but hard to escape in this day and age. I hope I can pass along to them the fine arts of relaxation, imagination, and self-reliance.

As Maureen frames it, her ability to resist the pressure of fads is an issue of self-confidence, based on her own experience of herself as a competent person in the work world. Now she feels pretty sure she can be a competent mom, without a lot of bells and whistles. And she aims to convey that self-confidence to her kids. Maureen's account repeats a point made by many new later moms, who described a similar trust in their own judgment around their mothering decisions. Maureen and her husband agreed from the first that she would stay home with their kids for as long as it made sense, and she expects to be there for a while.

Money (and Accounting Ability)

Many issues entwine around the theme of "home work." We all do some of it, and we all have complex relationships with the many aspects of that work—many of our mothers defined themselves in terms of what their homes looked like, and we can't escape having some identity issues at stake around the topic (sometimes imitative, sometimes reactive, sometimes both). Men often have high standards for home upkeep as well, along with some identity-based ideas of what work they should and should not do. Changing the patterns can mean deep psychological upheaval.

The issue of money compounds the complexity of our feelings about home work. Once a parent leaves the workplace, the power balance in the house often shifts toward the one with the salary, which can mean a kind of psychological servitude, if the home parent feels the need to do all the care (even when she or he doesn't want to and the working parent could) or risk a backlash. Marriage expert David Popenoe finds that husbands and wives tend to want different things from marriage. "Women want the man to be a good communicator, someone who listens and expresses emotions. And men still want kind of a servant."[2] And that's not just men with stay-at-home wives. Old habits die hard. And money plays a big role.

If a mom decides to stay home with no income and no cash in the bank, there's the underlying threat, even if it's buried under lots of romantic talk, that the dad might dump her if she doesn't do (or supervise) all the housework and childcare. Of course, he might still dump her, even if she goes along with the roles. Even if your husband *never* would think this way, the dependent situation in itself carries a threat.

Some moms take on the old division of labor unflinchingly; for others, some sharing of home work, even if the mom is the one who's home all day, seems only fair. After all, if the logic is based on care (she cares for them because she cares *about* them), shouldn't the dads care too? And if the dad refuses to do work he could easily do and that relates to his own upkeep (like, say, unloading the dishwasher), it marks that work as degrading for the mom left doing it all.

Of course, working moms can be dumped as well (as can working dads), and there's plenty of politicking around home work within working couples—maybe more than in houses where the division seems more obvious. But at least the working moms have some funds to hand, and because the money dynamic differs, the dynamic around housework differs too. But it's always an issue of some kind. Sadly, the likelihood that a person will live in poverty in our country is much increased if she becomes a mother. Not only is the pay low, but staying home can mean big cuts in long-term earning ability and in payments into retirement and social security accounts. And after a divorce, women's and children's income often plummets, while men's income falls minimally, on average, and tends to rise again quickly.[3]

Many of the women I spoke with knew all this already and waited for kids on purpose to avoid having to be dependent. They invested a lot of time and energy in their jobs and their education. But while many women do stay at work when they become mothers later, others effectively retire into motherhood—leaving a career, sometimes for the short term, sometimes planning to step back in down the line in another field, and sometimes for the long haul. (One female police officer I spoke with did literally retire from the force after twenty years of service, with full benefits and a pension, to raise her young child and start a new [and flexible] business—putting to use the graduate degree she'd earned at night school. Not the usual definition of retirement, but an interesting variant.)

The new later moms who decide to stay home don't all have the same kind of experience with respect to money. For instance, **Valerie**, mom at 36 and 38, had always had family money, so choosing to stay home for a few years when her kids were young and then taking occasional contract work in her field did not affect her ability to make decisions around money in her marriage. **Colette**, mom at 40, left her career to stay home with her son for a few years (she'd always made less than her lawyer husband), but money wasn't an issue because, by the time she had her baby, both her parents had died and she had inherited a substantial sum. This is not a situation she would have chosen, but it affects the power dynamic in their home.

A third mom, **Ginger** (new mom at 39), keeps her own nest egg from a long and successful career, even though her husband makes plenty. Her savings don't play a big role in their day-to-day life, but it's a cushion for them and a comfort to her. Ginger, who left her job because of the grueling hours and the limited time with her child, felt deeply depressed in the time just before she quit. She finally told her husband to take a job offer that gave her an excuse to leave. And though she found the transition difficult, the effect on their finances was beneficial:

> I think my actually quitting at the time that I did contributed very much, in that old-fashioned way, to the bottom line, in terms of my husband's career. Because he was able to advance in a way that [he would not have] had I said, "No, we've got to stay here." It led to a series of events that were extremely profitable for him. So that is an issue between us. I say, "You know, remember buddy, it's my money too! Because you wouldn't have had X, Y, and Z, if I hadn't stepped out at a certain point." . . . I've enabled that to happen. And he realizes that. It bothered me to be in such a role. I thought "God, I'm doing the 1950s thing," you know. But I'm doing it with my eyes wide open, and I do have my own money.

Not everyone has big bank accounts, but many new later moms know money can be an issue, and they make a point of working that issue through before they decide to leave their own revenue stream behind.

❖ PROFILE: Ava, New Mom at 37 and 39

Ava grew up in a working-class family in the Midwest. Though lots of her friends were marrying and having kids right out of high school, she decided to move to the big city. Once she'd established herself in a job, she put herself through college at night. At 30, she met lawyer Brad, and they married when she was 33, at which point she made more money than he did. By the time they had their first child, she was 37, and they were firmly partners. In their partnership, she handles the money. Big purchases they discuss, but otherwise, the check goes into the account, he pays no attention to how much is there, and she makes all the household decisions and pays all the bills. Once she left work after her second child was born, she kept on handling it, both from habit and because she knew she wouldn't feel comfortable if she didn't. Ava explains:

> I know that there are women who stay home who don't know how much money their husbands make, and how much they have in savings, and are given an allotment of money—and I am floored. . . . When women don't know how much money their husband makes, they don't know how much is in the bank, they have no control whatsoever—I think that's dangerous. Because if you get into a divorce, you have no knowledge if he's been hiding money or anything like that. And I've just seen several women who've gone through divorces that have been affected by that. And I've also seen elderly women whose husbands pass away, and they know nothing about the finances. I've always determined that wasn't going to be a part of my mix. . . . Honestly, if I didn't have this control, I would probably be back in the office. I would be back working, cause I can't not have freedom to go out and buy things, if the money's available.

Being a later mom with a history of managing her own money and trusting her own judgment may not be the only factor that made Ava confident enough to work out that arrangement with her husband, but it was a factor. ❖

New later mothers who do stay home tend to be in a secure situation when they choose that option—they've often spent more time getting to know their spouse and establishing a partnership with him (or her) before having kids. They have assets and skills of their own to draw on, and they have a clear sense of who they are and what a good working relationship means to them. They know the value of compromising to keep the relationship going and of walking away if real boundaries are crossed.

The move to the dependent role often involves a sense of loss, even for these more financially established moms. Having a history of independence around monetary decisions can make it harder to adjust to consultation and compromise. And sometimes one person's move home means a big cut in the available cash—even though what remains is sufficient, that's not the same as abundance.

Both these reasons played in for **Patty**, another former big earner and new later mom, now staying at home for a while as a result of an entertainment industry layoff (that's still a fierce industry for women over 40). She made lots of money in her pre-kids days and remembers weeping when she had to ask her husband whether she could take $3,000 from the family account to attend a workshop, even though it was a discussion and in the end the decision was yes. She didn't like having to ask, and she didn't like diminishing the family's reserves. The unfairness of her job situation may have played in too.

Rowena (mom at 35 and 37 and retired lawyer) feels her marriage is a partnership, but she also noticed a change in the power balance when she left work:

> If a person is not going to go back to work, I think you have to find your source of self-worth another way. You have to be willing to be dependent upon your spouse's or companion's income, and for a lot of people, being a dependent is a tough status in which to place yourself. [I had issues with that], but not serious ones.

Each woman and each couple has to figure out what can work for them, and they need to be aware that there's likely to be a transition process into the new arrangement. The more up-front couples can be about their concerns, the better. Those who can set up an expectation of ongoing review and discussion about how things play out that allows for midcourse adjustments when things go wrong are more likely to avoid resentments on both sides.

Deciding to Stay Home

Sometimes the move to stay-at-home parenting happens upon the first child's birth, sometimes a few years later. National data on new later mothers' behavior patterns is rather sparse, but the 1990 and 2000 censi indicate that while they have young children new later moms tend to stay in the workplace in higher proportions than moms who start their families earlier. In 1990, by my calculations, new later moms whose youngest child was 1 year old or under were 15 percent more likely to work full time than moms who started earlier (51.7 percent versus 37 percent), and 12 percent more likely to work overall (76.9 percent versus 65.1 percent). A similar pattern held true in 2000. See Appendix B for more data and discussion.

At the other end of the children's age spectrum, the pattern shifted a bit. While both earlier and new later moms became more likely to work full time as their kids grew older, in 1990 earlier moms outpaced new later moms in this category—they were working full time in greater proportions than new later moms by the time their kids were 7 to 18 (55.4 percent of new later moms versus 60.5 percent of earlier moms). And overall, adding together both full-time and part-time workers, while earlier moms with kids 1 and under were almost 12 percent *more* likely to be at home in 1990 than new later moms with kids the same age, earlier moms with kids 7 to 18 were 6 percent *less* likely to be at home than new later moms with kids in the same age range. That pattern seems to have held true for moms in 2000 as well.

Staying at work when kids arrive, rather than leaving for a while and then returning, has effects on income long term (one year off leads to an average 20 percent long-term income loss, adjusted for education and hours, and two or more years leads to an average long-term loss of about 30 percent).[4] It seems likely that the difference between the work-status patterns of earlier and new later moms is based both on the greater clout the new later moms have accrued that allows them to flex around family more easily and on the fact that they have more investment in their work (in terms of length of service and sometimes education) and more to lose (in terms of salary, benefits, seniority, etc.) if they leave. All of these factors have effects on long-term economic status. Flexible work arrangements that allow furloughs or other time off around family care with benefits maintained should not interrupt work history and economic status in the same way that quitting does. It may be that many of the 55 percent of new later mothers with full-time work when their kids were 7 to 18 had more stable and better-paid positions (adjusting for industry) than many of the 60 percent of their earlier mom counterparts, just because they'd stayed in them.

One explanation for the new later moms' increasing tendency to stay home with older kids (27.2 percent at home with kids between 7 and 18 in 1990, versus 22.9 percent at home with kids 1 and under) might be that they are in a better financial situation to leave work at that point, having worked and saved for a long stretch. On the other hand, earlier moms who've been at home while their kids were young may feel ready for more contact with the wider world and an increased cash flow (34.7 percent of moms who started their family at 34 or earlier were at home with kids 1 and under in 1990 and just 21.1 percent were at home with kids 7 to 18). In addition, new later moms are older by at least ten years than the majority of earlier moms—and may be choosing early retirement as desireable in itself (like quite a few of their male peers, these days). On the other hand, the move home might also be a response to the pressures of juggling family and work in an environment that doesn't make that easy.

Whether she was a new later mom or an earlier mom, the more children a woman had, the less likely she was to work full time. But new later moms were still more likely than earlier moms with the same number of kids to stay at work full time in their children's early years (see Appendix B). A key difference in the groups in 1990 was that a much larger proportion of new later moms had one child than the moms who started earlier. That pattern may have changed since 1990, but the data are not available.

Following the pattern in the data, most of the moms I spoke with stayed at work with young children, but some stayed home from the start. A few of those who had worked when their kids were young then made the move to staying at home after their kids got older (for examples, see Julie's, Ava's, Patty's, Vivian's, and Linda's stories in this and the previous chapter)—some others may yet. Some went by choice, others due to a change in their or their husbands' work options (layoffs, relocation to accompany spouse, etc.). All of them leave open the option of an eventual return to work.

In a related dynamic, **Callie** (new mom at 35, widowed at 39) went from full-time to part-time lawyering when her daughter, Jenny, became a preteen and developed issues in middle school. Jenny needed her mom to be more present for her, time-wise *and* attention-wise, so Callie cut her hours and shifted to a job that didn't put her at the beck and call of her BlackBerry. Now when she's in the room with Jenny, she's more than just physically present.

There's a lot of debate about what social and personal factors fuel career women's decisions to stay home once they have kids, and I don't expect to resolve that here. From the stories I've heard, a variety of prompts can move women home.

Several of the women I spoke to left careers (in diverse fields) because, as in the *Times* Opt-Out article, they were asked to decide between working sixty hours a week or none at all. Others left because they wanted to be able to spend quality time with their kids while the kids were young, because they felt having one person in the family who was free of work demands would make the whole family's life less pressured, because they wanted to recapture their own childhood experience of a mom at home, or because they felt ready to leave their work situation and children provided a good reason to go (the "noble out"). Or they left because of a combination of these or other reasons.

Are they foolishly risking being sidelined in the world of established work rules, as some have recently argued? Or are their choices telling us something about the inadequacy, for women workers, of the way business is organized—as if all the workers were still 1950s family men, with wives to do all the child-minding and dinner-getting? That day is gone, and until creative and real solutions arrive to make business work for families, some women will keep voting with their feet. Maybe we need to stop thinking in such narrow categories about what constitutes a career.

❖ PROFILE: Vivian, New Mom at 35 and 38

Vivian and Sven married when she was 32 and he was 30. She had an MBA and a Masters of Engineering and was something of a perfectionist in her work at a civil engineering firm. Sven was still doing his medical residency when they had their first child, when Vivian was 35. Given her travel and work schedule, neither parent had much downtime, so Tommy went to childcare twelve hours a day. Despite her limited time with Tommy, Vivian loved being a mom, and she and Sven decided to have a second child soon after. They knew something had to change, so Vivian spoke to her boss about a job share. The boss agreed in principle, but in reality the firm had no idea how to make a job share work. Vivian and her partner were to split a job, each working two days alone, with a third day overlapping. But they had separate assignments that neither could complete in the time allotted, and they both ended up quitting in frustration.

Once at home, Vivian the perfectionist put her skills to work homeschooling her kids for a few years. Eventually they transferred the kids to their local elementary school, and Vivian looked into going back to work part time. By now her surgeon husband had a full calendar, and the consultancy work she was offered involved traveling.

It was going to be a lot of time and a lot of traveling. It was up to me—I could have done it like once every other month, or whatever, and on the face of it, I was excited to get out and be with people and do something kind of higher level. But being away from the family was not working out . . . unless I went full time and got full-time nanny help.

She didn't want to go full time, and they didn't need the money.

In the meantime, Vivian got very involved in community life—she became a church leader, a Scouting mom, and an environmental activist. She's felt less of a pull toward the work world than she once did, and she's learning to appreciate the value of community work. Her husband, on the other hand, isn't always so sure about her situation.

It's a very touchy subject in that, when he says something, I take it as, "Well, why aren't you working?" where I think where he's coming from is more of a loving place, like "Are you going to be sorry when you look back that you didn't pursue something?" He's like, "Just make sure that you're not going to be sad that, when the kids are gone, that you didn't pursue your career fully."

He wonders if she would do the same if she had girls—would she want to model the opt-out for them? And sometimes, she's not so sure he doesn't mind. But, she notes,

The other thing I have to realize is, he knows no other life than a working life. And what I'm finding is there's a pretty rich—there's a lot of things to do, and the community needs a lot of things, and the children, not just my children, you know, when I'm working as a Scout leader, I'm helping other children, when I help out at the school, I'm helping other people too, so it's not just my children that my energies are helping. And it's hard for him to know.

When she was working, she had a similar view:

[It was hard] for me to know, before I started doing this sort of thing. I mean, you think less of people who don't work for money, but you have to have a lot of self-confidence to know that that's not true. If you've never had the experience, maybe you just assume everybody else's opinion, that this is kind of secondary to the real working people, but it's really not.

So where the rigors of the corporate schedule pushed Vivian out of the workplace, the pleasures of family life and the community work she's found keep her at home. ❖

Though I heard some complaints about how the moms who stay at home don't arrange meetings so that working moms can attend, most working moms know that the moms who stay home and have time to volunteer at school are doing their whole neighborhood a service. They are a huge part of the value-added in many schools—public and private—and will continue to be until the working world shifts to the point that parents (of both sexes) have the chance to take off work for the occasional field trip. And it's the value-added dimension that moved several of the moms I spoke with to choose the stay-at-home life.

❖ PROFILE: Rosemary, New Mom at 35, 38, and 39

Rosemary and Harry started dating when they were both 27 and married when they were 32. She was traveling a lot for work as a technical adviser, and he was working hard, too. There just wasn't time for kids. But, Rosemary explains, she realized eventually that "I didn't want to be out of town for the rest of my life, so I thought, 'I'm not going to do this. I want to do something else.'" They had been talking about kids, and once they decided to have some, they got busy. They were 35, and she could hear the clock ticking ("loudly"), and, "I mean, I knew I wasn't going to stay at that job, so it was a good time jobwise as well to do it." And one month shy of her 36th birthday, they had their first baby. Having left her tech job, Rosemary planned to stay home for a year with the baby and then go into teaching. But she found the home life very absorbing, and they decided to have another baby—who arrived two years later when they were 38. Then they decided to have a third; it all happened very fast, and at 39— nearly 40—they had their third and final baby (they considered maybe going for four, but three felt right, and Rosemary didn't want to push her good luck).

Looking around her, Rosemary has noticed that, in her set,

> people who work full time are not having three, but people who work part time are going for a third one. So that's been interesting and fun to see. So there do seem to be quite a few of us who got started late but decided to keep going and have one more. Although I do think people start getting nervous [about birth defects] when they hit about 40.

(It makes a certain sense that people with at least one parent at home might have more children than others, but of the eleven women in my study who had or were about to have three or more kids, four were at home and seven were working full time when they had them, and of the four, one has since returned to full-time work.)

Rosemary likes being at home with her kids, because "we enjoy spending time together." As a result, she feels she knows a bit more about what her kids are thinking and what's going on with them. She can be there to guide and to cushion their lives in a way she could not if she were working. She plans to stay at home until her youngest is in kindergarten and then start teaching. Having watched her mother struggle to get back in the workforce after years away, when her father died unexpectedly, Rosemary has no doubt that she will go back—after what will have been a nine-year hiatus. She has no doubt she'll find a job, given the endless demand for teachers. ❖

❖ PROFILE: **Dolores, New Mom at 36, 38, and 40**

Dolores always knew she wanted to have lots of kids and stay home with them. She was an only child and wanted to do things differently—she wanted a crowded Thanksgiving table and lots of layers of connection. At college she got a design degree and then worked in sales, and she enjoyed it for the time being. When she fell in love at 26, she thought she'd be starting the family soon, but it turned out the boyfriend wasn't ready for a family yet, and he didn't expect his wife to stay home when he *was* ready. So, they broke up. Dolores kept on working and got involved in another serious relationship, but they, too, had different ideas about family. Finally at 34, she met Brian, who was great and who wanted the life she wanted, and they knew right away they were it. When I interviewed her, she was living her dream and loving it, with two small kids and one more on the way (the third arrived a few months later).

For Dolores, the decision to stay home happened early. But finding the right guy took a while, which turns out to have been a good thing in her view:

> I love it that I worked so long. I mean, I really do. I guess if you had asked me when I was 17, "Do you think you'll work after college for 15 years?" I'd be like, "No, I'm going to get married and have some kids." But once I got out into the world and just experienced everything, I mean, I had a great time. I really probably wasn't ready to settle down. . . . I was like going out with friends. Going to the rodeo. I'm a very social person. And from 18 to 35, I was out and about all the time.

Now she's more of a homebody:

> I'm real happy to be at home and go to bed at nine. We can still do
> fun things together, my husband and I, go to parties and go to foot-
> ball games. We still get a babysitter and go out. It's just not as much,
> and I don't feel like I have a big—I don't feel like I've missed any-
> thing. Because I've kind of done it all. And so we're real happy just
> to go to a little restaurant with the kids on a Saturday night and rent
> a movie. It's nice.

Dolores expects to stay home at least until her kids are in school. At
that point her options will be open, so her future might include a return to work, either part or full time, or it might not. ❖

Clearly, parents feel differently from one another about how they want
to raise their children. Everyone isn't the same, and no one way guarantees success. The issues involved aren't limited to which option
makes children brighter or more emotionally secure. Both options, and
options in between, can create happy, smart kids. Stay-at-home moms
can give their kids a luxury that the kids of moms who work don't
have—the luxury of time and attention, two things that the modern
world is radically short on. When a mother takes pleasure in spending
time with and interacting with her children, writer and psychologist
Daphne de Marneffe argues, she creates a reciprocal dynamic that
plays an essential part in introducing a child into the experience of
pleasure and enjoyment of life.[5] Who'd want to undermine that? The
key is to find what each mom's pleasure is—so that she can share it
with her child.

Ava, a bit of whose story we heard a few pages back, tells me that
she stays home for two reasons. First, she's "just happier" being at
home and readily accessible to her kids at all times. She makes a point
of saying that she doesn't know if there's any benefit beyond that; "kids

are going to make it regardless." Second, she sees a benefit to being there to monitor and provide a safe haven for her kids and their friends; it's a complicated world, and it's easy for kids to get drawn down wrong roads. "My hope is to be that safe haven and to be the policewoman, because I can be pretty strict."

Part of her pleasure is derived from community-building. She sees her role as supplementing the work of the mothers who've remained in the office, and she's started a neighborhood mothers' breakfast group with the aim of putting more moms of varying job status in touch with each other, so they can pool resources.

There has always been variation in the amount of time spent among mothers, children, and "allo-mothers" (what anthropologists call people who care for the baby when the mother is away—a group that includes grandmothers, babysitters, and teachers, among others). Just being in the same room with her child all day, for a woman who doesn't want to be there full time, would negate the "pleasure sharing" effect. On the other hand, a woman who might like to stay home with her kids doesn't always have that option. There's a lot of social energy spent on making moms feel guilty for not staying home, especially with very young kids, and conversely, on making moms who do stay home feel like traitors to the cause of women's advancement (and where do stay-at-home dads fit in this argument?). Both blame-throwing approaches overlook the extent to which mothers' decisions around their children and families deserve respect and support rather than lectures and admonition. Rather than blaming the moms, it's up to us to present parents with good alternatives, so they can make real choices for the good of their particular families and communities.

Changing Gears

Sometimes it takes working moms a while to adjust to the new life at home. **Abby**, mom at 35 and 38 to two kids who are now teenagers, has been at home since she left her law partnership soon after her second child was born. Like Vivian, she, too, had to choose between seeing her child ("sometimes I wouldn't see him for a week") and keeping her job. Like Ava, Abby does the finances at home. And she doesn't cook well or even often. ("My husband asks me if we're *having* dinner, not what's for dinner.") But while she loved being at home with her kids and not having the stress of work, she did have an identity crisis:

> There are so many brilliant women out there who choose to be homemakers, but you feel like you're judged: "What do you do?" "I stay home with my children." So I had that problem. When people asked me what I did, it would be hard for me not to say, "I used to be a lawyer." . . . I think a mom identity is pretty hard for women who have worked. And yet, I *loved* it. . . . I loved just raising my kids, every minute of it. I've never missed work for that reason.

But sometimes women find that staying at home just isn't what they thought it would be, and they can't adjust to the change. So they go back to work.

❖ PROFILE: Linda, New Mom at 35

When I first spoke with Linda, she had a 1-year-old and worked full time in a corporate finance office. She looked forward to the day when she would be able to quit her job and stay home, as her mother had. Linda had great memories of her parents' active involvement in her childhood activities—they hadn't missed a performance or a game. She wanted to be able to do the same for her son.

When I spoke to Linda two years later, she had fulfilled her plan and was at home. Her husband had made a tidy profit in a business deal, and they had been able to afford to lose her income. But now she was planning her transition back into a job—a part-time job now, but a job.

Although she loved spending time with her son, life at home hadn't been as satisfying as Linda had imagined.

She missed the mental and social activity of the work world. And the dynamics of her marriage had changed—in some positive ways (her new flexibility allowed the family to accompany her husband on business trips now and then), but also in some ways she didn't feel entirely comfortable with. For instance, she now felt much more hesitation around spending money—not because he pressured her about it, exactly, but because she put pressure on herself.

> When I was working, I would like to go into Target, and I'd buy something, and maybe I didn't need it, but I didn't feel guilty about it. And now I sit here and every time I buy something I scrutinize it, "Does Sam really need this? No. Do I really need another pair of black shoes? No." Where in the past, when I worked, I sometimes justified it as, "This is why I work, to buy something." So I'm actually having a harder time with it than he is.

Whereas her sense of ownership of the family funds had weakened, his remained strong: when he wanted a fancy new bike, he bought it, reasoning, "I work, I made that bonus, and this is what I want to do with it"—the same sort of rationale that Linda used to offer. Since she didn't make the bonus this year, the balance shifts. This is not a problem specific to any one couple; it's a standard dynamic, and one that only changes with a lot of honest talk and hard work, if it changes at all (see the section on peer marriage in the next chapter).

In terms of her son's needs, the part-time route seems best to Linda, because she still wants to be available as needed for him—but she doesn't think he should be at home with her exclusively. After spending his early years at home first with a nanny and now with mom, he's rather shy, and she thinks more interactive school experience will be important for him.

Ironically, Linda finds that, while her husband was initially resistant to her quitting, she now has had to convince him of the merits of her part-time plan: "He understands, because he realizes the troubles I'm having with adapting to staying home. But he likes the fact that I'm home for Sam, he likes the fact that we've gone with him a couple places when he's out of town. We're more flexible for his schedule."

But she is going back, and she'll be able to build on her established reputation to fashion her new job on her own terms. ❖

Stay-at-Home Moms and the Clout Effect

The clout effect has its clearest benefits in the business world, but it also works when moms stay home. Over the last decade, we've seen an increase in cultural respect for mothers who don't have other jobs; the efforts of new later moms have contributed to this trend. Quite a few new later moms worked throughout their twenties and thirties and have opted to "retire" into motherhood or to work part time, something they can now afford to do because they have their own savings and the expanded salaries of their partners. And these stay-at-home mothers, used to respect at work, are demanding and getting a new respect at home and in the schools.

Sometimes stay-at-home moms go public with their critique of the status quo, as did Ann Crittenden, a journalist, Pulitzer Prize nominee, and new later mom who took years off to raise her son. Crittenden is tuned into the nuances of the evolving public debate over women's rights and roles. She couldn't help noticing the inequity displayed on her social security balance sheet, which showed zeroes for the years when she was at home raising a child, the child who would one day be paying the social security of people in the standard work economy (including those who had never had kids). As she looked around, she noticed a number of other disparities in the treatment of mothers in U.S. society—disparities not in evidence in many other Western countries.

Crittenden went on to write *The Price of Motherhood,* a powerful analysis of the economic situation of mothers that excites almost every mother who reads it. "After fighting hard to win respect in the workplace, women had yet to win respect for their work at home," she wrote.[6] But due to her efforts, and those of many others, it now seems that respect in the workplace is at last serving as the basis for claims to respect at home. Crittenden's ability to crystallize the issues surrounding the inequitable treatment of mothers (with regard to childcare options, work, power dynamics in the home, divorce settlements, and so on) comes not from her being the first to recognize the inequities (millions before her have known things were wrong) but from being able to combine that recognition with a competence gained through her experience in newsrooms presenting arguments clearly. Her work history won her a respect that got her words a hearing.

This marks Crittenden as a member of a revolutionary generation of mothers—mothers with credentials, accrued as proven members of the standard workforce. An articulate mother, with the cultural capital requisite to winning listeners, Crittenden speaks to an audience of women with similar capital and expectations. These women are alert to the debate and are themselves raising questions, including: Why isn't motherhood (and all the management skills attendant thereon) valued as a credential? (Crittenden's latest book explores this issue further.) Why can't work schedules be flexible to accommodate the needs of children and parents? Why aren't dads more overtly encouraged to take childcare seriously? What about universal preschool and a decent wage for childcare workers?

In fact, many of the participants in the current motherhood debates, on all sides of the issues, are new later moms or had otherwise established themselves in their careers before having kids.

Taking a more experiential approach, writer and new later mom Anne Lamott (35 at the birth of her son) has also helped change the terms on which motherhood is discussed. Her 1993 book *Operating Instructions* was an early entry in the now flourishing baby book market—notable for its down-to-earth presentation of the pains as well as the joys of motherhood (and the way those two can flip within moments). Lamott's worldly tone and experience allowed her to approach motherhood without the anxiety about looking competent and completely content that younger moms often feel. She introduced a new frankness about motherhood's combination of difficulties and satisfactions—demythologizing in a way that opened motherhood to more realistic discussions. A similar frankness now animates the conversation on hundreds of mother blogs, where mothers from all over the nation and the world discuss all aspects of their experience. This conversation runs on a mother's terms, not terms foisted upon her.

Revaluing Women's Work

Along with the work of mothering, many mothers also hold down paying jobs outside the home. African American women sometimes note that white women who juggle family life with full-time work today imitate the lives that black women have long juggled, of necessity.[7] The difference lies in the range of jobs that women (of all races) now choose from. Where it used to be the case that "women's work" outside the home closely resembled the work moms did at home, nowadays the range has expanded and continues to expand.

As the definition of what work women can do has changed, all the other assumptions about who does what work and how it's valued are shifting, too. People have begun to realize that, if you want good childcare without constant turnover, you have to pay the workers a wage that will attract a skilled group in the first place and then keep them loyal to their jobs. In a roundabout way, raised pay for childcare workers means raised respect for the women who do it for free at home. And the flextime discussion involves recognition of the importance of caring for children.

Recently, philosopher Linda Hirshman, in her manifesto *Get to Work*, slammed stay-at-home moms as laggards and wastrels who squander women's opportunity for advancement in corporate America by opting out of careers just when they are poised to rise to the top.[8] She portrayed staying home as caving to the pressure of an antifeminist backlash in the wider community that asks women to live throwback fifties lives, which effectively slow everybody's progress instead of moving us forward. Without that siphoning off of talent, she reasons, what I've described as a "trickle up" of women into upper management might be a gusher. Even more recently, Leslie Bennetts has offered a similar argument.[9]

In fact, the new later motherhood trend is a means by which many working women, via the clout effect, do manage to combine work with raising a family. But that pattern is not of interest to everyone, and Hirshman's polemic overlooks the fault in the system that makes it hard for many mothers to find balance. Many women don't want to wait to start their families, and as we've seen, even if they do wait, sometimes the clout effect isn't enough to support continued travel up the work ladder when there are kids needing attention at home.

One new later mom I talked with, **Gloria**, told a story of her first year working at a corporate job. Though she had scored highest in all the tests among her incoming group of workers, she discovered one day in conversation that she, the sole woman in the group, was paid several thousand dollars less than her coworkers. Shocked (and armed with the knowledge that this was illegal), she asked her employers for an explanation. They had none, and they immediately made up the difference in salary and back pay to her. In the years following, she sailed on up the ladder with a smile.

Gloria's story is an example of the working of old assumptions that women's work, whatever it was, just deserved less. Sometimes you'll hear it linked to ideas of a family wage (men should make more because they're feeding a whole family—whereas women who work aren't?), but those arguments seem to spring from much older prejudices against women's work. They're the reason why secretaries get less than truck drivers and cleaning ladies get less than handymen, in spite of their "comparable worth." Ideas of gender and economics are so intertwined that it's hard to tell which comes first—and so you have to address both at once to make change. Pay women more for all the jobs they do *and* make more kinds of work options available to them.

Hirshman argues that, by aligning themselves with body-care work and effluvia (as in diapers, bath scum, and throw-up), women who stay home are perpetuating the low ranking of all women's work. But the equation works both ways. By perpetuating the low ranking of care of all kinds, we make it harder for women to climb the ranks at work. In a direct link, trashing stay-at-home moms and their work negatively affects our view of childcare workers in general and makes it harder to argue for the raises in pay that make it more likely that skilled people will take those jobs and stay in them long enough to provide the consistency that families want for their babies. After all, they aren't bad jobs; they're only badly paid. And less directly, the low ranking of traditional women's work draws down the ranking of all women's work, by association. We all have to pull together here—not so that we can succeed within the available options, as working women on the male model or as nonworking or badly paid working women on the old female model, but to write some new options into the structure of work and family life. The new later motherhood contributes one new option, but it has its drawbacks, and it's hardly sufficient to the needs of all. The restructuring process *is* under way, but it has a ways to go yet.

All of which reminds me of Pammy, the girl in the epigraph. When my daughter's playmate remarked that "mothers are servants," I smiled and kept moving. Though fairly new to the planet, she was already packing a lot of cultural baggage and making an association that caregiver equals low-status work that many others have made before her. Pammy wasn't differentiating between moms who stay home full time and moms who hold other jobs too; she paints us all with one brush. In one respect, Pammy just had it wrong—I offered that treat because I wanted to, not because anybody paid or ordered me to do it. Pammy is a bright girl, however, and not rude. She called it like she saw it—and though nowadays dads do a good measure of service work too, apparently that wasn't what Pammy had seen. She saw a gendered task split, and she ranked the mom's role lower.

Still, one way to gauge that home work is getting more respect than it used to is that *more and more men are seen doing it.* We all know the status losses associated with working in a field not seen as appropriate to your gender, particularly for men working in traditionally "women's" fields (think of the male nurse jokes in the movie *Meet the Fockers*). But as more and more men take home work on, the ranking shifts, and the status of home work rises further so that even more men can afford to risk doing it—publicly and privately. It's a dynamic system. Again, the shift is gradual, but it's there. Not only do more and more men do more and more housework and childcare (seeing it as "only fair," since their wives also work outside the home for pay), but more are choosing to be househusbands who take primary care of their children. It turns out men like caring for kids, once the status barriers come down. Maybe soon they'll be lining up to take family-friendly flex options at work. Once more of the barriers fall, maybe the Pammys of the world, and all of us, will come to value home work more highly.

CHAPTER 5

All in the Family

Changing the Ways
We Live and Love

At 40, it better be your *life, or what else?*

—CECILY,
writer and mom at 40

I f you're a new later mom, you've pretty much figured out who you are by the time you have kids. It comes with the territory that you've handled a fair number of situations, some of them difficult—so you know how you respond. You've learned a few things in your job and in your personal life, so you're likely to be fairly sure of yourself. Here's **Dorcas**, quondam TV commentator, currently staying at home, and mom at 38 and 40, now 44:

> I think that hitting 40 was a huge milestone. I don't know what happens at 40, but . . . for me and for most of my friends, it's just so liberating. . . . I mean I just feel good. You're not . . . intimidated by anything. You just say "This is who I am, take it or leave it; I don't have time to worry about pleasing everybody."

Today's later moms have life experience as well as job credentials and accrued accomplishments like no generation of moms before. And that affects the way people relate to them, including people in their most intimate relationships. Maybe especially them.

In the past forty years, the range of relationships that grown people can have in public has expanded quite a bit. Often that change seems linked to just how grown these people are. As women and men enter parenthood later in life, they know themselves better and can construct situations that suit them. Many of the women I spoke with participate in new relationship dynamics that seem directly linked to having started their families later, including peer marriage, a tendency to more stable marriages, higher rates of marriage or partnership, a loosening of the custom of marrying older men, a tendency to spend time together before having kids, more involved dads, and lots more onlies—all these trends frequently involve new later moms, though not in every case. On the other hand, some new later moms are single (15 percent), but single later moms tend to be in much more secure financial and social situations than single moms who started their families at a younger age. And, often for logistical reasons, lesbian moms seem overwhelmingly to be later moms, though as we'll see, the logistics behind that tendency may be changing.

The New Traditionalists

New later moms tend to arrive in the delivery room with rings on at a rate much higher than younger moms (where 85 percent of new later moms in 2003 were married when their children were born, 82 percent of teenage moms in the same year were not). That isn't accidental. Here's **Rosalind** (married at 39, new mom at 40, formerly in sales, now staying home with her daughter):

> Even as I got older, I just couldn't see [having a child] as a single person. To me, the idea was having a family, not having a child. . . . Surely I would have lamented not having the childbirth experience

and that kind of thing, but to me it wasn't going to be meaningful unless it was a family—husband and kids.

Deborah (corporate executive, married at 36, mother at 37 and 40) feels similarly:

I never wanted to be a single parent . . . because I grew up with a mom and a dad and values that my parents instilled in me. [I feel that] it helps; it's important if two people are there to raise a child. A father is a very important person in a child's life. . . . But you know a lot of women who can afford to now and who are older, but because they're older they waited—they're having kids without a husband. And [before I got married], I even thought about adopting a child when an opportunity was presented to me, but I thought long and hard about it and chose not to. Financially I could have handled it on my own.

Though some later moms do decide to go it alone from the start, most of them have partners. That's because many waited on purpose to find the right mate—if they'd been open to parenting solo, they could have started sooner. You could call these new later moms "the new traditionalists."

In the same vein, though the data on this are skimpy because the U.S. government stopped tracking national rates of marriage and divorce in 1995, the marriages of new later moms seem less likely to end in divorce than marriages in which children were born to younger moms. State and CDC survey data do show that early first marriages (teens and early twenties) are more likely to end in divorce than first marriages between people in their mid-twenties,[1] so the states with the youngest average age at first marriage are also the states with the highest divorce rates. Though we don't have specific stats on marriages in which children are born to women 35 or older (or on how that intersects with the age the marriage was entered into), we do know that money and maturity affect marital stability. One recent study indicates that middle-class women with jobs are less divorce prone than middle-class women who stay at home.[2] New later moms tend to have college degrees and to be married to men with college degrees, and marriages between two college-educated partners last longer than others. Money makes a difference here, too (degrees mean you're more likely to have a job that pays a decent wage, and that on average means less abuse, less drug use, less strife), and shared interests and shared work (both at home and outside) can keep things dynamic.

Also, later marriages in which first children are born (as opposed to later marriages after you've already had a child) tend to be entered into both on an informed basis (by that point, you've probably made a few mistakes in love and know what you can and cannot live with) and on a committed basis (women who have kids later often waited on purpose to get things right, and after waiting so long, they report feeling committed to working to resolve marital problems rather than moving on to the next candidate). As **Sharon**, now 51 and mother of four, including a set of triplets at 40, puts it,

> I think one thing about being 50 and looking at this, maybe if I were 30 and my kids were these ages, you'd think, well you've got a long, bright—you've got a long time. At 50, I'm thinking I'm buying the last couch for this house, and I don't want a new husband. I want this relationship to work, he's a good, good guy, and I need to make this relationship work, and I'm more interested in making that happen, putting in the energy.

Sharon had an earlier marriage without kids, and she knows how moving on can go. She and her husband have put a lot of work and love into their family, and she can see the time, in the near future, when they'll be alone in the house again: "And we will have done all this great stuff; we've raised these really great kids; we've had all these great experiences and done great things with them, learned so much and then to not be together? That would be, that would just be the worst tragedy. . . . It was my life."

These dynamics are interesting for what they tell us about family circumstances and about what women are aiming for when they decide to wait. Though it's no guarantee of the long-term involvement of a dad with his kids, marriage does signal the likelihood of his sustained involvement, as well as the likelihood of a stable family environment. And there is a greater probability that married parents will be solvent and able to supply their kids with the many goods and services that make up a middle-class life. And dads who are intimately involved in their kids' care will feel less interested in leaving the family in the first place and less willing to impoverish those kids via an unfair settlement if divorce does happen.

It makes sense that people who marry later will have a clearer sense of what they want in a mate; likewise, people who marry earlier, but who wait to have kids until a few years into the marriage, will have a firmer sense of what they've gotten into and that the marriage is likely to last. Similar dynamics affect the marriages of people who have early "starter" marriages—marriages that involved no kids—who then go on to begin a family in a second marriage with a new partner.[3] I say your first spouse should count as an education credit.

While growing numbers of women are choosing the new later motherhood road if it's open to them, for many reasons that road is *not* open to everybody. Once it is an option, whether it feels right is another issue.

Then there's the fact that fertility declines with age, meaning that delaying involves a risk—though exactly how much risk has not always been clearly represented in the press. Some women don't feel willing to take that risk; for others, the compromises involved in *not* taking the risk feel equally or more problematic. For everybody, the important factors are having a realistic sense of that risk and knowing what the alternatives are if your fertility runs low.

Many women wait because they haven't yet met Mr. (or Ms.) Right, and they're not willing to compromise on a wrong partner just for the sake of being married on a conventional schedule. Or, if they have met the love of their life, they feel that it's important for them to spend time as a couple before they branch out. Here's **Margaret**, mother of three (at 37, 39, and 42):

> Well my husband and I got married, also late for me, I was 32 [he was 28], and we always knew that we wanted to wait to make sure that we knew each other before we had children. So we spent about five years married, traveling, and just relaxing, happy hours with friends. And when I turned 35, we knew that it was time that we should think about it.

Of the partnered women I talked with, nearly 60 percent (58.1) had been with their partner four or more years when they had kids, and a little more than 35 percent had been together six years or more. Fifteen percent had been together ten years or more—the couples at the upper end had been together fifteen, eighteen, and even twenty years, before deciding to have kids. These are interesting numbers because they indicate that these couples were not all marrying in order to rush directly into parenthood. And most of them were not delaying due to fertility issues.

Sometimes the wait had to do with overcoming personal barriers: **Stephanie** (public relations consultant) and Mark married when she was 23 and he was 26. Now 51 and 54, they had their first and only child when she was 38—a fifteen-year wait.

> I've often questioned myself about why I didn't consider it a primary need at that point in my life. First off, I was very career oriented, very driven, you know, had a need to achieve and work hard. . . . But I also think a big piece of it was, while I consider myself to have had a very happy and fun childhood, I had a younger sibling [who] was

very hard to manage as a child and my mother had great difficulty with it, and I think I didn't see her as having such a great time being a mother. So it, you know, it didn't inspire me.

[But after a while I wondered], was I missing something? And we also felt we had been married so long without things changing, you know, that we wanted something different in our lives.

The long interval in a happy marriage gave Stephanie the time to draw back from her mother's experience and feel ready to engage as a mom on her own terms.

Sometimes there was no sense of urgency or perhaps a lack of awareness that fertility declines with age. Notes **Deirdre**, former marketer and mother at 39 and 42, who married at 35 after having known her husband for five years, then waited another few years before trying to have a baby, "there was no sense of worry about not being able to conceive. Because the buzz [that it might be difficult] just wasn't in the air in those days. So luckily I conceived very quickly, probably the first time. Even with my second child, I was very lucky."

Ann, a designer who had her one daughter at 41 and then encountered secondary infertility when she tried for a second, had been with her husband for ten years before they started their family. She explains her wait:

I was too busy having a good time, basically is what it was. And I worked hard. I worked a lot. There wasn't really a whole lot of time left except a whole lot of work and fun. . . . But anyway, finally, we went off the pill. Got pregnant right away, then had a miscarriage at ten weeks. Then I thought, "It wasn't meant to be. I shouldn't have." I went back on the pill. "I'm not supposed to have a kid. It's too late. I'm too selfish, I'm too, whatever." Finally, I thought—I hadn't really resolved it. I thought, "I really *do* want to have a kid. I really want to have one, or maybe even more." So, I went off it again. Got pregnant again, and now I have an almost 7-year-old. Wish I hadn't waited so long.

Because of the experience of women like Ann who encountered age-related infertility, most of us have now heard about the fertility risks of waiting. Those risks are not only documented, but sometimes exaggerated in the press. But if you're clear you want children and your circumstances are what you want them to be for starting your family, it makes sense to start sooner rather than later, if you want to bear a child or several children. If Ann had started at 35 or 38, she might now be the mother of two kids. But hindsight often skews the realities of the pressures of life in the moment.

Often women who wait sense that families formed later are more likely to hold together and that they (with or without a spouse) will be better able to raise kids in a financially secure environment. If they do find the right partner, then two emotionally, educationally, and financially established parents can offer their kids additional advantages. In today's divorce-prone world, many women wait, at least in part, because they seek to increase the likelihood that their union will last and that, as a result, they can offer a strong support network to their kids.

Peer Marriage

I guess I see, just looking at my parents' marriage, where my mother stayed home; I felt like she didn't have a say, or as much of a say as I do, in decisions in her marriage. And I think it was partly because she wasn't a financial contributor.

—DOMINQUE,
mom at 37 and 40 and chemical
engineer, working part time

Sociologist Pepper Schwartz wrote the book on *Peer Marriage* in 1994 when the phenomenon was still new. She described a trend toward marriages of "equal companions." By that she meant couples that did not rely on prefab gender roles to define their jobs or their spheres of influence within the marriage. They tended to contribute similarly in all areas of work and play within marriage. Peer husbands did about the same amount of housework as peer wives, and peer wives made about the same amount of money and worked as much as their husbands. If one person didn't work outside the home, the pair made sure that the worker did not take control of the purse or scorn the home work. Dr. Pepper describes peer marriages as the road to deeper intimacy and true companionship:

> [Peer] couples were distinguished by more than their dedication to fairness and collaboration; the most happy and durable among them also had refocused their relationship on *intense companionship*. To be sure, they shared child raising, chores and decision making more or less equally and almost always equitably. . . . [But] the point of the marriage was not to share everything fifty-fifty. Rather the shared decisions, responsibilities and household labor were in the service of an intimate and deeply collaborative marriage.[4]

Schwartz identifies four characteristics of peer couples:

- The partners did not generally have more than a 60/40 traditional split of household duties and child raising.
- Each partner believed that each person in the couple had equal influence over important and disputed decisions.
- Partners felt that they had equal control over the family economy and reasonably equal access to discretionary funds.
- Each person's work was given equal weight in the couple's life plans. The person with the least glamorous and remunerative job could not always be the person with the most housework or childcare.[5]

As a result of this companionate and equitable dynamic, peer couples connect in a different way from couples who split the world into separate spheres:

Peer couples experience much more of each other's lives than do traditional or near peers. Because they share housework, children, and economic responsibility, they empathize as well as sympathize. They experience the world in a more similar way, understand each other's personality more accurately and communicate better because they know each other and each other's world better and because equal power in the relationship changes interaction style. They negotiate more than other couples, they share conversational time, and they are less often high-handed, dismissive, or disrespectful than other couples. They choose to spend a lot of time together.[6]

Because they're not the norm that most people grew up seeing, peer marriages take work. Both partners have to reinforce peer behaviors and to complain when the dynamic falls into traditional patterns.

Though it's not a necessity for a peer marriage, Schwartz notes that many people in peer marriages came there later in life after being disappointed with earlier, non-peer relationships. Many of the peer husbands had enjoyed being in a traditional marriage "up to a point. Then they reported being either bored or overwhelmed with responsibility."[7] And the peer wives sought a real partner, one who didn't leave them feeling lonely and misunderstood after the initial euphoria of new love wore off. "Age," Schwartz explains, "seems to tame men's preoccupation with work and control, and it gives women more courage, self-confidence and direction."[8]

On the down side of peer marriage, Schwartz lists lowered ability for one partner to pursue an extremely high-earning, time-intensive job (you have to be there to be a peer); tamer sex lives (or maybe not); and the costs of having to fight social pressures to conform to the stereotypes (those pressures may be less today than in 1994). Although partners decide for themselves whether their relationship is or should be peer, the groundwork for peer couplings sounds a lot like the circumstances of the majority of the new later moms I've spoken with.

Most of the women I met have an education level and job experience similar to their partners, and many bring home as much or more in salary as their husbands do. Many did spend a lot of time as friends with their partners before they became parents, a quality that Schwartz notices can help partners resist pressure to take on prefab roles when kids do arrive.

When neither partner is dependent on the other for survival, the power dynamic shifts. The husband learns to share the power of the purse strings, and the wife moves out of the role of supplicant. Says **Susan** (writer and new mom at 40), "It's a real position of strength to have your own money. . . . I never have to ask permission. We just discuss expenditures, but I never have to ask permission to buy a pair of shoes or anything—and that's great."

Sometimes there's chafing during the learning process—if some aspect of peer-ship doesn't get fully learned. But when the full dynamic is in place, it means that no one feels resentful because they're stuck with an unfair dose of an unpleasant task—or if they feel they are, they can complain and work to change it.

If you don't feel as though you *have* to stay, you can have a different kind of argument—one in which you feel free to stand up for what you think, and win or lose on the merits of the case you make rather than on the basis of whose voice is louder or who has the power of the checkbook. And likewise with the kids—if a dad feels tuned in to his kids' lives, he can contribute to discussions about their rearing in newly informed ways.

Remember the women in Chapter 1 talking about wanting to avoid feeling trapped, as their mothers had been? A peer marriage, especially one in which you earn your own income, is frequently the way out of that trap. **Jeanne**, a scientist married to another scientist and mom at 38 and 41, explains her sense of the dynamic:

I think education and knowledge and having met all the people I've met, having traveled as part of my career, has developed me. I wouldn't be the person I am now, I wouldn't have the confidence I have now, if I didn't go through that. So I changed tremendously after that, maybe age too—but I think it's just meeting people, being in the situations I have been in that's made me what I am now. I would be a very different mom, I think, if I had my kids earlier.

I am now more assertive than I was prior to going through my education, I have more confidence. And I can live on my own, don't have to have my husband to support me. That's a very strong statement I can make. So that probably affects my relationship with my husband.

Even if one partner is working less than the other, as is the case for **Dominique** and Bill (both in the oil and gas industry, she part time, he full time), the terms of discussion differ from those in which one person couldn't make enough to support herself if needed.

I think [my work experience] makes me more of an equal partner in the marriage. Maybe just back to the confidence I have, and the fact that I *could* have an income level equal to my husband; I think that gives me some clout in negotiations with my husband or coming to compromises. Just everyday compromises—should we buy a couch, should we not buy a couch, should we move to Houston, should we not move to Houston. I think it gives me some credibility in my marriage. And I think it probably makes our marriage stronger because we deal with each other as equals.

The element of threat that has deformed many marriages over the ages goes away when neither partner can trump with the money card. Both sides find they can listen and, more often than not, alter their behavior when called for.

Couples in peer marriages report the highest proportion of shared household responsibilities (whether or not they have household help). If you're both working the same hours, it's hard to see why one person

should then come home and do all the home work on her own. Says
Margaret, human resources manager and mother of three:

> My life is so much easier [than my mother's was], because of my
> husband. You know how—now, when you're older, you know how
> lucky you are, and I am. . . . My father was sort of the old Hispanic
> style, where my mom would work all day and then come home and
> have to fix dinner. And only *she* could fix dinner for him, and then
> she had to serve him. . . . My husband is, a lot of times I say we're
> not fifty-fifty, he's sixty, I'm forty. He's not picky about things, he's
> very laid back. Much more laid back than I am. . . . He takes the
> kids to the doctor. He takes them to school. I mean, we go back and
> forth. He has no problems taking them *all* to get their hair cut, he
> does it all. And my father did not do that *at all*. So I don't have the
> burdens that my mom did. I think that's a major, major difference.

Not that all couples do exactly the same things. **Marcy** and Dan
(parents when she was 39 and he was 37) have their own split, based
on what each one feels most strongly about:

> I think it's pretty even, although my husband does the grocery shop-
> ping, sometimes with the kid, as in last night. And we sort of split up
> the cooking, although I really detest cooking, and I'm not good at it,
> so I tend to do a lot of dishes, a *lot* of dishes—he makes a lot of
> dishes, but he'll get something decent on the table. I do all the laun-
> dry, cause I'm—the typical gender sniping, "because I want my
> clothes to come out the color they went in." And it could be taught,
> I know. So I think I'm pretty fortunate about the division of labor.
> And we probably should try to hire somebody, with [our son's]
> asthma the dusting is kind of a big deal. But I think it's pretty even.

Sometimes jobs don't allow for an even division. Sven (dad at 33 and
36), husband to **Vivian** (stay-at-home mother and engineer, mom at 35

and 38), is a surgeon and is in the operating room early and late. He doesn't do much housework, but Vivian says he is there for his kids:

> He's a very involved father. So, you know, he doesn't coach any sports teams, but every time that he can be there, he's there. And both my sons are big chess players, and I don't play chess at all, so they have this big chess thing going. And he is very, very good—he takes them, he's a wonderful father. And that's kind of what his free time is about, is spending time with kids. And if they have time off at school, he'll take time off at work to be with them. So he plans his days off at work to be with them. So, he's great. He doesn't really have that kind of time, but every free moment is with the kids.

Yvonne's husband Nick (she was 37 and he was 48 when they had their baby) sold a successful business and took off five years "to develop a relationship and be supportive of me. He stayed home with our daughter [now 2]." Now that their daughter is in preschool, he's starting a new business that he really has a passion for. "It's his turn." Yvonne also runs a business and reports that, apart from childcare, their household work split is "probably sixty-forty his favor."

It isn't always so nearly even. Sometimes that's a problem, and sometimes not. **Deborah** and her husband Phillip (now both 41, both 37 and 40 when their kids arrived) both work between forty and fifty hours a week in administrative positions. She explains their situation:

> He helps with baths, and I mean, you know, he's a good dad. He does one half of the drop-off or pickup. If one of the kids is sick, we alternate whose turn it is to stay home with them. [But] I don't think it's fifty-fifty, I think more of it is on me. Because I take care of the food and the cooking and buying their clothes. But I want to do that, and it's never been an issue. I can't say it's fifty-fifty. He helps a lot, but I don't know of any relationship where it's fifty-fifty. . . . I never

believe it's ever fifty-fifty. Someone always seems to have more of the responsibility.

As all householders know, housework isn't just cleaning and grocery shopping—there's a whole layer of management too. "Right," says Deb,

> and that's me. I make sure that—you know how fast kids grow out of clothes, and my husband wouldn't have a clue. Now I've gotten it down to where I know my son—depending on where we buy his clothes, what size would work for him. If I buy it at Baby Gap or Gymboree, it's a different size than if I bought it at Children's Place. And half way in between at his six-month mark birthday, I know he's switching into a new size, but my husband doesn't know stuff like that.

Deborah gets up early to get the kids ready for school and then she drops them off. Phillip picks them up. At night, she cooks dinner. He does the dishes and plays with the kids while Deb puts her feet up, because by that point in the day "I'm tired!" They divide much of the housework, but in many respects, they've chosen a traditional gender split. Says Deb:

> I want to do it. And I have girlfriends who are single, and you know, women's rights, who say, "You shouldn't. . . ." And I say, "I do what makes me happy." I like to be the nurturing one; I like taking care of my family. That's a role I chose for myself, and it's not one that was forced upon me. I chose it. I'm very strong willed, and they know that. And if I wanted to, I could change it, but I don't want to, I love it the way it is.

Though for several years Deb has consistently made considerably more money than her husband, she accedes to his judgment on major purchases:

Our central air-conditioning went three weeks ago; I wanted to just buy a couple of window units and stick them in and be done with it. But he decided it would be better in the long run to replace it. And since that was a lot of money, I could say that, "Yeah, I'm okay with the decision. Fine."

There's a big difference between "I'm okay with the decision" and "Whatever you say."

Not everyone loves the more traditional gender split. Some wish their spouses were more open to sharing the household burdens. For instance, **Stephanie**, now 51 and the mother of a 13-year-old, is married to 54-year-old Mark. While her husband does all the cooking and food shopping, beyond that he doesn't pay attention to the household management details. When he comes home,

he kind of goes off the clock. Every evening I see my husband sitting there watching primetime television and reading newspapers and for some reason my day doesn't become mine until ten o'clock at night. I don't know why. I'm not conscious of it, but I'm doing things that are all very practical. I'm not sitting there manicuring my nails, or looking at pictures that I just, you know, took from the camera or anything. There's always some sort of purposeful activity and then, by the time my time is my time, I'm too tired to read the newspaper because it will put me to sleep, so. . . .

Deirdre, another new later mom from the early nineties, now 54, analyzes it this way:

Even though this is evolving, and on paper we're very different in gender roles than our parent's generation, we grew up in our parents' times, and those were the models we had, and we're still struggling, like in [Mark's] subconscious, it's the traditional model he's trying to follow still and he's not really bending on that at all. So we're caught between two generations.

It's an ongoing evolution, but the peer marriage model is the prime ground for pushing forward.

Peer marriage is a work in progress—according to the women I talked to, the split-up of housework can play out in many ways. Almost all the partnered women had mates who shared in the childcare more than *their* dads did. A fair number said their husbands did the housework and childcare 50 percent of the time. But most women said they did more, sometimes unwillingly, and sometimes happily. The more men get used to doing housework and to viewing their spouses as partners, the greater the ease with which divisions fair to both will be struck.

The Older Woman

He is two years younger than me. . . . All the wives that I've been meeting of my husband's colleagues are all older. And not just a little bit—I thought two years was a big deal, but it's really not—at all!

—VIVIAN,
stay-at-home mother and
engineer, mom at 35 and 38

Many factors play into the way power balances are struck in a marriage. A person's sex, earning power, parenting skills, attractiveness, and knowledge all contribute something. So apparently can age—or why would close to 80 percent of married women who have their first child in their twenties have older husbands? Eighty percent is an enormous majority, and the pattern draws not just on custom but on the reasons behind the custom. A relatively youthful woman tends to be less skilled than an older man, justifying the division of their labor into the private (unpaid) and public (paid) markets. Since she would make less anyway, it makes sense that she be the one to forgo income and do the childcare. And if *older* is linked to *wiser* and/or *more educated*, then her financial dependency would be reinforced by an intellectual dependency too. "Father knew best" in the fifties. He claimed to anyway, because he was older, more educated, and richer. That linked pattern still holds in many American households.

As I took notes on the families of the women I interviewed, the pattern fell apart. At one point, 45 percent of the women were older than their husbands! When I checked the national data for new later moms, the breakdown was forty-sixty. A similar breakdown happens when you sort by education. As the split approaches fifty-fifty, age seems to be less and less a factor in the choice. These people are older or younger because somebody's got to be one or the other, not because they're following the old role model.

What are the virtues of marrying a younger man? Well for one, they're cute and they won't sag so quickly; but more significantly, it means you're less likely to be widowed in old age. We hear a lot about the proliferation of elderly widows, and it's usually attributed to the fact that women outlive men (in the United States, women on average live to 80 and men to almost 75).[9] The fact that women tend to marry older men exacerbates the problem—of course older husbands tend to die sooner! Add that to the fact that women tend to live longer, and there's the groundwork for a long widowhood. Women who marry younger men can increase the odds of having a long-term companion.

Marrying an older woman benefits the man, too, if he's looking for a peer marriage. The likelihood that he will not have to bear the burden of supporting the family alone is greater if his wife is more advanced in her career. Even if she's going to stay at home, she's likely to have more savings, as well as retirement and social security accounts.

Marrying a younger man also decreases your likelihood of infertility. New research indicates that the ages of the men and women involved combine to determine the in/fertility of the couple.[10] Younger dads may benefit the kids genetically as well—recent research links autism and schizophrenia in some cases to having an older father (though that's not the only cause) but finds no link to maternal age.[11] Two of the moms I spoke with reported having a child in the autism spectrum.

Marrying a much younger man may also involve risks—especially if other factors that tend to link with age (like earning ability and education) are also skewed. Over the three years of this study, I learned of three new divorces (three other women were already divorced from the father of their children at the time of our first interview). One of the new divorces involved a wife nine years older than her husband. She was also much more educated and made much more money than her spouse. Though they had started out optimistically, he ended up very resentful of her, and their divorce became extremely ugly. On the other hand, three couples in which the husband is ten or more years younger than the wife, whose education and earnings are on a par, have had long and happy marriages.

A fifth couple with a ten-year age difference had equal levels of education but widely disparate salaries. **Libby** and Damon went through a bad patch and considered separating. But before they started dividing the furniture, Libby realized that she really did not want that to happen and that she especially did not want their daughter to grow up without her dad in the house. Recognizing that she had been assuming that her opinion counted more because she made more money, she began instead to treat Damon as a respected and beloved equal. As Libby described it, their difficulties melted away as a result—confirming that the marital power balance is determined not only by who has what attributes but that love and perseverance can play a role too.

Gay Moms

Most of the lesbian moms that I know fall in the 35 and above category. . . . Mostly I think it's because (a) alternative reproductive methods were not available, and (b) we didn't know anyone who was doing this, ten years ago. So we didn't really consider it something

we were ever going to do. Or we didn't have the means to do it, and
so we didn't consider it.

—LOUISE,
mom via sperm donor and
adoption at 40 and 43

Gay women have been parents for ages, but most often they were the parents of kids from hetero unions entered before the mom came out. An out gay woman didn't generally think of herself as a potential mom until recently because it just didn't seem like an option physically; because "mom" often wasn't the image many gay women had of themselves; and because the world was not very receptive to gay families. With the growing openness about gay relationships and the availability of sperm donation and adoption, gay women can explore family options as they never could before. And very often, for the time being anyway, gay moms are new later moms.

This seems to be partly because it wasn't an option when they were in their twenties, so gay women in their thirties and forties today have only recently been able to become moms—later by default. And for many, the process of claiming and coming to terms with sexual orientation takes time.

I spoke with several gay moms who had come to motherhood by various routes. All were in couples. **Cecily** (writer and new mom at 40 via sperm donation) reflects on her own journey to motherhood:

For me, I think I probably had to get to a place of comfort with my sexuality before I could take that leap [into motherhood]. Because certainly it requires coming out like every second of the day. When you're a gay mom, there's no hiding. "Oh, does your child look like your husband?" or "Oh . . . whatever." When you're with a child in the world, people want to know about the dad. And there's no dad, so it requires coming out so much. And also, it means at every juncture that I see a mom and a dad and a child, I'm reminded that I'm not a mom and a dad and child. So I think I had to get pretty comfortable with it. Some of the comfort comes from four thousand years of therapy, and the other just comes from, you know, really like, "Back off, it's my life now." It took forty years, but I think at a certain age it matters less for family things what the world thinks. At 40, it better be *your* life, or what else?

Gay women face the same pressures to establish themselves at work before starting a family as do other women. As with their hetero peers, starting later means gay women have established themselves as individuals, with the kind of personal authority that allows them to be clear on what they want for themselves and can make them confident advocates for their kids. (Starting later can also, of course, mean a decrease in fertility. Cecily's partner, in her early forties, has tried to become pregnant via sperm donation without success so far.)

Louise (architect) had a baby at 40 via sperm donation. Then her partner Alana had a baby three years later, when she was 38, using the same sperm donor. Their kids are biological siblings as well as siblings by affection. Louise and Alana have both adopted each other's birth child—a step many gay couples take to ensure that if something happens to the biological parent, the other parent can keep the family going. Without that adoption, the child could lose not only the parent who died but the remaining parent at the whim of disapproving family members or judges.

Some lesbian couples choose to share the motherhood experience by having one mom serve as the surrogate, carrying a child made through a combination of the other mom's egg and donor sperm. (Since they both have a physical connection, they both can answer firmly "I am" to the irritating but persistent question, "Who's the 'real' mom?") Some share parenthood of a child born from one mom by adopting the child legally as a second "unrelated" adult, or through less formal arrangements. Clearly, there's a maze of legal issues here, just as there is with surrogacy and donor genetics in the hetero world.

In addition, there can be a complex of new emotional issues brought up around balancing the roles of two moms, especially if both partners have different experiences; for instance, if both try to become birth mothers but only one succeeds, or if one partner's child has a known donor and the other's has an anonymous donor (so there's a difference in access to the biological father, if they want that later). As with all relationship issues, different couples will come to terms around these issues more and less harmoniously.

Though Louise didn't think about kids as an option until she was 36, she sees that pattern changing already:

I would expect there would be quite a number of 35-and-above first-time moms [in my online lesbian parents group], and there certainly are. But one of the things that we're noticing is that there are certainly a number of younger women who are suddenly joining our group, and what's interesting about that is that when *we* were younger it just wasn't an option.

Gay women who choose to become moms seem to want to do it for many of the same reasons as straight women. The pivot is being in a bonded relationship with people whom you love and feel committed to and who love you back in a committed way. Cecily recalls very specifically what awakened her desire to be a mom:

What happened for me at 36, . . . my mother was diagnosed with ovarian cancer, and my very beloved grandmother suffered a cerebral hemorrhage and was dying for a period of months. The other thing, perhaps more significantly for me, it dawned on me, wow, these people are not going to last forever. And in fact, the unique, incredible relationship of motherhood, grandmotherhood, and daughterhood could end. And in fact, the only way to keep motherhood in my life was to become a mother. That really was the major turning point.

And then at 36, when all that happened, in actually the same couple months, I think I felt desperate to keep a mother around, and lo and behold, it was going to have to be me.

It took her a few years to work out the logistics. Since she's become a mom, she understands a lot more about her own relation with her mother, who felt distressed about her daughter's being gay primarily, Cecily thinks, because she didn't want her to miss out on the experience of being a mom. "I think that she just felt it was the most immense love a person could experience, and she wanted me to have that experience. . . . I think the moment when my daughter was born, I started to get it. And then I continue to get it as the days go on."

Caroline (writer and mother via anonymous sperm donation at 38 and 41) and her partner Bridget (adoptive mom at 39 and 42) got married in Massachusetts when that became an option. Caroline wanted kids because she had a lot of siblings and a happy childhood and

that whole family life experience is something I value, and more or less wanted to replicate. But not nearly to the degree—two is plenty. But I'm very, very close to my sisters and my brothers and my mother and my grandmother and my extended family, and it just means a great deal. As much as I have many close friends and a lot of social acquaintances and an active social life, I would say that my relationships with my family are some of the most meaningful in my life.

I haven't asked gay women friends of mine point blank, but my sense is that their sense of what their life can include has just expanded, and they would never discount the possibility now. In the last six years, I know twenty gay women who have decided to have families, some with partners, some without. It's like "this is my right, this is my desire," and it's not even a blip.

They're all over 35.

Nell (business owner and new mom by adoption at 40) has legally adopted the child her partner carried. She, too, speaks of motherhood in terms of continuing family connections.

> When I was coming up . . . I had a large family; I had lots of siblings; we had the neighborhood thing; but then we sort of lost it. My whole coming up thing was trying to hold onto things that were meaningful in my family, like my grandmother's baking. . . . I was interested in carrying that tradition on, and I was interested in, you know, *communities* is the only word I can think of.

As a teenager "I had worked with my grandmother two summers learning how to bake some stuff. . . . I was learning her family recipes." As a mom, she loves handing that knowledge down to the next generation.

> I try to show her what I'm doing, like on Saturday morning we'll make biscuits, . . . and I love it that she says "Biscuits" and she's two years old. . . . But what's nice about being in a place in my life and in my career that I can actually spend an hour on biscuits instead of "Got to hurry, got to make these biscuits in five minutes." It's like, okay, we'll take the whole morning to make biscuits and let her get biscuits all over her.

Whereas Cecily, Caroline, and Louise used unknown donors, Nell and her partner used a known donor. They wanted to expand their daughter's community as well as provide answers to questions about her dad in years to come. In doing so, they risk that the man involved might decide at some unpredictable point to try to get more involved than the couple wants. Knowing him, they trust that he will respect their wishes, and they do have a legal contract (though even those aren't entirely dependable). It's worth any risk, however, because they know their daughter will have questions that only he can answer.

Notes Caroline,

> I would say the one thing that comes up fairly consistently [in dis-
> cussions with other lesbian moms] is, how are we going to deal with
> the Daddy question with the kids. And everyone kind of has their
> own way or plan, but no one has really—because all the kids are
> *young,* so far no one has had to really do the full process. So I think
> it remains to be seen.

Sperm and egg donation offer a new freedom to parent outside of a relationship with the provider of the genetic material, and the sudden expansion of families formed by these means creates a much more open and
supportive environment for families formed in these new ways. But there
remains a yet-to-be-wrestled-with hornet's nest of identity and relationship questions to be addressed by these children in the next few years.[12]
Sometimes the issues come from unexpected directions. As Caroline discovered sometime after her first child's birth, donor babies
sometimes have numerous genetic half-siblings:

> I made the mistake once of telling a friend of mine, who used an
> anonymous donor for her child too, and I told her my sperm donor
> number, and she went online and *found* two parents of half-siblings
> by [my children's] donor. I was so annoyed. It felt like an invasion of
> my privacy, very much a boundary crossing. And yet, that's the issue,
> you know, it's like this public domain kind of weirdness.

Unexpected family can be a good thing, for health reasons and for
emotional links. Sperm and egg donation facilities generally ask donors
whether they're willing to be contacted by their progeny once they
reach 18, and about 90 percent say no. Some moms (like Cecily and
her partner) make a point to choose donors who say yes—in case their
kids do want that option. Louise and Alana felt no interest in having
their children know the biological father when they started out.

We used a cryo-bank that did not have "yes" donors. . . . We didn't
even think about that, all we were thinking about was, possibly we
were being selfish, but all we were really thinking about was that this
was going to be our family, and that surely we would explain to our
child where he came from, and that a nice man that wanted to help
people create families did give his genetic material, you know, and
probably in a much nicer way explain this, but we didn't really think
that this child is going to be questioning his identity for his entire
life. So this is going to be something that we'll have to deal with.

It takes a while to recognize and come to terms with all the complexities a new technology introduces. But once she thought about it
for a while, Louise decided, "We don't have the opportunity for our kid
to have any contact with his donor, so at least we should probably find
out if there are any siblings to be in contact with." She joined a registry,
and they did find a half-sibling, and the two families got in touch. "And
I met them. I had a conference in [their state] last February, and I met
them, and they were really nice, and then we went back as a family in
May and met them again. So I anticipate that we will stay in touch
with them and be quasi family over the years."

The questions sperm and egg donation raise aren't so different from
the questions adoptive children have encountered for ages. Donors terminate any claims to parental rights in a way similar to what birth parents do when they give children for adoption. Down the line, children
will decide for themselves whether they want to try and find out more.

Divorce, New Later Motherhood Style

Though divorce may be less likely for people who start their families
later, it does happen. As I mentioned earlier, three of the women I interviewed were divorced from the father of their children when we first
spoke (two of those were remarried to new husbands), and three more
divorced during the three years of the study. While overall 6 of the 113

women I spoke with had divorced their children's dad, 27 of them (about one-quarter) had had earlier "starter" marriages, without kids, that ended in divorce prior to the marriage in which they had kids. These early marriages without kids served as training for what not to do in selecting a mate the next time. It didn't guarantee success (three of the divorced moms had also had a starter marriage), but in general people reported that they found it educational. In **Kelly's** case (banker and new mom at 43), both she and her husband had been married before, "so we knew what didn't work, in a big way." Armed with that knowledge, they could focus on the more effective range of relationship strategies.

Charlotte (mom at 37 and 40, now 54) was in the process of divorcing Tom (also 54) when we first spoke. They had been married for twenty-five years and began having kids ten years in. They made equivalent salaries, he as a lawyer and she from her own legal services business, and had a very ample family income. In spite of all that, he found a new love and moved out. Though he loved his kids, he had worked seven days a week and had not been much involved in the nitty-gritty of family life. Charlotte did all the childcare and activity planning. ("He would frequently say, 'So what are y'all doing this weekend?' [and then] pick and choose the activities that he was interested in to come participate.")

Charlotte didn't like the change, but a year and a half later, she's moved on and has a new beau. Tom, on the other hand, has broken off with his romance. She could remarry, but she doesn't think her kids need a new dad now, so she will wait a while. She's not looking to start a new family ("That opens a whole set of new challenges that won't be something I have to deal with, because at 54, I'm not having any more children!"), and she doesn't need a new husband to pay her bills. Her business has always done well, and in the past two years she's grown it further.

Charlotte lives on the other side of the anxiety about being trapped in a marriage without funds of your own or of being destitute if you divorce. Charlotte recalls having seen a number of divorced moms . . . who haven't been financially in a situation to maintain the same lifestyle. And that's very difficult to watch, because the mom and the kids are at a real disadvantage and frequently what happens is daddy goes and remarries and has children again and the first children are left behind.

She's glad that wasn't the case for her kids, and she likes it that her 14-year-old daughter can remark, "I guess you waited to have kids later because you wanted to be able to support 'em when you had 'em!" Charlotte, whose mother had three kids by the time she was 18, can nod and smile. And now that she's divorced, her ex actively shares the childcare for the first time and gives her every other long weekend off. If you have to divorce, an income of your own cushions the blow.

If you've been involved in a peer relationship, the likelihood is greater that your ex has been very invested in his kids and won't want to toss them into poverty just to punish you. Pepper Schwartz predicted in 1994 that peer dads would be less likely to divorce because they were more involved with their families than many traditional dads, and that peer moms would be less likely to divorce because they want to hold on to an involved dad for their kids' sake. It seems likely that, when divorce does happen to a peer couple, the terms of the breakup would be of the kinder, gentler sort. A dad who knows his kids and has been involved in their lives will want to do right by them. That was the case in the two instances of peer divorce that occurred in my study set.

New Later Single Moms

The dating scene was really nothing for about five years, and I realized, I told myself I wouldn't panic until I was 35, and the day I turned 36, I decided to just skip the guy part and get pregnant. So I investigated what it would take to do that by artificial insemination, and I succeeded. . . . It was hard, in fact it was extremely hard, but

it was very much, you know, worth doing. I finally bought a house,
rather than figuring I might move at any moment in time. Just de-
cided, well no, this is going to be it. So that was wonderful.

—VERA, new mom at 37

The world's views on single motherhood have changed a lot in the
past few decades because women in general have more options. The
level of mainstream acceptance that single moms experience varies
widely according to their ability to support their kids on their own
and to care for them consistently. Though some visibly much-older
moms get raised eyebrows (are you going to be there for your kids
long term?), many of the women I've talked with sense, like **Lucy**
(physician and single adoptive mom at 40 and 42), that "people view
older moms as more mature, more ready, wiser. Maybe more stable."
And that goes double for single moms, since it's doubly hard to
mother solo. Younger single moms may not face the kind of moral
censure that Hester Prynne did, but they may face disapproval from
middle-class taxpayers who think, as **Deb** puts it, "they are not responsible enough, and they're going to be on the system to help them
take care of their kids."

The difference is mainly socioeconomic, but it overlaps with the
moralistic, as **Andrea** (government official and single mom at 44) discovered in a direct way when she was weighing whether to adopt or
bear a child on her own:

I remember, I was very active in my church in a girls mentoring program, and one of the rules they have for the mentors of these girls is
you may not have any children out of wedlock, because we are raising girls, we are mentoring girls, and so it kind of pissed me off! I actually did quit because during the year that I was really thinking
about it, I thought, "What if at 43 years old, 42 years old, I just decided I was going to have a baby, are they going to put me out because I decided to have a baby and I'm 43 years old?" And so I quit

the program because I was really seriously struggling with that. And then I decided to adopt and they said, "Oh Andrea's so wonderful, look she adopted a baby! Come back!"

The church might have welcomed her back even if she'd decided to bear a child, but it is certainly easier for some people to feel comfortable with a single adoptive mom than with a single bio mom. Adoption so clearly crosses the line from the old sense of "sin" into what looks like obvious virtue.

Eleven of the 113 later moms I spoke with were single when they became moms, and of those eleven, eight adopted. It's hard to know how that proportion (eight to three) relates to the proportion of adoptive to birth moms in the wider world of later single motherhood, since adoptions don't track easily. We do know that about 20 percent of new later moms who give birth are unmarried women, though the birth certificate doesn't tell us if they're in a committed partnership. It also certainly doesn't tell us if they marry after the birth—as four of the eleven initially single moms I spoke with did. There's no reliable source of data on the numbers of adoptive parents in the United States of any age or status, let alone of later single adoptive moms.

However a woman comes to single motherhood, once she's there, she'll have many things in common with other single moms, including an even greater tendency to avoid risk than partnered parents: "I'm afraid of not being there for him, you know, being the only parent." On the other hand, single-from-the-start moms have it easier in some ways than single divorced moms, at least in the view of **Casey** (new adoptive mom at 44, who divorced her husband to start a family after it became clear that he had changed his mind about wanting one): "There's only one set of rules to go by. I see some of my friends who are divorced, you know, going back and forth, juggling the two houses, and 'he lets us do that when we're over there,' and that kind of thing."

Single-from-the-start moms also lose the built-in male role model. Some, like Andrea, make a deliberate effort to compensate:

I wanted my son to make sure that he had some male figures in his life. I remember reading an article, when I was going through the adoption process, about Nell Carter who had two adoptive boys, and they had eleven godfathers between them, and so I said, "Hey that sounds like a good idea," and so I got three godfathers for my son, and that was a good thing because people are busy with their own lives, they don't have time for your life all the time. And it worked out really well, because one of the godfathers, right after the christening [got too busy with personal issues], and one of the godfathers lives out of town, and comes and goes as he can, and one lives here and is very, very active in his life.

This strategy isn't exclusive to new later moms, but they may have a better chance of knowing a range of responsible men in positions to commit to a godchild.

Amanda, an IT staffer who adopted as a single woman at 45 after being widowed in her thirties (her late husband hadn't wanted kids, and her own health problems had led her to a hysterectomy), also set up a network, for different reasons:

I figured the issue, and I was pretty much right, was going to be a balance issue between our needs—her needs and my needs. And that time was going to be a biggie, and that I needed to take good care of myself, so that I would have something left to take care of her with you know. And I knew that it was going to be hard, and you know, basically what I did is I had a network—close relationships. I ended up finding grandparents for her [Amanda's own parents were very elderly and far away], actually they are my friend's parents. . . . They were ready for grandchildren and just fell in love with [my daughter], and it's just like we just all connected that way, and you know she goes over there still. They pick her up in the afternoon, one day a week usually, and they go play and have dinner, and then we pick her up in the evening—you know that kind of thing. I had a support system, and I also had really good babysitters and stuff like that, so I could continue to take good care of myself.

The "we" in there includes Amanda's new husband, whom she married when her daughter was 5 and she was 49.

While several of the single-at-the-start moms I interviewed ended up marrying later, having a child isn't always conducive to finding a partner. **Lucy**, physician and adoptive mom at 40 and 42, responds to a question about whether she dated soon after she'd adopted her first son:

Occasionally. Yeah. Hard. Especially like within the first six months after he was home, I didn't want to be gone from him all day, and then be gone again. So what I would do was, if somebody wanted to have lunch with me on a Saturday, we'd do that and my son would come. And it takes a special kind of guy to have the baby there too.

At that point she imagined possibly marrying, but she worried:

Sometimes when I meet somebody, and I'm thinking, "Well you know, I really kind of like this person," and I start planning out in my mind like how it would work, I think, "Oh my god, it would be such an undertaking." . . . Like, I love [my son] I'm sure more than anybody loves him. And to have a man come in, I don't know that he could love him the way I do, and I'm not sure I could tolerate that.

On the other hand, she knows from her own experience of adoption how affection can grow for a new person. When I heard from her again shortly after her second adoption, her schedule was packed, and dating was not on her radar.

Only Children

Everybody else wants us to have a second child. . . . Why is that just the thing? And we are perfectly fine with just the one.

—NELL, entrepreneur and mom at 39

I have regret over not having a second child.

—OLIVIA, former career woman, mom at 39

And I feel very relaxed in that, if we did not get pregnant, we've got one great healthy baby, and if we did get pregnant, that would be great as well.

—DELIA, financial analyst and mom at 37,
now 40 and considering another child

For ages, the common wisdom held that being an only child meant being a lonely child, a potentially spoiled and selfish child, with any number of other problems to boot. But as more and more people have just one and find they turn out just fine, attitudes have changed. Predictions are that 30 percent of families started today will end up with one child, total. A good portion of these will be the families of new later moms (though many younger moms and dads are choosing that route, too).

In the group I spoke with, a little less than half (fifty-three people out of 113) had one child at the time this book went to press, out of whom six are actively trying for a second, and ten may try (by birth or adoption) in a few years. Ten of the fifty-three tried to have a second but ran into secondary infertility (that's when a woman has had at least one child by the usual means, but then can't have another with her own eggs). These women either didn't want to or couldn't try fertility treatment or adoption, but they would have loved to have had another. Ten of the fifty-three had step-children, and four of those were raising their step-kids along with their bio kids. Some of those with step-kids would have liked to have had a second bio child, but given that they were already supporting several kids, the finances didn't make sense for their families.

Several others with just one child in the household might have liked to have had another child but didn't feel financially or otherwise prepared to follow up on that. **Roberta** (businesswoman and new mom at 40, now 42) would have liked to have several but doesn't feel that makes sense for them now:

> I mean this is my one regret about having waited so long to have a kid, is how old I am now. Cause this is the stage where people have second kids. You know, people who are younger than I am. But you know, my back hurts. I don't relish the idea of chasing after a kid who's just learning how to walk. . . . I sort of feel like, we finally have some equilibrium, and it's financial equilibrium and in our marriage there's equilibrium and we've bought this house and there's enough room for all three of us in this house. . . . There's a big part of me that says, "Enjoy this! This is good, this is working."

As with many others in the study group, Roberta's expectations around family (including timing and size) evolved over the years to suit the changing realities of her family and work worlds.

As we saw in the last chapter, **Linda**, mom at 35, remained full time in the corporate world for two years after having her baby, but then quit to stay at home. One year later, she's tired of the home life and looking for part-time work. Though she had hoped to have a second child, she's changed her mind on that, too:

> Honestly, my husband is more against it than I am. But to be honest, I think he's right. He feels that one child is kind of all we can handle. He's also very selfish—he has hobbies he wants to do, and he also loves his son a lot and wants to spend time with him. And he feels like, when we have one child, we can incorporate all of that

and also have time for us. And he feels like we have a happy marriage. But a second child would put pressure, stress on our marriage, and also take away from the time.

Quite a few of the moms I spoke with went into parenthood planning for two but experienced the first one as both an enormous pleasure and an enormous time and energy consumer. The thought of having another receded. **Nell** and **Allison**, lesbian partners in both life and business and moms to an amazing 2-year-old (via sperm donation and adoption), had imagined that they would each have one child biologically. But that view changed quickly. Nell explains:

Everybody else wants us to have a second child. [Laughs] I mean they are very adamant about it—"So—when?" I'm like, "Why?" . . . "You have one kid, when's the next one coming?" Why is that just the thing? And we are perfectly fine with just the one. So I think in the end, we respect so much more how much work it is that it's, like, Oh—could we do two? Sure. But it would affect everything—you know, more.

Allison agrees:

Financially, emotionally, physically, it's a lot. I mean we get nostalgic about it as we see her growing up. There was one day [we] were having a discussion, and Nell [thinking ahead] says, yeah, "Soon she'll be 8 years old. . . " and I got a little teary, and I'm like, "We need to have another baby." But you get over that really, really quickly.

Nell and Allison have a very large and active pool of friends and coworkers in their business who love their daughter and give her a community that ensures she will never be lonely. In this world where onlies proliferate, the chances for frequent playdates with other onlies proliferate, too.

Here are some of the reasons I heard for stopping at one child: life feels full with one; financially, two would be too many; secondary (age-related) infertility; spouse didn't want another child. As **Audrey** (mom at 40) recounts, though she and her husband are both over the moon about their daughter and she was eager for two, she stopped asking, "because my husband—you know, that has to be a two-party agreement and that never became a two-party agreement—my husband didn't want to. And so . . . I begged and pleaded for a while, and then I gave up." Some moms simply felt that they didn't want to start fresh with a new child after a certain age (people vary on what that age is), since they'd be older than they'd want to be by the time the child got to . . . (pick any milestone).

Some reasons I heard for having two or more: anticipation that child number one would like to have a sibling (generally based on the parents' own experience) and wanting to provide a long-term family network. As **Raina** (writer and mom at 38) notes,

> You could die. On a good day you live another forty years and you're 80. On a bad day, you don't, and so then she's in the world by herself. And especially since we're in a situation where you move for jobs, so you're not around your family, . . . it would be nice to provide her with the possibility of another person who would be invested in her.

On the other hand, **Marcy** points out, "You shouldn't have a second only for the idea that they're going to be best friends, cause they might not be." And prime among the reasons for having two: loving being a parent and wanting more of the experience.

Having fewer children than they ultimately preferred was the drawback to later motherhood I heard mentioned most. **Kim**, urbanist and scientist, now working part time from home and a mom at 39, is a very accomplished person who was surprised to experience motherhood as "really the best thing that ever happened in my life." Though she and her husband did not actively try for a second (he had older kids from an earlier union), "we didn't do anything to prevent it from happening. And if it had happened again—matter of fact I did get pregnant and miscarried—starting younger might have increased the odds that we would have had another child. And I'd have loved it."

Paradoxically, the enormous pleasure these moms experience connects directly to the circumstance in which they had their children. They were in comfortable circumstances, and they'd realized many of their dreams. Would they have felt as blissful earlier on in their careers? Kim the biochemist reflects: "I never imagined an experiment going like that, and then have it just come out so wonderful. I mean she is truly a gift. . . . And if I had been younger, I don't know if I would have recognized that. It might just be because I'm older that it had this effect on me." And Kim takes the gift very seriously and nurtures her daughter with exceptional thoughtfulness and care to amazingly good effect.

Another reason there are more onlies, and another sort of paradox, may be the more-involved dads. What Linda describes as "selfishness" in her husband, though she doesn't condemn it, others might call a form of time defense. In the days when dads were less involved, multiple kids might have relatively little impact on a dad's work options. For today's more-involved dads, limiting the number of kids may be key to ensuring that there's some time left over from child-related activities to spend on work and leisure. The same is true for women, but many are socialized to fit the kids in no matter what. Many men approach involved parenthood from the other direction: they're trying to add that in to a career-focused socialization, whereas the women are trying to figure out how to add in the career. Linda's husband, an environmentalist and outdoorsman, may not want his family to be his only occupation outside work and may want to devote more time to a job that he worked hard to get and makes a good living at.

The greater willingness of dads to voice concern about the time demands created by multiple children opens the way for working women (like Linda) to admit to having similar concerns. And sometimes moms do lead the way on that front: **Marie** (businesswoman and mom at 38) is clear that she wants just one, though her husband would like to have several. In such debates, one parent may just win out over the other, who may end up regretful. Or, as Audrey did, the parent who wants more may conclude that, if both members of the couple aren't on board, there's no use worrying about it and move on to enjoy the happiness that they have as a threesome, which may turn out to be plenty. Audrey concludes, "The only footnote to all of it is it just gets sweeter every day. [Having a baby is] the best thing I ever did. And for me personally, I did it at the right time."

The later parents of onlies tend to spend a lot of time with their kids and can put a lot of thought into raising them because, in general, they have more time to spend on that than do parents with more kids. As a result, onlies often do well in school and in the work world.[13] Since new later parents are given to doing a lot of research on parenting methods, they generally know they need to actively counter the built-in tendency to overdo for their kids. Reflecting on her only daughter's life, **Olivia** (now 48 and mother of a 9-year-old) stresses that she is aware her daughter lives in an enriched environment and that she needs to let her work things out for herself sometimes:

> I think she's a really pretty happy kid. . . . I mean, she was a wanted child who we adored from the get go. And the danger is smothering her and not allowing her to suffer. . . . We have that issue of privilege—economic privilege, but [also] the bathing in all this attention, [so we are careful to] hold back sometimes. [To let her know] that life isn't going to be these two totally devoted parents all the time. And helping her to solve her own problems, that's the key, to not do it for her. . . . The danger is when there's two parents [and one child, she can say], "Mom I forgot my homework." [And I can say], "All right, I'll drive you back to school," cause I can. Cause I don't have 500 kids that have to be fed. . . . Now my mother had to say, "No fricking way, dear!"

So Olivia didn't forget her homework. Now she's taking care to teach her child not to forget either.

Olivia and Jim also make a point of not losing their life as a couple:

[Parenting] was the best thing that ever happened to us, still is. We absolutely are madly in love with our daughter and find the whole experience of parenting joyful. . . . The couple—I mean obviously the marriage changes and stuff, but we were really happy and antic-ipatory, and it was just great. It solidified us as, you know there are many issues that we differ on that—I think frankly having a child ce-ments you in a certain way, it does. . . . And we worked at being a couple, still maintaining some coupledom separation, because with an only child you could just be morphed into this threesome and stop existing as a twosome. . . . I need to remain somewhere a cou-ple. [So] we go on dates. We have to carve it out, it has to be really conscious. We have to make time to talk and not about Judy. "How are we doing? What are you doing? What's your life like lately?" It's a very conscious effort.

Some couples choose onlies; some end up with just one by default. Attitudes toward the default differ: while some women mourn the loss of that dream and then move on, others feel the pain more long term. Of the women I spoke with, three—**Alicia**, **Olivia**, and **Ramona**— stressed that they missed having a second child and that they'd been misled by the media (and in one case, by her doctor) into thinking that fertility would last longer than it had. **Alicia** (lawyer and bio mom at 39) started trying to have a second at 40 without success. She and her hus-band tried egg donation, and when that didn't work, they went on to adopt a second child (at 44). Alicia feels very happy with her family but still regrets not having been able to carry a second child to term.

Olivia (bio mom at 39, now staying at home) explored egg donation and adoption after not getting pregnant the standard way when she tried again at 42, but neither felt quite right for her. Ten years later, she still feels the loss of the second child she'd hoped for. Ramona (new mom by egg donation at 40, former teacher, now SAHM) went into early menopause in her mid-thirties. She would still like to have a second child but isn't interested in undergoing the rigors of fertility treatment again. She would like to adopt, but her husband (who calls their daughter the "best thing we've done" and now can't believe he had his doubts initially about the egg-donation process) isn't there yet.

Several other mothers of onlies I spoke with would have liked more but have come to terms with having one. The huge majority of these moms (whether they came to that state by choice or by default) are living very happy lives. **Gemma** (arts administrator and new mom at 40) would have liked a second child, but she loves her threesome and the balance of family and work in her life:

> I'm happier than I've ever been in my whole life and that's saying a lot. I'm not really a happy person—I never found it appropriate to strive for happiness. I mean, life is life, and happiness to me was like a by-product. But I've just been going around these past weeks saying, "I am so happy." And I think it has to do with the family thing. And both Lincoln and I have had major professional growth opportunities in the past two years, and it's just great! And financially things are good. . . . And, it's great!

Kelly (banker and mother at 43 of a honeymoon baby), who didn't consider a second, echoes Gemma as she speaks of life with her husband and 10-year-old:

> I'm as happy as I've ever been in my life. When I get home on Friday—I still look forward to Fridays, because I call and I say, "Okay. What time are you going to be home?" And you know, . . . it's like I'm drawing up the gate. . . . It's just [the three of] us. We order in or maybe we'll go out for dinner, but it's just us. We make no plans for Friday night. It's just great.

New later motherhood, like most things, includes trade-offs, but the trade-offs they'd encountered made sense to the great majority of the women I spoke with.

Because real-life circumstances play a big part in determining what kind of family feels right for you, there is no perfect family size. For many reasons, onlies feel right to more and more moms and dads these days. Outside the family unit, they will also affect the life of the nation long term: there will be even fewer children to fund the social security of the generations above them than there are now. On the other hand, these children of parents dedicated to nurturing their creativity and educating them extensively may just have the innovative wherewithal to create new sources of value and systems of social support in the years to come.

Peer marriages, respected single and gay moms, more marital stability, more financial support for kids—these and other new family dynamics affect not just the families that enact them but all of the rest of those in the community who observe and interact with these families. The learning that results about what works and what doesn't expands and evolves everyone's sense of what family can be. Though every family form involves its challenges (isn't that part of the definition of *family*?), the changes in family dynamics associated with mothering later have many positive effects for all members of the family group.

CHAPTER 6

Sarah Laughed

Who's Fertile and How

> *We're not clueless; we know that fertility declines—*
> *from the minute you drive off the lot, basically.*
> —ROBERTA, new mom at 40

Genesis 18:10 [And the Lord said to Abraham] Lo, Sarah thy wife shall
have a son. And Sarah heard it in the tent door, which was behind him.

11 Now Abraham and Sarah were old and well stricken in age; and it
ceased to be with Sarah after the manner of women.

12 Therefore Sarah laughed within herself, saying, "After I am waxed old
shall I have pleasure, my lord being old also?" . . .

21:5 And Abraham was an hundred years old, when his son Isaac was
born unto him.

6 And Sarah said, God hath made me to laugh, so that all that hear will
laugh with me.

Lately, fertility anxieties haunt the dreams—waking and sleeping—of
every adult woman who hopes to someday be a mom. Women
hear from all directions that fertility wanes fast, especially for women
over 35. Odd that against this background of unease, so many post–35
women who want kids end up having them.

More than 594,000 babies were born to women 35 and older in
2005 (that's one in every seven babies). How does that fit with the

lonely sterility story that gets blasted at women repeatedly? A general confusion over who's fertile and who's not and what that means for family down the line pumps up the general level of female anxiety.

Progenitrix

To begin putting this picture in perspective, let's back up a few millennia and remind ourselves that, while the trend to new later motherhood is recent, its poster girl hails from ages back. The mother of the Judeo-Christian tradition, as well as of her boy Isaac, **Sarah** was the wife of Abraham. Together they were the first of the Chosen people, and from them came all the rest. According to scripture, it took them quite a while and some stress to get their family started, because the first thing we learn about Sarah is that she "was barren; she had no child" (Gen. 11:30). Then, as you may recall, after extensive travels and some experimentation with an early version of egg donation (see the story of Hagar), the situation changes and Sarah laughs. In fact, she laughs twice: the first time she laughs to scoff when she hears God telling the 100-year-old Abraham that she will bear their child even though she has been barren all her life—and is well past menopause. The second time she laughs for joy after the birth of their son.

Family dynamics play big roles in many religious narratives, and the story of Sarah and Abraham's near miss at continuing their family line increases the sense of the importance of that line. Sarah's post-menopausal pregnancy—literally miraculous in the basic sense of that word—puts the paradigm of later motherhood at the root of Western culture. Several of the moms I spoke with made the Sarah connection in a very positive way. Though apparently Sarah's infertility had no basis in age (she starts out barren), the miracle was nonetheless that she had a child after menopause, when it had "ceased to be with Sarah after the manner of women." Sarah provides a distinguished pedigree to new later motherhood, if a complex one.

Whereas Sarah's drama depends on contrast with most women of her day, who generally started young, nowadays much has changed, and many women start their families later—at or after 35, whether by birth or adoption. For the most part, modern-day Sarahs come to motherhood without intervention, but sometimes they use fertility technologies (even postmenopausal birth, a kind of scientific miracle, occurs with increasing frequency via modern egg-donation technology). Over the past few decades our culture has transitioned, like Sarah, from skepticism to acceptance and to a lot of happy laughter.

On the other hand, not all the results of waiting are joyous; unlike Sarah's sudden transition into pregnancy, the technological fertility journey can be hard and long. And some women don't succeed—sometimes for identifiable and predictable reasons, sometimes not.

Ball of Confusion

This unpredictability plays a role in contemporary women's anxiety, but it's not the only factor. The hammering women get from media stories about infertility also plays a role. Partly that's to do with the pleasure people take in negative stories. Not only do we thrill to stories of danger and loss, but somebody must get pleasure from the whole narrative of judgment and vengeance (back to the Old Testament connections) that blames working women for their ambition and sees a justified punishment being meted out when they find out (too late!) that what really mattered most to them is now out of their grasp. Or almost. The punishment narrative ran the storyline in Sylvia Hewlett's *Creating a Life*, which directly linked high-achieving women with infertility and warned younger women not to trade their hopes of family for lonely success. Hewlett's evidence was deeply flawed,[1] but that book and the spirit of exaggeration that animated it set the tone for much of the discussion that has followed.

Then again, while these stories go overboard, *some* counterbalance to the frequent announcements of births to celebrities over 44 seems called for—those stories go overboard in the other direction, rarely mentioning that egg donors and much money and effort were involved. Today, both sides of the fertility spectrum get skewed in the media and the common lore. People seem to think simultaneously that *nobody* can get pregnant after 35 and that *everybody* can. It does seem difficult to strike the perfect balance between alerting women to the real effects of decreasing fertility and unnecessarily alarming them.

❖ PROFILE: **Maureen, New Mom at 41 and 42 (nearly 43)**

Maureen had an absorbing business career and a few boyfriends over the years, but none of them serious. She'd always hoped to marry and have kids, but she wasn't unhappy with her situation. In fact, sometimes she found it scary that she wasn't more worried, since that might mean she wouldn't try as hard to find Mr. Right. But she did notice that, with the years, the type of man who attracted her was changing. And suddenly, a man she'd known slightly for a while without a passing thought started to look increasingly adorable. So she talked with him at some length at a gathering, and he asked her out.

> We both knew instantly on the first date that 'okay, this is it.' And we both say that to this day, and we don't know what greater force was steering this relationship. But it was very odd to me, but maybe it's just age, maturity; we were at the same stage of life; we were both ready at the same time. It could have been a number of things, but it all clicked really well.

Maureen and Bart got married when they were both 39, having already discussed the possibility that they might not be able to conceive and having agreed to adopt if that was the case. Maureen herself had been adopted and felt very strongly about it—Bart had no qualms.

But fertility reigned in their house. Maureen checked with the doctor right after the wedding, and he advised them to give it three months on their own and then come back for a revved up treatment. He detected a fibroid in her uterus, removed it, and not long after that they were pregnant. Two months later they miscarried, but the pathology report suggested it was a fluke, and the doctor suggested they keep trying. A month later they were pregnant again, and their son arrived when Maureen was 41.

Maureen and Bart knew they wanted two kids, and again they expected they might end up adopting. Maureen was nursing, and it took about six months for her period to return. She never went back on the pill, and within a few months she was pregnant again. Their daughter arrived right before Maureen's 43rd birthday.

This is just one of the many stories of successful fertility without treatments I heard in the course of my interviews (though the removal of the fibroid would count as a form of fertility maintenance and may have played a part). But as Maureen and Bart knew, infertility was a real possibility at their ages. And most of the stories in this chapter will look at cases where infertility did play a role. ❖

What Are My Odds?

If you're 35, you're probably fertile: A study from the 1950s indicated that, while 11 percent of women could have no babies after 34, the rate rose to 33 percent after 39 and 50 percent after 41. Though this data may not accurately reflect the current fertility scene, no more reliable data for women 35 to 50 is available today. Some recent results do corroborate the trend of the 1950s study for women 35 to 39, however. Data collected at seven European natural family-planning centers in the late 1990s (the European Fecundability Study) indicate that about 90 percent of women *not already known to be infertile due to pre-existent issues like endocrinal disorders or surgery* who try to conceive between 35 and 39 will become pregnant within two years. That's if they use natural family-planning methods (charting temperature and cervical mucous to more accurately predict when ovulation happens and to shorten time to conception) and have sex at least two days per week.[2] Roughly 82 percent will become pregnant within one year.[3]

Given the restriction to people not already known to be infertile, these estimates fall on the high side of what would be the case for the whole population of women 35 to 39. But they do indicate that women in this age range are generally fertile. And, of course, while the study averaged together all women in the 35 to 39 range, people at the lower end of that age spectrum have a bigger chance of success than people at the higher end.

If you're 43, you're probably *not* fertile: Data is limited, but chances both of becoming pregnant and of carrying to term diminish quickly after 41, though the chances with a donated egg stay the same at all ages (about 50 percent chance of success per try). In the fifties study, 87 percent of women could have no babies after 44. Past 43, it's only the anomalous who become pregnant with their own eggs, though it definitely does happen sometimes. In the course of my study, I spoke with two women who had healthy children without intervention at 44, and one who did that at 46.

How useful is all this information to you? **Roberta,** a successful East Coast professional who married at 39, found it of limited utility:

> I spent a lot of time looking at those numbers. You could be perfectly fertile at 40 or you could be not fertile at all at 40. But the numbers don't mean anything about you. . . . I think that I knew very well what the deal was. But there was maybe some hubris about my physical condition. I've always been very healthy.

But overall good health doesn't guarantee trouble-free fertility. Eggs keep their own calendars. When she started trying at 39, Roberta did encounter difficulty getting pregnant. She and her husband employed IVF, and they went on to have a healthy baby when she was 40. So her sense that she could have a child at 40 held true, but some technological assistance was called for.

All fertility statistics should be viewed skeptically, because there's lots of heterogeneity among individual women and among populations and because all the available data is imprecise. But having a general sense of fertility's progress over time usefully informs a woman's thinking as she makes choices that will affect the timing of her family. We do know that women's fertility starts declining in their late twenties.[4] The current understanding holds that women are born with their lifetime supply of eggs.[5] Every month, menstruating women lose eggs, and progressively more of the eggs that remain lose viability over time. In terms of fertility for women in their thirties, what goes down isn't so much the likelihood of ever getting pregnant, but the likelihood of getting pregnant in any one attempt. Most women will still get pregnant between 35 and 40 if they keep trying, but it sometimes takes longer than it does for younger women.

While most discussions of infertility focus on women, the European study suggests that *male* age also affects the fertility of the couple, beginning in a man's late thirties. That study suggests that a 35- to 39-year-old woman with a partner 40 or older goes from an 18 percent likelihood of infertility in the first year of trying to a 28 percent likelihood.

The European statistics can't serve as an overall guide because the study included only outwardly healthy people with no previously known infertility conditions, and it only tracked the odds for getting pregnant, not the chances for carrying to term. But it does find that roughly 50 percent of women 35 to 39 who fit their criteria and who don't get pregnant within one year will do so in two.[6] The study's authors recommend that the one-year cutoff for an infertility diagnosis be extended to two years for women 35 and over.[7] They suggest that women consider not going directly to fertility treatment in their late thirties if they don't get pregnant within a year *and* if there are no other indications of infertility. Instead they advise that couples keep trying for another year, using natural family-planning techniques.[8]

The recommendation to wait another year will not compute for many people—after all, if it doesn't work in two years, you're that much older when you start treatment, and you have that many fewer viable eggs. On the other hand, trying longer skirts the risks inherent in all new treatments, sidesteps the expense of IVF and other fertility technologies, and avoids the higher probability of multiple births often associated with these procedures. I am not a physician and make no recommendations here for anyone's choices around pregnancy and whether or not to employ assisted reproductive technology. My attempt here is to get some perspective in a realm where we generally don't get much. Given the experience of many of the women I spoke with, one reasonable route for a couple with a woman 35 or older who hasn't gotten pregnant after six months of trying would be to consult a good doctor to discover whether there are diseases or structural issues involved and, if so, to seek treatment for those. Once that's clear, each couple can work out for themselves (in consultation with their OB/GYN) the best way to proceed.[9]

Since a woman's monthly chance of conceiving goes down as she ages, the total number of her own genetic children that she can bear without intervention from that point forward also goes down. When a woman has a limited number of fertile years remaining, and if it takes her two years to get pregnant each time, she can bear fewer kids overall than if it took her one year per conception. But if the aim is to have one or two (or even three) kids after 35, it doesn't really matter that a woman no longer has the capacity to have six. Keeping in mind that every woman's body works on its own timetable and that there are no guarantees, we can say that the more children a woman wants, the more difference starting later can make. The eight women I spoke with who had three or more kids with their own genetic material all had their first at 37 or before (five started at 35 and one at nearly that). Sometimes the limiting effect of starting later isn't so much biological as it psychological—not everybody feels prepared to have several kids in quick succession.

Where Did We Get Those Odds?

Why can't we get precise statistics on fertility? Nobody knows exactly at what rate fertility declines or if it's the same average rate all over,

because doctors can't mandate that a big group of people have unpro-
tected sex constantly for the sake of an experiment. Most people
today use some form of birth control unless they are trying to get pregnant. A woman gets diagnosed as infertile when she and her partner
have been trying consistently to conceive for a year, without success
(barring a male infertility issue). Infertility is not the same as sterility,
so infertile women *might* very well have children with technological
assistance—or more trying. And then different people "try" with more
or less efficiency, and that's hard to gauge in a really rigorous way.

Part of the decline in fertility with age has to do with the fact that couples tend to have less sex as they get older. Sad but true. The European
Study found that fertility increased dramatically when people went from
having sex once a week to twice a week. (That's because the time of possible fertility around ovulation—the fertility "window"—is six days, so if
you have sex on two days during one week, you'll hit that six-day spread.)[10]

The closest thing to a thoroughly controlled experiment of women's
fertility documented so far—the fifties study referred to earlier—involved a Protestant religious sect called the Hutterites. As a rule, the
Hutterites of the period essentially tried to have as many kids as they
could, year in and year out, as a religious duty, and the community supported all children equally so having more didn't draw down the family
resources. A study based on Hutterite data indicated that the infertility
rate (deduced from when each woman had her last confinement) was
3.5 percent at 25, 7 percent at 30, 11 percent at 35, 33 percent at 40,
50 percent at 41, and 87 percent at 45. Thirteen percent of them had
their last baby between 45 and 49, and nobody had a baby after 49.[11]
The average woman in this group had eleven babies! (And unlike in the
general population, the women tend to die earlier than the men.)[12]

These infertility numbers may have been low relative to the general
population at the time, and they may be low now, but we can't prove
that because the records of any group of people today would be skewed
by the many forms of birth control in use. Besides that, unless people
are impelled by a religious enthusiasm like the Hutterites, there's no

way to guarantee that even a totally "natural" population won't skew the data by simply exercising restraint in the bedroom at the prospect of too many children. One researcher I spoke with noted that, given that no rigorous studies have been done on fertility in women's forties, it's also possible that the onset of age-based infertility might have occurred *earlier* among the Hutterites than it would among the rest of the population, due to the wear and tear on the women's reproductive systems from having had so many babies. But there is no direct evidence of that.

What about Fertility Tech?

Fertility technology comes in many varieties, but it works in two basically distinct ways: with a woman's own genetic material, or with someone else's.

Fertility technology can assist some women who are having difficulty getting pregnant to do so with their own genes, but it's less effective the older a woman (and her eggs) become. Among the techniques commonly employed to this end are

- *intrauterine insemination* (IUI—a sophisticated version of the turkey baster that directly delivers sperm to womb);
- *hormones* that stimulate egg production (like Clomid or Gonal-F); and
- *in vitro fertilization*, a process in which a woman takes drugs to stimulate production of as many eggs as possible in one cycle, which are then removed from her body and mixed in a beaker with sperm (her partner's or a donor's). Some or all of the resulting embryos are then reintroduced into her womb in the hope that they will implant.

These methods all work more or less effectively depending on each person's age and health. Table 6.1 shows the most recent (2004) stats from the CDC on IVF with a woman's own eggs.

TABLE 6.1   2004 Non-donor IVF Success Rates by Age of Woman

	<35	35–37	38–40	41–42	43–44
Fresh embryos from non-donor eggs					
Percentage of cycles resulting in live births	36.9	29.3	19.5	10.7	3.9
Percentage of cycles resulting in pregnancies	42.5	35.5	26.5	17.3	8.3
Frozen embryos from non-donor eggs					
Percentage of transfers resulting in live births	30.6	27.7	23.1	18.7	14.6[a]

Source: All data except that for 43- to 44-year-olds comes from the CDC's annual ART report, *2004 Assisted Reproductive Technology Success Rates: National Summary and Fertility Clinic Reports*, December 2006, p. 81, available at http://www.cdc.gov/ART/ART2004/. IVF statistics on 43- and 44-year-olds are in the Society for Assisted Reproductive Technology Clinic Summary Report, which includes data on most but not all U.S. fertility clinics and which is available online at https://www.sartcorsonline.com/rptCSR_PublicMultYear.aspx?ClinicPKID=0 (all accessed June 19, 2007).

[a]While frozen embryos are less likely than fresh to succeed for women 37 and under, frozen embryos are more likely for women over 37 because they were formed with younger eggs.

These data do *NOT* represent the overall fertility success rates for all women at these ages, because only women who are having difficulty try IVF. Rates of success go up with repeated attempts, but there is a ceiling.[13] The average IVF cycle in states that do not mandate health insurance coverage costs about $12,000.

If a woman's own eggs do not create embryos due to her age, she may employ egg donation—which means carrying an embryo made through an IVF process where another, usually younger, woman's eggs are substituted for a woman's own and mixed with her partner's or a donor's sperm. When the process succeeds (and when a partner's sperm is used), the woman ends up giving birth to her own genetic stepchild.

Once a suitable donor is identified (usually a healthy woman in her twenties, possibly with characteristics the parents-to-be find particularly desirable), she and the mother-to-be undergo simultaneous hormonal protocols to precisely synch up their systems, so that when the donor ovulates, the mother's body will be ready to receive and implant the embryo. The process is successful 50 percent of the time with fresh eggs in women of all ages and 30 percent of the time with frozen eggs (if a woman has a uterus, she can at least theoretically bear a child at any age via egg donation with the right hormone treatments). Egg donation is not generally covered by insurance and costs about $20,000 per try. As with non-donor IVF, rates of success do rise with repeated attempts, but there are no guarantees; it is possible to spend a great deal of money and emotion in this pursuit to no avail. In 2004, 13,722 donor-egg transfers occurred (that's not the same as the number of women attempting, because some were repeaters) among women of all ages (there is no breakdown by age of mother, so we can't tell how many were undertaken by women 35 or older). About 6,042 were successful (some of which involved multiples).[14]

Counting Up: Who's Fertile Later?

Clearly, quite a few women are fertile later, since in 2005 one in every seven children was born to a mom 35 or older (more than 594,000 babies born to about 577,500 moms).[15] Of those, a bit less than one-fifth (111,190) were born to moms 40 and older.[16] In 2004, about 4.4 percent (or 25,800) of the 585,000+ babies born to moms 35 and over arrived with the help of IVF.[17] Those mothers constituted about 3.3 percent of the pool of moms 35 and over who gave birth in that year.[18]

Not all of the 577,500 or so women who gave birth at or after 35 in 2005 were new later moms, since some were having a second or later child after having had their *first* kids before 35. But the big number does give a clear signal that fertility doesn't disappear at 35. And since plenty of women who *could* have kids later, in the sense of physical capacity, don't choose to do so, the number only hints at the possibilities for later fertility if everybody were trying.

Most women have already finished their family-building by 35. In fact, 53 percent of married U.S. women between ages 40 and 44 (and

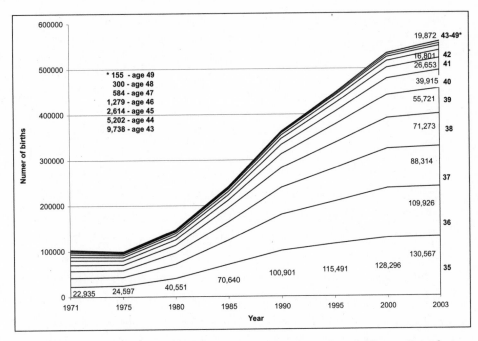

FIGURE 6.1   Number of U.S. Women Giving Birth at 35 and Above, Cumulative by Age of Mother. CDC Natality Statistics, 1971 to 2003. Decimal numbers on right are 2003 data.

45 percent of married woman between 35 and 39) have chosen actively against trying later by having had their tubes tied or a hysterectomy or other sterilizing operations, often for contraceptive purposes, and/or 14.5 percent are married to men who've had vasectomies.[19] When I cited that 53 percent figure to a friend, she found it amazing that so many women would undergo elective surgery (it's not elective for all the 53 percent). But for many women it's not an additional surgery, it's done at the same time they deliver what they've determined will be their last child, and often they're already under anesthetic and prepped for a C-section.

Figure 6.1 illustrates the numbers of women 35 and older giving birth, by age, from 1971 to 2003. The numbers inset in the graph on the right are the numbers of women who gave birth at that age in 2003.

This figure documents the increases in numbers of births to mothers of every age from 35 on up in the past twenty-plus years. It does

NOT document the relative ability of women at these different ages to become pregnant. At the same time that there are substantial increases in the number of kids born in each age band over time, within each year category there is a notable relative decline in the number born with each gain in age. This reflects some combination of a drop in biological ability with age *and* a decrease in the pool of people interested in having kids with each added year. Recall that more than 45 percent of married couples are sterilized by the time they reach 39 because they feel they have enough children. There are plenty of others who use birth control to prevent the arrival of additional kids at that age. The older you are when you try for kids, the fewer peers you have trying along with you.

Raw birth numbers show the volume of people involved. But given that the population has grown over the years, it's more reflective of the real shift to chart the change in the *birth rate* (that's the number of babies born per 1,000 women in an age category). See Figure 6.2 for birth rates by age of mother. The CDC also publishes birth rates in five-year age bands: Whereas in 1978 (the low) 18.9 babies were born to every 1,000 women 35 to 39, by 2005 the rate had more than doubled, soaring to 46.3. Likewise, the number of babies born to women 40 to 44 jumped from 3.8 in 1981 (its low) to 9.1 in 2005. This is due to improved fertility technology, better medical care overall, and most of all, the fact that more women try later than used to.

Among 30- to 34-year-olds, the number went from a low of 53.1 babies born to every 1,000 women in 1975 to 95.9 in 2005. On the other hand, the birth rate to 25- to 29-year-olds has stayed fairly steady over the past thirty years (115.6 in 2005), and the birth rate to 20- to 24-year-olds has declined (102.2 in 2005, down from 131 in 1972).

The little downturn in the birth rate visible on the left of Figure 6.2 in most of the age bands between 1971 and 1975 shows the tapering off of the *old* later motherhood—when women who had started young kept on having more children well into their late thirties and beyond (like my grandmother who started at 25 and had her eighth and last

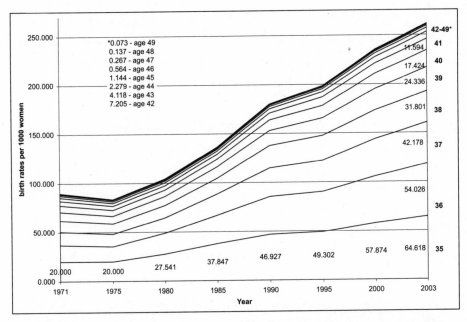

FIGURE 6.2   Birth Rates for U.S. Women 35–49, Cumulative by Age of Mother. Birth rate per year per 1,000 women in each age band. CDC Natality Statistics, 1971 to 2003. Decimal numbers on right are 2003 data.

child at 39). From 1975 onward, the growing effect of the *new* later motherhood trend on the birth rate is clear in each age band. The same dynamics apply in this chart as in the earlier one: the decline in numbers with each gain in age combines a biological decline due to age (especially in the upper age ranges) with a lessening of the pool of people interested in having kids with each added year.

Non-Age-Based Infertility

Apart from age-based infertility, there are several other kinds that can affect couples of all ages. Some are caused by ailments that affect women's reproductive organs, some occur because of structural problems, some are attributed to "male factors," and then there are the "unexplained." The standard wisdom holds that 35 to 40 percent of non-age-based infertility is due to "male factors" (mostly to do with low sperm count or low sperm motility—sperm that swims upstream too slowly to get any action with the egg), and 35 to 40 percent is due to "female factors" (like tubal blockage or uterine fibroids or cysts). The remaining percentage is due to a combination of male and female factors or the "unexplained."

For male factors, doctors often work on improving the delivery of the sperm to the egg, sometimes with IUI and more rarely (and much more expensively) with *intracytoplasmic sperm injection* (ICSI). In this process, they actually cull through all the sperm and choose the one that looks the most promising, and they literally inject it, with a micro-needle, into an egg in a petri dish. There is ongoing debate about the possibility of global environmental damage to sperm, but no clear verdict.

PROFILE: Vanessa, New Mother at 41 without Aid, but Her Husband Had Fertility Issues

Vanessa (lawyer and new mom at 41) was ready to get pregnant once she'd found the man she wanted to have a baby with. Her younger and very virile mate slowed the process when they discovered early in their romance that he had varioceles—varicose veins of the testicles, a condition that basically cooks the sperm and renders them useless for purposes of fertilization. Vanessa saw a certain irony in the fact that at 40 she'd picked a younger partner with a fertility problem (his sperm count was 600,000 where fewer than 20 million gets you counted infertile). But she loved him, so he went for surgery with the expectation that, if everything went right (which it might not), the sperm count would move up to a workable number over an eight-month period. When his doctors heard the age of his wife, they suggested that they move directly to IVF with ICSI. Vanessa found the dynamic infuriating:

> My husband was the one with the documented fertility problem, . . . but it was always about me. You know, they were like, "Well, you're so old . . . ," and they're showing me all their charts and all their graphs,

which have downward slopes [after 35]. So this first doctor gave us this whole speech about how probably I was way past all hope. So he was like, "Let's just go and do a little ultrasound and see how many eggs you have left." And a great thing did happen, we took this ultrasound and the doctor was like, "Wow, your ovaries look like they're 27." And that was very nice to hear, but it still didn't make him think that we should not go forward with some treatment like this.

So they signed up for the IVF, but nature smiled, and before Vanessa started the drug regimen, she turned up pregnant, just three months after the surgery. And she and Vince are now the happy parents of a bouncing baby. ❖

Non-age-based infertility in women can be due to acute pelvic inflammatory disease (PID), which develops in about 20 percent of the infections caused by sexually transmitted diseases like chlamydia and gonorrhea. The CDC reports that more than 100,000 women become infertile each year as a result of PID.[20] Women who've had PID and the scarring in the fallopian tubes that can follow may require surgery or other alleviation if they want to get pregnant—and sometimes that doesn't work. The faster you treat chlamydia and gonorrhea, the less likely you are to segue into acute PID.

Infertility can also be caused by endometriosis or polycystic ovarian syndrome, conditions that, like PID, can block pregnancy but don't affect the egg supply. Or there might be structural peculiarities with the organization of a woman's particular set of organs that she doesn't know about until she tries to get pregnant. These conditions are not related to age either and can often be successfully addressed through surgery or drug therapies. But not always, and not always right away. (And if you can't afford more than one treatment, knowing that a problem probably could have been fixed with a few more attempts doesn't help you much.)

All of these scenarios, as well as the unexplained infertility that has always been a factor for a small number of women (like Sarah), can drive a woman to fertility treatments in her twenties and early thirties. They aren't age related, but if they aren't addressed until a woman's later thirties or beyond, the time of treatment may delay the process to the point where age-related problems do kick in. Leaving any of these conditions untreated over a number of years may cause it to become worse than it would have been if it had been treated earlier.

Three of the women I spoke with discovered they had endometriosis around age 35; they had it treated and went on to become pregnant without difficulty after that (two had three children and the other had two). One of these women, **Nora** (teacher and new mom at 35 and 36), is now 58. She had known the man she married since high school, and they married when she was 29. They didn't start trying for kids until she was nearly 32 because they wanted him to be far enough along in his medical residency that they would be able to afford a house by the time the first baby arrived. When nothing happened in two years, they went in for testing and found she had rampant endometriosis. She had the extra tissue removed, and immediately all systems were go. Almost one year to the day after the surgery she delivered her first son, and six months later, she was pregnant with her second.

Another of the women I spoke to was treated for polycystic ovarian syndrome and became pregnant at 37 without further difficulty. A fifth had fibroids removed and then quickly became pregnant without difficulty at 38. A sixth had severe damage to her fallopian tubes, and though she might have gotten pregnant via IVF, she decided not to try that and went the adoption route to family instead.

Is Infertility on the Rise?

The many stories circulating about fertility problems and treatments may give you the impression that the incidence of infertility is rising. On the other hand, a 2002 CDC report says that infertility has actu-

WHAT ARE INFERTILITY SERVICES?

According to the CDC, 11.9 percent of women aged 15 to 44 in 2003 reported using an infertility service in their lifetime. By "service" they mean advice (6.1 percent had sought this), getting a test on either member of the couple (4.8 percent), ovulation drugs (3.8 percent), medical help to prevent miscarriage (5.5 percent), surgery or treatment for blocked tubes (0.7 percent), artificial insemination (1.1 percent), or assisted reproductive technology (ART) (0.3 percent). (For the breakdown by age group, go to their Web site.)[21] Different people use different combinations of services.

All these statistics *sound* interesting, but they don't convey much firm information. They don't tell us why people sought services (did they have a specific problem for which they sought advice, or did they go in order to find out in advance how to "try" most effectively because they were worried by all the infertility buzz?). These numbers don't tell us how many women resolved their infertility with the birth of a baby, or how hard they had to work for such a result, or at what expense.

There's not a lot of reliable information on infertility available. The CDC keeps fairly detailed statistics on ART, but there is no information on the actual success rates of women with tubal blockages or endometriosis or of those who used Clomid or Gonal-F and IUI or surgeries. So we can't tell how many of the babies born to later moms were preceded by an infertility experience or an infertility treatment. And if people don't have the money or the insurance coverage to pay for services, it doesn't matter to them what the success rates for treatments are. The infertility advocacy group RESOLVE states on its Web site that roughly two-thirds of infertility cases resolve with the birth of a baby.

ally declined substantially in the past twenty years, though that report has been disputed.[22] If you're confused about fertility, it's probably because you've been paying attention—the messages out there are mighty mixed. Though the *use* of fertility treatments is rising, there's no evidence that the intrinsic span of women's fertile years has changed much over time. While advancing treatment options can expand the span for some, the blockage of fallopian tubes brought on by pelvic inflammatory disease or endometriosis can impair it for others. Then there's the male infertility element.

So if women aren't more infertile now than in the past, why are the numbers of visits to fertility doctors rising? In part because more people start trying for children later in life, at ages when fertility rates have always been lower. In addition, more fertility treatments are now available so more people seek them out, and there are more fertility doctors.[23]

That last item may seem to argue circularly. But while the rise in the number of fertility doctors responds for the most part to a rise in demand (caused by the first two points on that list), it is also a response to the potential for profit in this area. Fertility clinics are an enormous boon to the infertile, but they are, after all, businesses as well—as Debora Spar points out in her recent book—and businesses seek to expand the market for their services where possible. The reigning mood of fertility anxiety encourages women to visit doctors at the slightest sign of difficulty. Doctors need customers (the average fertility clinic needs to perform three hundred to four hundred IVFs at about $12,000 each to break even, and most are run for profit).[24] Spar explores the complexity of the current fertility market—noting that, while doctors do work to get their clients good results, they may also profit from prescribing treatments that have a great likelihood of failure (like IVF for women who are unlikely candidates) but which couples will step up to pay for, sometimes repeatedly, because they live in hope. Sometimes the couples won't take no for an answer, even when doctors try to dissuade them. And, of course, there's always a chance that it will work, though that chance might be slight.

Doctors may also profit from prescribing unnecessary treatments to women in their mid-thirties who are driven to their offices by the anticipation of failure—some of them will really need help, and some of them might well get pregnant if they kept trying a little longer.

The tangled dynamics of the current fertility scene jumble together the parents' desire for a child and the doctors' and the pharmaceutical companies' joint motives—both to assist potential parents and to make a profit. Some people *are* infertile early, and it's hard to say firmly who fits that description, so it's hard to blame doctors for taking an aggressive route. But we might hope they would avoid fanning the flames of anxiety and work instead to develop and convey clear information on fertility.

Sometimes they do the opposite. While some clinics are very straightforward about fertility knowledge on their Web sites, others seem to aim to create an emergency mood, as part of their promotion of services. For instance, at least one online site presents an intentionally misleading table comparing the fertility rate in earlier centuries in Europe to the fertility rate in the twentieth-century United States, under the heading "relative fertility rates." No note is made of the fact that the U.S. data reflects the effect of the use of modern birth control! That information would make a difference to a worried person looking at a table that tells her that, while in "16–19th Century Europe" 55 to 70 percent of 35- to 39-year-old women were fertile, in the "Modern USA" only 18 to 25 percent of women in that age group are fertile. Whereas in the table being "fertile" means having borne a child (what other data could be gathered from the sixteenth century?), the presentation of the table (in the midst of a discussion of fertility decline) is intended to suggest that it documents the *ability* to bear. The data itself may not be altogether inaccurate as regards actual births, though it is very generalized, but the context in which the table is presented suggests that women's ability to bear children—the other, more abstract kind of fertility—has decreased enormously in the last century. The table includes a footnoted comment that the "older data is likely to include substantial inaccuracies." No note appears on the huge inaccuracy created by the presentation of the modern data.[25]

Another clinic site declares without qualification that 30 percent of women are infertile at 35, though that percentage is disputed. This kind of imprecision anticipates and contributes to the sense of emergency felt by anyone who finds herself not getting pregnant when she counted on it, increasing and spreading that anxiety. Though fertility technology does great things for many couples, since clinic Web sites with information on infertility generally sell infertility services, their vested interest makes their claims potentially unreliable. As ever, prospective buyers need to be wary of the data they find online. A clinic's "success" rate can be hard to rely on, since some clinics screen patients on purpose to exclude women they think might not get pregnant. Spar explores many of the complex market factors at work in the contemporary "Baby Business" and concludes by calling for a national debate on whether and how to regulate its many sides. Such a debate would mean more informed attention to the complexities of what we know about fertility rather than continued promulgation of media stories about an infertility crisis for women in their thirties.

On the plus side, and paradoxically, the anxiety that all the recent attention to infertility has created means that women in their mid- to late thirties (and later) have become very proactive in seeking medical intervention early, if they see the least hint of a problem. That proactivity may have a positive effect on overall success rates, though it might also mean that some people will progress more quickly to treatments that are more aggressive than are actually called for by the symptoms (and pay more for them, both in hard cash and in the physical and emotional expense). The balancing act for doctors and for informed patients involves combining vigilance about signs of real trouble (which can be gauged with more and more precision by attentive doctors, though by no means absolutely) with an openness to trusting nature when there is no such sign and the woman's age supports that trust.[26]

PROFILE: Meredith, New Mother at 40 without Aid and at 46 via Egg Donation

Meredith, a banker, met the man of her dreams in her late thirties. She'd had a lively career and hadn't felt ready to settle down much before then. They both wanted a family, and she turned up pregnant the usual way soon after the honeymoon.

Their son was born happy and healthy, and eighteen months later they decided to try for another baby. Given their easy experience with the first pregnancy, they had hopes the second try would go smoothly too, despite knowing that their infertility risk had increased. When it didn't happen right away (Meredith was 42 at this point), they went to a clinic where they were diagnosed with "secondary infertility." Meredith tried IUI and then one round of IVF. When those didn't work, the doctor recommended that they try egg donation. Hoping for other options, Meredith switched doctors. She spent two years doing rounds of fertility drugs and monthly IUI attempts. The doctor thought that was reasonable given her history of easy pregnancy and delivery at 40. At 44, she tried one round of IVF with ICSI. When that failed she went to egg donation. It took her that long, she said, to get over the "ego stuff" that made her want to see her own genes in her baby.

Once on the egg-donation path, they soon found a donor they considered ideal (a graduate student), but the woman kept going out of the country at key times. After nine months they decided to go with the next reasonable alternative, which turned out to be an artsy and athletic woman in her twenties who had had two kids in her teens (proven fertility!) and who had recently completed her high school diploma. Meredith and Roger are now the happy parents of a very lively young girl who provides them with a built-in fitness plan.

From one perspective, Meredith's story might sound dismaying: a series of expensive and trying failures (not only emotionally trying but difficult also in terms of the mood swings the fertility drugs brought on and the pain of daily injections) leading up to an even more expensive late-life success. From their perspective, however, Meredith and Roger did just fine. They did what made the most sense for them at each stage, were in a position to afford the treatments, and were in the vanguard of an evolving communal experiment that is leading to ongoing improvements in the technology. They had a clear sense of purpose with each step, and now having resolved the situation in a very modern way, they are enjoying the family they had hoped for. ❖

For most people, Plan A is a bouncing baby by the usual means. If you run into infertility, and treatment doesn't produce a baby, the next options for those with the means are adoption or egg donation. For **Ramona** (new mom at 40), who had her first and (so far) only baby through egg donation after lots of fertility treatment, the physical experience of being pregnant felt important:

> I got to be pregnant, and I got to give birth to this baby. So that, I think, helped me work through some of the loss that I felt as a woman, because I could still do these sort of womanly things that connected me back to my body, which I felt had sort of abandoned me during this whole process.

The opportunity to experience pregnancy that egg donation provided meant a lot to Ramona. For some, the fact that the child is genetically connected to one parent also feels important, sometimes for reasons of bonding or of continuing the line and sometimes just to have a firmer sense of the child's genetic background.

❖ PROFILE: **Raina, New Mother at 38**

Raina, a writer, married artist Sam at 32. They started thinking about kids when she was 35. *Thinking* about kids, but not acting upon that thought right off, because she had fibroids—uterine growths that can cause severe pain and interfere with pregnancy if they grow too large. Fibroids can occur in women of all colors but are especially common in black women. They can be treated holistically, with laser surgery that could make kids less of a possibility, or with a much more invasive traditional surgery ("basically like a C-section, where they just cut you open and take them out"). Raina's doctor was very pro-pregnancy but also very conservative about surgery, so they tried cutting dairy and other such routes. The fibroids didn't cooperate, growing and hurting and buckling Raina over in public places. She finally had the surgery, took a year to recover, then she and Sam started trying to get pregnant when she was 37. They had no problems and had their daughter at 38.

Raina and Sam loved the family life, but Raina did not enjoy the physical side of childbearing. She gained a lot of weight, and it took her three years to get back to where she recognized herself. Her baby didn't sleep well for the first few years, and Raina's job was at a very demanding phase, so there was no chance that she would be spending any of her spare time at the gym. It all added up to a situation where Raina's ideas about family size shrank: "I don't think we will have more children, because I don't think I can do the three-year thing again." Much as she would like her daughter to have a sibling, she thinks it doesn't make sense for her and her husband now. She thinks people should keep that in mind as they think about planning a family:

> I didn't want to be in my mother's situation, where I was dependent on somebody else for grocery money. And so in order to fix that, this is the situation you get in. But it also means, you have a smaller family and you do things differently. . . .
>
> I mean, the thing you can't do is ask people to grow up fast. And I do think it's more important to be mature, than not to be mature [when you have kids]. So in that sense, I feel like, if you feel capable, then you can do it, but if you don't feel capable, then you shouldn't do it. But if you do feel capable, you should understand that if you do it earlier, you have more choices in terms of what your family looks like.

Although Raina did not encounter age-related problems with egg quality, resolving her medical situation meant that her family was delayed longer than it otherwise might have been, and her age along with her demanding job situation ultimately affected her decision about the number of her kids. ❖

Proactive Fertility

One of the effects of delaying—due either to awareness of infertility's decline or to an impatience to have kids that grows with age—is a growing tendency among later parents not to wait a full year to find out if they're infertile. If things aren't happening early on, many women head to the doctor for immediate treatment. That was the case with **Dolores**, who knew she wanted several kids when she married at 35:

> When we didn't get pregnant at first, it was just sort of like—I was 35 and I thought, you know, I had talked to Carter, if it doesn't work in six months, I'm going to the doctor, because I don't feel like we have a whole bunch of time to be waiting around if there's a problem. And so I was very proactive. I mean, the sixth month I was in the doctor's office. And it turns out that I had endometriosis, so I had to have a laparoscopy. Yeah. Surgery. And he went in and cleaned it all out. And then he wanted me to be on the pill for a while, cause he wanted to shut down my ovaries.

Dolores then had a hormone shot to "jump start the ovaries" again and used IUI to deliver the sperm directly to the uterus. Dolores and Carter had their first baby when they were both 36, then went on and had a second healthy baby without any medical intervention at 38 and a third at 40.

Proactive moms-to-be like Dolores drive up the number of infertility doctor visits. But they also drive up the success rates.

Miscarriage and Multiples

Fertility problems don't just mean inability to become pregnant. The term can also describe difficulty in carrying a pregnancy to term. As women age, their rate of miscarriage (or spontaneous abortion) rises. Whereas 10 percent of women in their twenties miscarry, 30 percent of women over 40 do. Among older women, pregnancy rates are lower and miscarriage rates are higher than for younger women.[27]

Quite a few of the women I spoke with had experienced one or more miscarriages. **Sharon** suffered three miscarriages in her late thirties. As she approached 40, a doctor suggested she try a fertility drug (she can't remember why, since she hadn't had trouble ovulating), and within days she conceived triplets whom she carried to term without problem. ("You know, in my mind, my three babies that couldn't come individually came together. So it was a full circle kind of event for me.")

Miscarriages occur either because the embryo has genetic problems or because the womb isn't supporting the pregnancy, for example, when pregnancy hormones aren't at the right levels to provide the environment for a stable implantation. Many miscarriages occur in women of all ages before they even realize they're pregnant, and most others occur before week twelve. Miscarriages at an advanced stage of pregnancy are often experienced as especially difficult.

Women miscarry at all times of day, sometimes after physical exertion, sometimes not. **Ruthie** (teacher and new later mother by adoption in her forties) described sitting behind a desk in a classroom, realizing what was happening, and calmly telling her students that class would be ending early that day. They departed cheerfully, and Ruthie, after waiting a few minutes, wrapped herself and her emotions up in her big coat and left too, with her privacy maintained.

Multiple births are another fertility effect more frequent in later mothers. Not only are multiples more common as the result of fertility drugs and IVF (often several embryos are transferred at once to ensure that at least one will implant), but twins naturally occur more often among later moms. I spoke with five mothers who gave birth to twins and one who had triplets. Two of the moms had twins naturally (at 34 and 42), one employed IVF with her own eggs (at 39), and the other two used donor eggs (at 45 and 46). In addition, I spoke with one mother of adopted twins. All the parents of twins experienced fatigue—especially in the early days. Sharon, the mother of the triplets, already had one child and describes the experience of multiples as

> a fairly traumatic event in a family. It was traumatic for each of us in our own ways. It was traumatic for my husband. While he was very positive about it in the initial stages, I was very fearful of the risk then of having triplets and having lost three and knowing that to lose three at once now would really you know be—I had already battled a couple of depressive episodes with the three pregnancy losses, and then to battle—if I were to lose those three, I wasn't sure where I'd end up.
>
> And then [my older child was only] 5, and it was a huge event to have happen in her life that I think we've continually dealt with over the years, with having her view the triplets not as an invasion of her life, but—they're here and they stay and you wake up everyday and they're still going to be here. And it's not their fault there's three of 'em, and they're three very individual kids. They don't look alike at all. And they don't act alike. I meant to have sheep—people who would get in the car when I said.

In addition there's the logistical challenge of managing all those people:

> Management, logistics, and the logistics of what it meant to our lives, too, is we had to hire more help. I wasn't used to having help around, managing other people in our lives. . . . Babysitters that don't get along with other babysitters. Skills I didn't necessarily have

before I started on this whole thing of really managing such a large group of people. . . .

Privacy is a big issue, and boundaries is a big issue, because the onslaught is so constant. And the thing I always say about mothers who have one baby at a time is at least you get to have some sense of satisfaction. I'm so grateful for the fact that I had a single birth before I had the triplets, because once you have multiples, you are in the realm of never having people satisfied all at one time. There's always somebody crying to be picked up, fed, changed, whatever.

And that goes on in different manifestations for years. In the long run, Sharon and her husband have adjusted and have found the challenges of parenting multiples hard but satisfying. They are very involved parents, but they've also had a lot of help.

Apart from the logistical issues that arise once multiples arrive, multiples involve higher rates of pregnancy problems, of premature birth, and of other difficulties for babies and mothers. The extra care preemies and ill babies require costs a lot—costs borne by both the families and the hospitals. On the other hand, for many struggling with infertility, multiples speed the journey to their optimal family size. As **Marina** (new mom via egg donation at 46) noted, she didn't intend to have twins, "but I was glad that I did, cause we would have not had another one." Lately, the rate of triplet or higher multiples is declining. As embryo transfer techniques and live-birth rates have improved, few doctors transfer more than three embryos at a time, generally with the expectation that fewer will implant, and some couples choose to transfer no more than two.[28]

Fertility Ethics

Parenting teems with ethics issues, and fertility technology adds a whole new set to the mix. New options for genetic testing mean that couples of all ages will become more and more engaged in ethical discussions around fertility and eugenics, but older couples face a greater likelihood of having to decide whether or not to bear a child with genetic abnormalities. The chances of giving birth to a child with Down syndrome, for instance, go from a 1 in 1,250 chance when a woman is 25, to a 1 in 400 chance at 35, a 1 in 105 chance at 40, and a 1 in 30 chance at 45.[29]

Older couples are also more likely to find themselves in the position of choosing whether to reduce a set of multiples in utero—not only are multiples hard to handle once they're born, the health of all can be compromised in utero by their drain on the mother, and reduction is sometimes the only way to ensure the survival of any. Where some see a black and white question ("it's our baby and we'll deal with it"), others see a question to be considered in light of the effect it would have on the family unit as a whole. Will the emotional and financial expense be fair to the other children? And whether or not there are other kids, will the parents be able to cope? Obviously, the decision is best made by the couple, but whatever the outcome, the decision-making process often occurs in the realm of the hard.

If a couple employs IVF or egg donation, often involving fertilization of more eggs than the couple chooses to use, they may have the embryo-in-the-freezer dilemma. The question of the fate of frozen embryos has received some recent press, but the images we're proffered of leftover embryos available for "adoption" in the womb as "snowflake children" leaves out the fact that most of the 400,000 embryos stored in cryo-banks are made from somebody else's older eggs and that they are the least likely candidates for implantation, the ones not chosen for the first go-round. Would it be "ethical" to ask women to undergo great emotional, physical, and financial expense to attempt to carry embryos most of which will not prove viable?

Roberta, a woman with a cache of frozen embryos and one wonderful child, pulled together several intersecting ethical concerns when we spoke:

Those embryos have taken on a whole life of their own, which I could never have anticipated when I got into this. You know, I am adamantly pro-choice, I have never believed that, you know, embryos at conception have lives, identities, whatever. And yet, these embryos are my child's siblings, and he came from that batch of embryos, and he is, you know, a miracle. And so his own person and so completely himself, and so it's very hard for me to just walk away or give them to science or let them suffer freezer burn or whatever happens to them. I feel really conflicted about them.

There's no guarantee that these embryos will develop at all or, if they do develop, that they'll be healthy. But they might. Roberta, who has a very absorbing job, isn't sure she wants another child anyway, and if she and her husband (who does feel ready) decide to have another, she's thinking adoption might be the more responsible road:

I feel like God gave us this miraculous child who is beautiful and smart and capable and funny, and you know, why tempt fate? Why— the world is full of children who need homes. I'm 43 years old. Like, let's not—let's not get the balance completely out of whack here. That's kind of where I am on that—none of it's rational.

She doesn't find it easy to discuss this with friends:

It's really a complicated thing, which is sort of left out of a lot of the discussion of all these fertility things. Just because it's so complicated, you can't really talk about all the sides in any real way, and so it turns into a caricature quickly, if you start talking about it. And so people don't talk about it.

But it's a question that quite a few couples do encounter.

On the other hand, not everybody feels connected to embryos. One mom by egg donation views the fate of the remaining frozen embryos as not hers to determine: "They're not my eggs; it's my husband's deal." Her husband has just completed the paperwork to offer the eggs to infertile couples who can't afford the full egg-donor process but want to bear a child.

Dolores, mother of three, has no frozen embryos, having gotten pregnant the regular way each time. She and her husband approached later fertility with a clear sense of what they wouldn't do: they wouldn't spin the sperm to determine the child's sex, and they wouldn't do any medical testing "because my husband is very clear on the issue that if we had a special child, we'd just have a special child. We wouldn't terminate." Their more established financial situation means that they could afford the costs involved if such a situation arose. But many others do choose to abort fetuses with abnormalities or to employ pre-implantation genetic diagnosis on IVF embryos to avoid age-induced or hereditary chromosomal disorders.

The new possibilities of human intervention in the essential levels of the fertility process create whole new realms for debate. Along with questions around the interventions themselves come a host of different but also ethical questions. What are the ethics of cost? Does the fact that we *can* do certain medical procedures at great expense mean that we *should* do them? If so, how many times per person (for instance, how many IVF cycles should one couple be allowed)? And who should pay, the individual or the insurer?

If, in the face of the complexity of such questions, it comes to seem that the easiest way to deal with these ethics issues might be to evade them by "simply" starting your family earlier, if you happen to be in a situation that allows that, what are the ethics of having children you don't feel ready for or don't yet want? In the past there may have been only limited options for "choice" around when to have kids, but once the choice *does* exist, is it possible ethically to behave as if that choice did not exist and to go back to the old pattern? As always, ethics means decisions that have to be made in the complex context of the world as the decider encounters it, not in a simplified version thereof.

PROFILE: Natalie, Mother of Twins at 39 via IVF

Midwesterners Natalie and Charles met in college, and they married when she was 26. He joined the service while she worked in various jobs, full time at first, then part time when she started studying toward a graduate degree. They always planned to start a family and began trying when she was 30. When it didn't work after a year or so, they went in for exams and were told they had "unexplained infertility." In spite of the name, the doctors came up with many explanations and treatments. Natalie had several small surgeries to correct minor abnormalities, and they tested Charles's sperm, but couldn't find a problem. Religious people, they turned to natural family planning. When that didn't work, they tried several cycles of IUI with Clomid. That didn't work either, and they were finally told they needed to try IVF. Natalie didn't like the idea.

> I don't know if I'd call myself, like, fanatical or anything, but I'm a very religious person, and I had a big ethical problem with what would happen to the embryos through the whole process of in vitro. Because it's physically very hard on the woman—you're getting your system pumped full of tons and tons of hormones and things to get your system to do things it's not used to doing. And then once you have the embryos, their situation is kind of precarious: they're in a petri dish or they're being, you know, put inside you. And it's very difficult.

They turned to domestic adoption, with Natalie very enthusiastic and Charles not so sure, but that attempt ended on a sour note. Not long after, they ran into friends who had gone through IVF successfully with a doctor they loved. Natalie and Charles also liked him, and when he, too, recommended IVF, they decided to try it. They reasoned that if they didn't, they'd always wonder. It did work on the first try, and they had twins.

Natalie was like a number of the women I spoke with who reversed expectations and came to later motherhood *after* a history of early infertility. In several cases, it may have been *because* they waited that they were able to have kids later—the technology had evolved only recently to help their fertility issues. In Natalie's case, the technology was there earlier, but it took her a while to come to terms with it. Since her religion is built around family, she concluded that it made sense that she use the means available to build a strong family life. ❖

How Old Is Too Old?

In November 2004, New Yorker Aleta St. James made headlines by having twins just three days shy of her 57th birthday. Two months later, Adriana Iliescu, a Romanian children's book writer, became the world's then-oldest known new mom at 66 (since then, a 67-year-old had twins). Both women were first-time moms and single, and both used donor eggs and donor sperm. Though some commentators disapproved, especially of Adriana, many people cheered Aleta (the sister of radio personality Curtis Sliwa and herself something of a public figure). Her doctors commented on her excellent physical condition. "You'll see, in another 10 years, what I'm doing will be normal," Aleta noted with a smile.

These stories aren't normal yet—and in spite of Aleta's forecast (she's a psychic), they may never be. But while they're unusual, both share something with the experience of many women today—most women wait longer for family now than their mothers did. The question many critics raise about these even-later moms has to do with longevity—will they reliably be around to raise their kids into adulthood? They expect to, but there's no guarantee. We'll see.

Insurance

Fertility insurance advocates argue that it makes sense because it meets needs: both the need of an expanding group of citizens who

want to have kids later (or whenever they encounter infertility) and
the need of society itself for an ongoing supply of new citizens. It can
be interestingly compared to the parallel coverage of normal birth
that most insurance plans now offer. Fertility insurance costs little
when it's spread across a big pool, but most states aren't yet convinced. So far, only fifteen states mandate that some form of fertility
coverage be included in health insurance. The options range from
full coverage in Massachusetts for women of any age, as long as they
get a doctor's okay, to states like Maryland and Arkansas that restrict
age or require that only married people using their own eggs and
sperm may benefit (effectively depriving lesbians and single straight
women). Some states limit maximum costs (ranging from $15,000 to
$100,000), and some write in no limits. In states that mandate full
coverage, the average addition to everyone's annual health bill was
$3.14 in 1995.[30] In states where coverage is not mandated and indi-
viduals pay all fees, women have tended to transfer more embryos in
each IVF cycle to raise the likelihood of success and avoid the cost
of another. As a result, the number of pregnancies and births involving multiples rises, and both health problems (for mothers and babies) and costs escalate. Insurance pays these costs up front, but we
all pay them later in raised rates. When women know they could
have a second cycle without big fees, they transfer fewer embryos,
and both problems and costs fall.[31]

Mandated fertility coverage means it's not just the rich who can
have babies if they run into infertility issues (whether due to age or to
other factors). The benefits to society would include an increase in the
happiness of citizens, a rise in the human capital of the workforce,
equalization of access to fertility treatment, expansion of the future
workforce, and the overall savings that would result if fertility prices
were regulated through the mechanism of state-mandated coverage
(an economy of scale).[32]

When Caroline had her first baby at 38, she had no difficulty (she got pregnant on the first try), but she had to use fertility technology because she was gay. She and her partner, Bridget, went to a sperm bank and chose a donor who looked like Bridget (people often think their daughter is Bridget's biological child). Since both of them were raised Catholic, they chose someone with a similar background for an element of familiarity in what was otherwise an intrinsically distant situation. Because Caroline felt that she would be supplying their child with plenty of creative energy, she opted for a donor who seemed more stable, even boring, for balance.

Thinking from the start that they might want two babies, they bought many vials of sperm from the same donor. (You have to think ahead in this arena, since there's no guarantee your donor will still be active when you're ready for a second or third child. In Caroline's case, the donor had indeed stopped when they were ready for baby two.) When Caroline started trying again at 40, pregnancy didn't happen right away. After trying IUI in an obstetrician's office for six months, she switched to a fertility clinic with two vials of donor sperm remaining. There, after a brief consult, the doctor told her that her ovarian reserve was too low and that IVF wouldn't work. Caroline then did a lot of research on the Web and began to doubt that doctor's interpretation of her results. She went to another clinic where the doctor gave her better odds, and she did get pregnant on the second try, under the influence of lots of egg-stimulating drugs, and with the last vial of donor sperm.

Though Caroline's treatments were covered by insurance in her state (which does mandate infertility coverage), today they no longer would be because they involved an anonymous donor. These benefits were cut from the plan because it was determined that women not married to men and using anonymous donors were making a social, not a medical, choice. This view assumes that if Caroline had sex with a man she would get pregnant. In Caroline's case, however (as in the cases of many older women using anonymous donors, whether lesbian or straight), infertility *was* a problem as well. ❖

Future Tech

The growing group of would-be later moms has a lot of money to spend, and the pressure of current and perceived future demand is fueling the proliferation of fertility technology research. Many of today's infertility problems may recede in the coming years—especially if the research also leads to reduced cost so that more women have access to whatever technology emerges as most effective.

Along with the research comes marketing—which can sometimes put the cart before the horse. Christy Jones made headlines in 2004 with a new company called Extend Fertility when she offered to freeze the eggs of women in their late twenties or early thirties for deployment at some unspecified later date (conceivably at 57 or 66, but the implication was late thirties to mid-forties). The idea was to make every woman her own donor—and to do an end run around the aging process that makes the eggs of older women less viable than they once were. Jones knew there was a market for this process because she'd done a survey of her fellow female MBA students at Harvard. Many of these women were approaching 30 and hoping to establish themselves in jobs before starting their families. Jones also wondered whether the perfect storm of committed romance, professional success, and fertility would come together in time to brew her a family using her own genetic material.

The only problem was that no one knew whether egg freezing would work (would there be a freezer-burn effect?). At $14,000 per try, it was a pretty expensive experiment. A year or so later, Jones married and announced plans to have kids in the standard manner, but two hundred women around the globe have since had children with frozen eggs, with only one known birth defect.[33] There aren't a lot of clinics trying this yet in the United States. The method sounds efficient and promising, and many women would be glad to try this route when and if the technology becomes widely and safely available. New speed-freezing techniques (vitrification) may be the way around the freezer burn, as might the use of less mature eggs that contain less water.

But why freeze just a few unstable eggs when you can freeze much more stable material for better effect? Ovarian tissue freezing has been used for women about to undergo treatment for cancer that might endanger their fertility. Instead of taking out the hard-to-freeze individual eggs, you slice out and freeze swaths of ovarian tissue (with many immature eggs and follicles embedded) for reimplanting when needed later on. Whether it will make sense for cancer-free women as well has yet to become clear.

Alternative avenues to fertility may emerge from unexpected directions. In 2005, scientists at Harvard Medical School announced a challenge to the understanding that females come into the world with their lifelong supply of eggs, which lose their magic as they age. Instead, they found evidence that the ovaries of female mice actively produce new eggs across their lifetimes, "upending," writes Natalie Angier, "a doctrine shared by reproductive biologists for eighty years: that a female mammal is born with all the oocytes and follicles she will ever have, and that her stock of eggs is steadily depleted until the procreation pantry is bare."[34] This research has not convinced many people yet, but if down the line human oocytes also prove to generate across a woman's lifetime, the next steps would be to re-explain female infertility at and before menopause and to work to control the generation of new eggs.

Then there's cloning—forbidden for the moment, but who knows how that might morph in the years to come. Given the potential popularity of designer genes, who's to say that people will even want to hand down their own characteristics in the years to come? The baby showers of tomorrow might come before conception and involve gifts of particularly prized genes or chromosomes—home-grown or store-bought—for which the parents had registered. Something like the gifts brought by the fairies (beauty, happiness, good fortune) for the baby in *Sleeping Beauty*.

As this book goes to press, the possibility that doctors may make stem cells from a woman's bone marrow into sperm bearing her genetic code boggles our basic notions of what differentiates men and women, and of who is essential to the continuation of the race.[35] This procedure would also open up new possibilities for lesbian family formation that circumvent the sperm donor complexity that many children of gay couples face today. Because only X chromosomes would be involved in their making, all of the children created through female/female genetic unions would be female.

Interventions into the old ways of reproduction frighten some folks, and there is conflict over infertility treatment just as there has been over contraception and abortion. But the demand and the many positive results seem likely to keep pushing research forward. Any or all of these experimental methods could be fruitful very soon, giving the next generation very different options.

If you want children, and you're thinking about when to start, you get to take all these factors into consideration: your own sense of when you'll be ready (in terms of education, maturity, partner, career, finances); your partner's readiness (where applicable); your sense of the odds for unassisted pregnancy at the age that you're ready; whether you would be willing to try (and, if so, afford) infertility treatments or adoption; and how you might feel if you ended up childless. Then there's the element of unpredictability in many of those factors. Each woman has to decide for herself when all the elements best configure for family. For those who don't feel ready to settle down, aren't in the career position they want to be in before kids, or haven't found life mates (and don't want to compromise in that department or parent alone, at least not yet)—for women in such situations, having children later is often the choice.

The question remains: How many women who want kids later (some in their late thirties and early forties, and some even after that) find themselves unable to have them unaided, and then either don't want to use fertility technology, can't afford it, or try it without success? We don't know how many fit this category because no such survey question has been asked in a rigorous way in a national study, but clearly there are a number of women. Some remain childless (or child-free—your language on this depends on the evolution of your attitude toward your situation), while others have gone on or will go on to adopt.

This chapter can't deal comprehensively with the amazing proliferation of issues on the contemporary fertility scene. Instead, I've touched on a range of issues, pointing to their multiple dimensions in the lives of real people and to their ongoing (and sometimes very rapid) evolution. Lots of people have kids later—most the usual way, some via fertility technology and adoption—and the set is expanding. The more solid information we all have and share, the more satisfying our choices around when to start our families will be. For later moms today, the fertility scene combines lots of old-fashioned, homemade babies with growing numbers of babies fashioned on new frontiers. They all meet on the playground, shouting and running around, with their later parents cheerfully in tow.

CHAPTER 7

Adoption

Expanding the Borders of Family

Infertility was the best thing that happened to me.
—MULTITUDES OF ADOPTIVE PARENTS

For some couples, unsuccessful infertility treatment means the end of the road to family; for others, it's one stage on that road. In one adoption study, respondents cited infertility as the reason leading to 80 percent of private adoptions and 50 percent of adoptions from foster care.[1] **Frances** and Roland (both professionals and parents by adoption at 40 and 45, respectively) met in college and married three years later when she was 22. Having found each other early, they planned to build their careers together and eventually to rear a family. They worked hard, their careers flourished, and when Fanny was about 31, they stopped using birth control. They didn't get pregnant. When she was 33, they consulted a fertility specialist, but he could find nothing wrong. They went down a fertility path that took them through endometrial surgery to the possibility of a uterine septum to IUI to IVF. Says Fanny, "Every time we tried something, [the doctor] was optimistic and he said, 'Things look perfect, you're primed, everything's ready to go.' And then when it didn't work, he always said, 'I can't believe it!' He was shocked himself; everything looked perfect. So it was always kind of a mystery."

It didn't seem to have anything to do with her age (her ovarian reserve and her hormone balances all seemed fine), but no other explanation presented itself.

Fanny got very involved in solving the mystery, trying several doctors to find one willing to give her individualized attention. Even with the right attention, the solution didn't emerge. Eventually the mystery got old, and Fanny and Roland started the adoption process. They experienced a few ups and downs on this new path also.

Open to any healthy child—any race, any gender—Fanny and Roland were soon matched with an expectant 24-year-old single mother of two kids, both of whom were being raised by their grandma. The three spent time together and connected, but at the point of relinquishing the baby, the new mother decided she couldn't. So Frances and Roland did some grieving, then decided to switch to an agency that did more screening and counseling of birth mothers.

A few weeks later, their new agency called and said they had a baby born that day available for adoption. Roland was out of the country, but Fanny got him on the phone fast. The birth mother had seen their profile and approved them, but didn't want to meet them. She was ready to move on. The law in their state requires that a birth mother wait forty-eight hours before relinquishing parental rights; Evelina was born on a Friday, and that Sunday morning Fanny picked her up at the hospital. Roland flew home that night to find a baby waiting. Says Fanny,

It was a very long journey to starting a family, then just all of a sudden it happened in a quick minute. She just fell into our lap really, and it really does feel like everything—I'm glad it happened the way it happened, and that I never got pregnant and that we waited as long as we waited. Because we both feel we have the right baby.

Even though she hoped to be a mom at 33, Fanny feels she's a better mom at 41. That has to do both with maturity and with "just being able to approach things with a little bit more knowledge and patience and also gratitude—I'm reminded every single second that this was a struggle to get this family, and I'm able to embrace some of the more difficult moments [as they arise] and accept them."

Quite a few of the women I talked with remarked on the preciousness of family achieved through big effort. Struggle might not be everybody's first choice as a mode of family formation, but it has its benefits. In the adoption world, it's not uncommon to hear infertility described as a blessing in disguise because it led the way to a happy adoptive family that wouldn't otherwise have existed. Many couples come to adoption after biological Plan A has fizzled. As one adoptive mom put it, "[D]eciding to adopt is not something that you come to easily. I think that as a woman, you have a desire to have *your* child." Many women look forward to the physical experience of pregnancy. If it doesn't work out, that's the point when the adoption option emerges for most. Once matched with a baby they love, most adopters see no reason to look back.

Jan (scientist, adoptive mother at 41 and 43) describes adoption as a kind of birth process: "The little picture is like our sonogram. The trip over is like labor, though the trip home is *more* like labor." And after the birth comes the bonding process:

> I remember after her first month home, staying home, that was a major life change. . . . Then she started to catch up developmentally, [and] I was starting to catch up as a mom. . . . Everyone was playing with each other, and she started to smile back. You fall in love with that little picture, but it isn't until [you get to know each other] that you really know. . . . And that's when I learned about Mother Bear. . . . It was just this global love. . . . I'm a mom, this is the best thing in the world. I had to grow into it.

Every adoption may contain an element of sadness, because it begins from a loss—a baby's loss of birth parents no matter the circumstances. Part of the joy of adoption lies in being able to assuage that loss and to create new sources of allegiance and delight for all the parties involved.

While many couples come to adoption after experiencing infertility, some couples adopt after having biological children. They've determined that they want to expand their family to include someone who is already on the planet and in need of family. Lately, because of a generally raised consciousness about the needs of children at home and around the world, a growing group (small, but avid) of both couples and singles are choosing to adopt without first trying the biological route.

Adoption is a hot topic these days for several reasons. Perhaps most noticeably, there has been a spate of celebrity adoptions. There's the recent popularity of Chinese adoption along with the backlash that sometimes flares up in response to that popularity—why aren't they adopting U.S. kids in need? There is a steady stream of stories about the problems in the foster-care system in the United States. Recently, some adult transracial adoptees, particularly those adopted from Korea in the seventies and eighties, have objected to international adoption as a practice in general.[2] There are ongoing debates and sometimes legislation and judicial rulings about gay adoption and foster care. And then, there are the evident needs of children in the United States and around the world, in regions devastated by war, famine, poverty, and disasters. It's against this background that later mothers and dads experience adoption today. In the following pages, we'll look at the wider context and the individual experiences of the adoptive moms I spoke with.

In 2001 (latest figures), 127,000 children were adopted in America (it's been roughly the same number since 1987—down from a high of 175,000 in 1970).[3] How many of them were adopted by new later parents? There are no statistics available on how many adoptive parents start their families at or after 35, but anecdotal evidence (and logic) suggests it's a good proportion. Though many families adopt after having had biological children earlier in life, many adopters are new later parents.

One woman I talked with got divorced in order to start a family. Having married with a plan to have kids, Casey's husband changed his mind a few years later. After arguing a bit, **Casey** realized she didn't want to parent with a reluctant dad, so she divorced him when she was 40. She put herself through a night school MBA program to boost her income and then adopted at 44.

Adoption rates have been historically hard to track, partly because not all adoptions are formalized in a court and also because for ages parents felt reticent about telling their children, and the world at large, that their kids were adopted. Some people sought children who resembled them at least partly in an effort to disguise their adopted status. But attitudes have changed recently, and we are now, as Adam Pertman puts it, an "adoption nation"—one in which most people, if they're not adopted themselves, either have adopted relatives who are known to be adopted without stigma or know someone involved in adoption.[4]

There are many kinds of adoption that encompass a range of experiences for all involved: some good, some not. As with all families, there are no guarantees on how things will turn out. That said, of the twenty-three adoptive moms I spoke with, most of them parents of kids 10 and younger, all spoke positively about the experience. All but two were private adoptions. Four were second mothers: lesbians adopting children who were either the biological or adoptive kids of their partners. Seven were single moms upon adoption. Viewing the experiences comparatively, **Mariam** (mother of one adopted and one biological child) concludes:

> When they're biological, there are some health issues, but you can tend to predict. When you don't know them, this is harder. . . . But even in hindsight, it wouldn't have mattered. This child has given us

the kind of joy we could never explain. With everything there's always [something unexpected]. Nothing happens in one line.

Parents of older kids from difficult backgrounds knew going in that managing the effects of trauma would be part of the job of parenting. Given that background, sometimes they have to struggle to stay positive in rearing their kids.[5] But they know that willingness to undergo that struggle is part of the importance of their being there for their kids.

Adoptions of young children may also involve difficulty—young children may have experienced trauma, too, and some children have difficulty attaching. Others have health and emotional difficulties, and there can be real pain for all in dealing with those issues. Some parents have difficulties as well. Adoptive families are just as prone to problems as biological families, and there are more issues to deal with around the loss of the birth parents and, if it's a transracial adoption, of the birth culture. Sometimes the adoption process breaks down in the middle. But the adoptive parents I spoke with were in happy families that worked around problems as most families do—with loving parents and children trying to do their best by one another.

The Adoption Options

Adoption matches children in need of parents with parents in need of kids. What could be simpler? Sometimes it is simple, but usually some complications emerge. All families have their complexities, of course, but the possibility of extra complexities sometimes makes people hesitate about adopting. In surveys, the percentages of people reporting that they had ever considered adopting far surpass the percentages of people who have actually adopted (nationally 2.5 percent of children are adopted).

When it comes to adoption, different questions occur to different people, but everybody has questions. Some are answered easily, others not. Once you've answered your personal questions, and you decide that adoption makes sense for your family, the next step is to determine which *kind* of adoption to pursue: a newborn, an infant, or an older child; one child or a sibling group; private agency or public services adoption; domestic or international; same color or transracial; special needs okay or not; open or closed? In general, the fewer limits you set, the faster your adoption can happen.

Speed (to referral and to finalization) figures large as an issue in the adoption world. Many people decide which kind of adoption to go with based on what seems most likely to happen the quickest, or with the least likelihood of interruption. For many, this has been a reason to choose the international route: adoptions from foster care in the United States have often been plagued by delays, private adoptions can break off if birth mothers change their minds, and there's the chance that no birth mother picks you in the first place. But many domestic adoptions go smoothly, and sometimes international adoptions break off due to sudden rule changes or other unpredictable circumstance. While everybody hopes for a smooth adoption process, it's understandable that something so emotionally important to all parties would involve ups and downs.

Sometimes the obstacle is money. Both domestic and international private adoptions cost in the range of $20,000. Most of that goes to the adoption agency that handles the paperwork, and the rest goes to the cost of the prenatal care for the birth mother or for travel and an orphanage donation if it's international. But after the initial outlay, some of that comes back, since all adoptive parents now get a tax credit of up to $10,000 to cover documented adoption expenses. Public adoptions cost little or nothing, and benefits (such as health insurance for the kids until they are 18 and sometimes college tuition) may also be offered, depending on your state.

Though descriptive data on *who* adopts is hard to track (and there are other difficulties around tracking data across states with different reporting rules), there is some data available through the U.S. Department of Health and Human Services. Of the roughly 127,000 U.S. adoptions in 2001, 39 percent came from the public foster-care system, 15 percent were international, and the rest happened through private agencies or other channels—involving either people not related to the adoptee or tribal or kinship adoptions (a large proportion of private adoptions were by step-parents).[6] Most private adoptions involve newborns, infants, and children under 5. Because it takes a while for parents to prove themselves unfit, most public agency adoptions involve kids over 5. The age of the kids involved affects many people's decision about which route to take to adoption.

The adoption landscape is extremely varied, and this chapter only scratches its surface.

Domestic Foster Care

Children enter foster care when their parents have been declared unfit—which occurs if they're found to be abusive (physically, sexually, or emotionally) or neglectful (failing to provide the basic care). Lately there have been around half a million kids in foster care each year. Each year, about half of them leave the system, and a new group of similar size replaces them. In 2003, 39 percent of the kids in foster care were white, 35 percent were black, 17 percent were Hispanic, and 9 percent were other races.[7]

Not all children in foster care are available for adoption—about one-fifth—since in many cases the best outcome for the child is that the family resolves its difficulties and stays together. Fifty-five percent of foster-care placements do end in family reunions. About 9 percent of the time, these reunions do not work out and children are returned to foster care. Of the 106,000 kids in foster care available for adoption in 2003, roughly 50,000 were adopted.

❖ PROFILE: Cleo, New Mom to Preteens at 47

Cleo has always been a caretaker and has long wanted to be a mom. For a few years she and her partner Wendy tended Cleo's grandparents (who were in their nineties), and after that they informally parented a teenage street kid for a year, offering him a home base and a sympathetic ear. But they wanted the full parenthood experience, so a few years back they put their names in the hopper with the state public adoption agency.

Open to a child or sibling group between the ages of 2 and 12, they learned a lot in the process about how public adoption and foster care work. If you read the news, you won't be surprised to hear that foster care has problems. There were 500,000 children in foster care in the United States in 2006, and many of them were in bad situations. For example, the states of New Jersey and Mississippi both made headlines recently for having totally inadequate foster-care programs, programs that cannot guarantee the welfare of the children they are meant to safeguard. (The average caseworker's load in one county in Mississippi was 130, whereas seventeen was the recommended limit.) Many other states have troubled systems as well, since money is short everywhere and the care of what are often poor people's children seems low on the list for funds.

Cleo soon learned that many children in foster care are on behavior-modifying drugs. Some need them, but others are medicated because it makes them more docile (handy for caretakers tending several or sometimes a dorm full of kids), and some, because foster parents are paid more to care for kids on medication. To really know what situations children are in, you have to bring them home, stop all medications, and begin diagnosing from scratch.

Cleo and Wendy expected it would be easy to find a child, given that they didn't care about age, race, or sex and were asking for an older kid in a world where babies are most in demand. It took more than a year. Cleo describes the matching process as similar to going to a dating service. Agencies are only supposed to send you information on kids who fit your profile, but you may have a caseworker who decides, "oh well, they said they wanted this, but I think they might be more interested in this kid or this sibling group." Periodically, you'll get an email or a fax with a picture of a child and a little paragraph of information, asking, "Do you want to see more of the file?" You work your way through to the right one, or in their case, the right ones. Cleo and Wendy eventually adopted two great tween-age girls—African American sisters who moved from separate foster-care situations to be adopted together. ❖

Cleo's girls had been in foster care for several years before they found their new home. The median time a child spends in foster care is one year, but 10 percent stay in as long as five years or more. Part of the slowness in moving kids into foster-care adoptions stems from the fact that the government works on the principle that the best outcome for birth families is that they stay together. This principle makes clear sense for most families, but not those in which kids are at risk or neglected. The law wants to find out for sure which are which—hence the long wait. More than a few families have welcomed a series of children into their homes, only to have one adoption after another collapse through no fault of theirs.

In 1997, a new federal law was passed to limit the time children can remain in care before their parents' rights are severed and they become available to be adopted into permanent homes. The change has led to an important increase in foster-care adoptions in many states (the number more than doubled from 1995 to 2000).[8] But many kids in need of permanent loving homes remain in fosterage. Singles and gay couples may adopt from foster care in most states, and many do, both because they are excluded from many other adoptions and because they are ready to parent hard-to-place kids. But some states, like Florida, prohibit gay adoption, which means that many kids remain in foster care there who otherwise would not. Evidence strongly supports the view that children do as well with gay parents as with straight, and certainly better in a permanent home with gay parents than in less permanent situations.[9] A recent ban on gay foster care in Arkansas was struck down on that basis.[10] Since they often come from troubled, sometimes traumatized backgrounds and are older, a good number of kids in foster care have special emotional and psychological needs and need warm, structured, supportive families. The government provides a variety of benefits, which may include, depending on your state, free psychological care and health insurance or even free public university tuition.

Transracial Adoption

In adopting black children, Cleo and Fanny, both white, represent a new trend in U.S. adoption. Even though it can take much longer to adopt a white infant than a black infant, white families, for decades, tended to avoid adopting black children. Part of this avoidance stemmed from varying degrees of racism in adoptive parents. Other hesitancy came from anxiety about having to deal with other people's racism (including family members') and the questions that arise around conspicuous adoption in a racially charged world; some felt it unfair to bring children into such an environment.

Another factor is that for a long time transracial adoption was hard or even impossible to do; in 1972, the National Association of Black Social Workers (NABSW) made a public statement discouraging interracial adoption and calling it a form of cultural genocide. Opposition to race crossing was reinforced at administrative levels as well as in the public culture. Many white couples were denied when they applied to adopt black kids. Some black people saw white adoption of black kids as an insult, suggesting that the black community could not take care of its own. Others agreed with NABSW that white parents could not adequately prepare black children to deal with the racism they would face on a daily basis. In one recent book of interviews with black adults who had grown up with white adoptive parents, the overall message was that thoughtful, loving parents—especially those who support their kids in making connections with their birth culture—give their children a good life, regardless of racial difference. But quite a few kids without access to a same-race community have found life hard and lonely.

Recently, some Americans of all colors have taken offense at international adoption, wondering why, for instance, Chinese girls seem to be welcomed into so many American families when there are so many needy kids in the U.S. foster-care system—both African American and white. One reason that Chinese and other international adoptions are chosen is that most involve infants.

The bias against white-black adoptions seems to be fading somewhat, and the number of white parents adopting black children domestically has climbed in the last few years.[11] More than one-quarter of the black children adopted from foster care in 2004 were adopted by white families—that's 4,200 kids, up from 2,200 in 1998. Transracial adoption from Africa has also been on the rise.

On the other hand, racial imbalances have not disappeared in adoption. A smaller proportion of black kids available for adoption in foster care get adopted than white kids. A recent media story pointed out that a steady stream of about five hundred American black babies are being adopted internationally each year, particularly from Canada, a country without the U.S. hard history of black-white race relations.[12]

Most commonly, U.S. transracial adoptions involve Asian babies. The trend began in the fifties after the Korean War when many orphans needed homes. Since then, more than 150,000 Korean babies have been adopted here. These babies' birth mothers were often (though not always) unwed mothers who sometimes chose to and were sometimes pressured into relinquishing their children. The babies were placed with families in the United States, often in very white areas of the country. Many of the adult adoptees now complain that, though they were loved, they were culturally isolated. As children, they suffered from the lack of contact with people who looked like them and who shared the culture and language they'd been born into, and they miss those connections as adults.

Many transracial and international adoptive families of young children today are responding to the negative experience that adult transracial adoptees have recounted. The adoption community now emphasizes the importance of keeping kids connected to their birth culture and to other people (including other adoptees) from that culture. Many families celebrate the birth country's cultural holidays. Others take language courses together so that children will be able to speak their home language, should they ever choose to return. Still others make a point of adopting more than one transracial child, so nobody feels racially isolated or lonely within the family group.

Will it be enough? A few holiday celebrations and a rough vocabulary don't equal an immersed cultural experience. There is, however, evidence that respect for the birth culture makes an important difference for children. The question will be whether the experience of growing up in a loving and culturally conscious transracial American family will make enough of its own lineage to ground a contented life for most adoptees.

Private Adoption

Private adoptions include step-parent and other kinds of kin adoptions as well as placements of infants and newborns with strangers who quickly become new families.

In the 1950s, when single mothers were frowned on, many women were pressured into giving up their babies for adoption, and many later regretted it. Adoptions were closed, and it was difficult for either children or birth parents to find one another. After a while, in reaction, a birth mothers' rights movement began. At the same time, with the advent of birth control and legal abortion, as well as the growing social acceptability of single motherhood, fewer infants became available for adoption. Women who did choose to give their kids up for adoption were in a position to choose their babies' new families. Within limits, they can often choose to what extent they want to remain involved with the child they relinquish.

Much of the difficulty in adoption springs from a tension among the needs of three constituencies: the children and both sets of parents. Many birth parents relinquish kids either because they don't feel personally ready to parent or because they don't think they could do as well by those kids as another more established family could. Some birth mothers don't want to stay in touch, but others want to maintain a connection with the children they gave life to. Many adoptive parents feel nervous about open adoptions. There is no one right answer, but many adopted children do want to know their birth parents at some point.

Would-be adoptive couples make picture books of themselves and their homes that include statements about their life philosophies. Several such books are given to birth mothers who then pick the family they want to parent their child. As **Paulette** (a black woman married to a white man, bio mom at 39 and seeking to adopt a biracial child at 44) described her feelings about a recent rejection, "It was perfect, but she didn't pick us! I am not liking this process!" Even with a rejection or two along the way, the process does go well for many. The difference can depend on some combination of the laws in your state, your openness to kids of various ages and backgrounds, and luck.

❖ PROFILE: **Penny, New Mom at 42 via Adoption**

Penny knew since she was 21 that she wasn't going to be able to have children—"little run-in with chemo," she explains. She was 35 when she married, after establishing herself in the petroleum industry and seeing quite a bit of the world. Penny was a little skeptical initially about adopting "because of all the horror stories you hear," but her husband, Leo, was family oriented (one of six kids). Penny herself came from a family of four loving siblings. She and Leo talked it through and finally she thought, "You know what? When I'm 65 or 75, I'll probably look at all the nieces and nephews and wish that they were all mine." The whole process took about two years, ending with a sudden, six-day "pregnancy": they got a phone call from the adoption counselor on a Tuesday, met the baby's birth mother on Thursday, the baby was born on Saturday, and they brought William home on Monday.

Penny's family has an ongoing relationship with the birth parents and *their* parents, and William sees his birth mother two or three times a year. He's beginning to ask questions like, "Mom, if I grew in Lori's tummy, doesn't that mean I should be part of *her* family?" Penny responds in terms like, "You're lucky you have two moms; you have a birth mom—Lori—and you have me." "Okay!" says the 6-year-old, running off to some other occupation. But eventually he'll want more detail. And Penny and Leo will explain that, when he was born, Lori was not ready to parent him, but that all four of his parents love him. Penny expects there will be lots of emotion to work through in the coming years, but they work at giving him an expanded sense of family to assist that process. Penny points to the fact that their son has many more than the usual complement of grandparents and great-grandparents, not only because he has twice the average set but because several of them have divorced and remarried. Penny explains that families are made in many ways, that what they have works for them but what other people have works too. Their family is active in their church, which includes quite a few gay and lesbian couples with kids, so that helps make the point. And though Penny and her husband plan to live a good long while, she likes knowing that, if that doesn't happen, their son will have lots of welcoming family for the rest of his life. After a career of traveling the globe at the drop of a hat, Penny's happy to be at home in the evenings with her family:

> I tell you, [kids] change your life. . . . In my youth, I was thrilled to travel, and sitting on a plane for thirty hours was nothing. And now, sitting on a plane for thirty hours is debilitating! . . . I never

thought that I could say that I'm happy to stay home. But I can say that, and it's because of this child, and my husband of course—I just want to be around them and trip on Legos in the middle of the night. ❖

❖ PROFILE: **Daphne, New Adoptive Mom at 56**

At 56, Daphne and her 43-year-old husband, Kevin, adopted a 6-week-old baby boy. Daphne is older than some grandmothers, and she's more energetic than most of her peers. Good thing, she knows. She makes her living in a field that requires lots of movement, so she's very fit. Her mother is a very energetic woman in her late eighties. Both of those factors were key in Daphne and Kevin's decision-making, with Daphne out of the usual range even for a new later mother. The fact that her husband was younger played in, too: they both expect to be around and healthy for a while.

It took them some time to find their child: four years into their process, they were referred the boy who is now their son. The birth mother did not look at adoption books and left it to the agency to choose. The process took time, but the result is the familiar "this is the perfect boy for us." Daphne, now 59, still gushes when she talks about her baby: "I feel like it's just the perfect match. I wouldn't have missed it for anything." The possibility of meeting his birth mom remains open, but the adoption does not include direct contact at this point. Their son is now 3, and he's keeping his parents hopping.

Of all the women I spoke with, Daphne became a mom at the most advanced age. But though she's older, her narrative echoes that of later moms who started in their late thirties and forties. It was all about readiness. Daphne started her career in one field and then realized in her thirties that she wanted to be in another field. That required re-training and delayed her thinking about family, though she'd always known she wanted one. Her lack of a partner played in, too. The men she chose to date weren't ready for family either ("which is why I kept choosing them"), and she didn't want to parent alone. It wasn't until her late forties that she met and married (at 49) the right guy. As she puts it, "I was not ready until I was older. . . . I think that at a certain age, you really become your own person. And it's a different age for everybody. For me, I was a late bloomer." Once she reached that point, she felt that motherhood was "an opportunity not to be missed, which is why I decided to go for it at this late date." Daphne has a younger spouse who can take over if anything happens to her, as do many older men who have kids later in life. ❖

International Adoption

International adoption has been on the rise in the United States in the past fifteen years. If you live in a big city, you've probably seen or met a few international families. Or you've seen one of the many recent stories on international adoption in the celebrity magazines. Why so many now? It's an issue of supply, demand, and process. Most countries, including the United States, if they allow adoption at all, handle it internally. The Hague Convention on adoption finds it most desirable for children to be adopted in their homeland in order to maintain connections with the culture they come from.[13] There is concern that internationally adopted children will feel isolated and lose important cultural connections if placed in a different country.

But war, famine, poverty, epidemics, disaster, or, in the case of China, population-control pressures mean that sometimes nations have more babies in need of homes than they can (or choose to) accommodate in-country. In the past few years, China, Russia and other Eastern Bloc countries, Guatemala, South Korea, and a few others have been involved in most international adoptions by U.S. parents. Lately, Ethiopia (where one in fourteen mothers dies in childbirth) has been expanding its international adoption program. That's the sad but clean part of the supply side.

Sometimes there's a dirty side. If a country has many abandoned babies and establishes an adoption system to meet those babies' needs, the success of the system may draw the attention of unscrupulous people with money in mind. If the government doesn't watch carefully, mothers may be pressured to relinquish their children, or babies may be stolen, bought, or produced on purpose for adoption.

The key to knowing the difference between clean and dirty adoptive situations is strict international enforcement of laws that ensure that adoption is in the best interest of the child, and that child trafficking plays no part in the process. Currently, such laws are more strictly enforced in some places than in others. The U.S. government is in the process of ratifying the Hague Convention on Protection of Children and Co-operation in Respect of Inter-country Adoption in 2008 and is encouraging all the countries it works with in adoption to do the same. But abuses occur, and much more international cooperative work is needed to make the system thoroughly transparent and reliable. Some people see instances of corruption as a reason to abandon the whole system, but that would be a real case of throwing out the baby with the bathwater, leaving many abandoned children without hope for the recourse that international adoption now offers.

While international (and domestic) rules forbid paying money for a baby, it is permissible to charge fees to cover the cost of caring for the child and to improve the lives of those remaining in the orphanage. The orphanage fee paid at each adoption (for example, it's $3,000 in China) is used for new buildings and more caregivers and improves the care of all the children remaining in that facility.

On the demand side of the adoption equation, many more families are interested in adopting infants than are available in the United States. And some families feel uncomfortable with the beauty-pageant or sales-pitch aspect of the process, where birth mothers select you on the basis of how well you present yourselves and your life in your adoption book. This may be especially true of older or single parents, who often feel at a disadvantage. Potential parents who seek an older child sometimes go the international route because they have had or have heard of other people who've had long delays or endless obstacles in the foster-care adoption process.

U.S. adoptions (both public and private) can occur on unpredictable timetables and can sometimes take years with no guarantees of success. Foreign adoptions, on the other hand, often happen in a predictable pattern and time span. With most foreign adoptions, there's small risk of a birth parent's sudden change of mind or of the sudden appearance of a grandparent. Because would-be adoptive parents in the United States have often heard stories about difficulties with domestic adoptions, many don't even explore the possibility of adopting here, either from foster care or through private agencies, because they don't want the emotional upheaval of disrupted adoptions. There are, of course, no guarantees in either realm.

PROFILE: **Monica, New Mom (in Her Early Forties) to One Girl from China and (in Her Late Forties) to One Boy from Ethiopia**

Monica, a lively blonde, worked and played throughout her twenties and thirties. Employed in an international industry, she traveled the world regularly and loved it. In the back of her mind, she knew she wanted kids eventually. Around the age of 35, she began thinking it was time to start that family, and since there was no man around who she wanted to start a family with, she looked into adoption. Then she met Rick, the man it turned out she loved and wanted to stay with long term. He wasn't ready for family yet, and they wanted to spend time exploring together before they settled down. They enjoyed each other's company and saw more of the world. She had a steady stream of increased responsibilities at work. They bought a house, fixed it up, then bought another house.

Finally, at 42, she knew she had to get to work on the family or she would miss it entirely. At their ages, she didn't think their chances of being picked by a birth mother were good, so they explored foreign adoption. China looked like the best match. Within months, they were the parents of 1-year-old Amaranth. Monica and Rick quickly discovered they loved being parents. They worked hard at their jobs but spent all their nonwork time on family activities. A few years later, they adopted again, this time from Ethiopia. Monica chose Ethiopia because she wanted a boy, and boys are hard to find in Chinese adoption. Also, the waiting time for Chinese adoption had increased considerably. Ethiopian referrals can come quickly, especially if you request a boy. In Ethiopian adoption, as in adoption worldwide, girls are much more in demand, for a variety of reasons.[14]

Monica and Rick worked to prepare themselves for the challenges they knew they'd meet in parenting an African boy in a white family in the United States. Though they were already a transracial family, their daughter hadn't encountered any particular notice in their community—Asian adoptions seem pretty common in their city. Other white parents of Ethiopian kids have told Monica to expect it to be different with a black son. She's hoping white-black adoption will soon be less of a rarity, so their family can go its way without too much comment. Meanwhile, she's honing her skills at communicating to passersby that, if they have something to say, they need to not say it in front of the kids. ❖

Ethiopian adoptions have increased in the last few years in large part because, as in China, the children are well cared for prior to adoption, and the system operates in a very straightforward and predictable manner. Many children are available because many Ethiopian mothers die in childbirth, and often there's no one in the surviving family able to care for or feed the babies. Others are relinquished because their families are too impoverished to care for them. Once orphaned or relinquished, they become wards of the state, which runs the adoption system. Children with AIDS or who are HIV positive live in different orphanages from those not infected. A separate program for adopting kids with HIV to the United States has recently begun. Part of the hope around adoption in impoverished countries is that the children who are adopted out will gain the education and resources needed to return as adults and help make things better for their birth country.

An open extended-family network is often hard to maintain in international adoption, which sometimes adds to the appeal for adoptive parents, at least initially. In the long run, however, they may find it a big loss to their children that they wish they could repair. Sometimes connections can be remade even across national borders. In Korea, birth moms relinquish their babies through a documented adoption process, so some Korean adoptees have been able to reconnect with their birth families.

The history of Korean adoption in the United States has paved the way for the recent influx of children from China and other Asian countries, but the Korean and Chinese situations differ. Korean birth moms relinquished their babies largely in response to social censure of single mothers, while the influx of Chinese baby girls began in 1990 when the Chinese government began to enforce its one-child population-control policy much more stringently than it had done previously. Lacking a national retirement fund, Chinese parents often depend upon a son to support them in their old age, and less materially, sons are often simply deemed preferable. For those reasons, some parents have chosen (or been pressured) to abandon their daughters so that they could try again for a boy. (In parts of the country where two children are allowed, many of the abandoned girls are second daughters, whose older sisters remain with the family.) As a result, many abandoned girl babies were left in orphanages with little hope of domestic adoption.

In Guatemala, where children often become available for adoption due to poverty, it's often the reverse—boy babies may be more likely to be relinquished because girl babies are seen as more likely to be a support to their families long term.

Not all cultures see adoption as an option. Muslim cultures generally don't allow adoption, though they do allow fosterage. When adoption does occur, the new family must be Muslim as well.

As countries become more wealthy, more stable, and more concerned with their global status, they may work toward cutting back on the numbers of children adopted out. After fifteen years of escalating numbers of adoptions (almost eight thousand in 2005), adoption from China has recently declined (to fewer than seven thousand in 2006), though the number of foreigners looking to adopt from China has continued to rise. The government seems to have been allowing more domestic adoptions while campaigning to change the bias toward boy children. In 2007, new rules were introduced that limited eligible foreigners to married heterosexual couples of good character between 30 and 50, in good health, and of substantial means. These changes put China's rules in line with many other countries' patterns, including the general pattern in private U.S. adoption.

The adoption scene can shift quickly as rules evolve in both sending and receiving countries. For instance, perhaps in response to adult adoptees' protests, Korean international adoption may now be on the decline. As of 2007, the country will begin to actively encourage domestic adoption by many means that weren't options before, including allowing singles to adopt and making direct payments to adoptive parents. At the same time, the speed and number of international adoptions from India, where millions of abandoned children need homes, seem to be increasing. The key for would-be parents deciding on which country to adopt from is that there be in place an ethical and transparent infrastructure and international supervision of the adoption process under the Hague Convention, to ensure that children's safety and best interests are paramount. The world badly needs to define and enforce rules against all human trafficking, and especially of children. Adoptive parents can be an active force in working toward that reform, both in the way they conduct their adoptions and in their activism post-placement.

International adoption addresses the crying needs of abandoned and orphaned children around the world as well as the needs of the families who welcome them. As in all families—adoptive and biological—the intention underlying international adoption is that the bonds and self-confidence established through a loving and thoughtful family life will serve the child well in facing the complexities of life.

PROFILE: Lucy, Single Mom (at 40 and 42) to Two Boys from Guatemala

Lucy, a doctor, was involved with a fellow doctor while they were both in medical school. During their residencies, they moved to separate cities and broke up after a year or so. Distance probably had something to do with the break, and so did the fact that he made it clear he expected that, when they had kids, she should be the one to cut back on work since his was the more lucrative field. It didn't feel so clear to her that this was the right way to make decisions about a partnership.

In the years following, she worked hard at setting up her practice and didn't meet anyone she wanted to start a family with. Suddenly she was approaching 40. Adoption had always attracted Lucy, so she looked into domestic adoption of an infant. The agencies she spoke with gave her the message that, because she was single, it was unlikely she'd be picked as a parent by a birth mother. Guatemala had a good record of speedy adoptions of young and healthy babies and didn't care about her marital status, so she put in her paperwork and was quickly referred a child. But just as she was preparing to go get him, Guatemala revamped its adoption rules and the process stalled. While she had been aiming to adopt an infant, Lucy's son (who had been in foster care with a loving family in the interim) was nearly two by the time he arrived in the United States.

Once he arrived they bonded immediately, and she can't imagine being without him. She keeps in touch with his foster mother and has links through her to his birth mother. When I first spoke with Lucy, she was just starting to think that Hector needed a sibling and that she would likely go to Guatemala again. Two years later, she adopted a second son. She's a busy mom, but a happy one. As she describes it, "when I adopted my first son, I felt like a mother, but now with two, I feel like we are a family." She describes their experience as "wonderful." If she were ten years younger, she might go for three.

As a single mom of one, she was able to go on an occasional date. With two, she hasn't had time to even think about it. Marriage is something she's open to, but she wonders whether a new man could love her sons as much as she does. As it happens, three of the eleven single moms I spoke to did marry after becoming parents. So it is a possibility. But for the moment, Lucy is happy with the family she has. ❖

None of the mothers I interviewed adopted from Russia, but that country, too, is a major sender of babies and older kids to the United States. Russia and other Eastern Bloc nations differ from many other countries in generally requiring two adoption trips—parents travel the first time to meet the child, and then if all goes well, they return a short while later to officially adopt and return home as a family. More than four thousand U.S. families adopted Russian children in 2006.

To understand the state of the often quickly changing international adoption scene at any given moment, would-be parents generally do lots of online research.

Gay Adoption

Gay parenting today frequently means that the parents involved are over 35 because it's taken them a while to come out and to explore parenting opportunities created by a combination of technological and social changes. Whereas a little less than half of straight couples (both married and not) are raising kids, one-third of female couples and a little more than one-fifth of male couples are as well.[15] As with hetero-sexual families, some involve adoption.

Gay adoption works in basically the same way for gay people as for straight. Cleo's adoption experience through the foster-care system ex-emplifies the way the process can work well. Most states allow adoption by gay singles (meaning people not in couples), but many refuse to allow unmarried couples to adopt, which would leave out gay couples in any state except Massachusetts (as of fall 2007). Florida, Mississippi, and Utah have laws forbidding either gay-couple or gay-individual adop-tion, and lately there have been attempts at legislating more prohibi-tions in other states. In 2006, those attempts failed as voters refused to deny families to waiting children.

Because they have so many kids in need, public child-welfare agen-cies often welcome gay parents. But private adoptions can be harder for gays. To adopt privately, gay people generally have to go back into the closet, at least as far as the adoption process goes.

The two-mommy dynamic also introduces a new adoption twist, both for couples in which one mom is the bio mom and for those where one mom has adopted a child as a single person. Two of the women I spoke with had adopted their partner's biological child in what is known as a *second-parent adoption*. Second-parent adoption, similar to step-parent adoption and legal by statute or custom in twenty-six states, ensures that kids raised in a family with two parents they love won't be sepa-rated from mom-number-two if something happens to mom-number-one. In **Louise's** case there were two adoptions in one day, since both she and her partner Alana were adopting the other's natural-born son. In being adopted the boys became brothers twice over, since they were already half-brothers via their shared sperm donor.

❖ PROFILE: Nell, Gay Adoptive Mom at 40

Nell and her partner, Allison, had also planned to bear one child each. Once they had the first, however, they realized two would be too many—not because they didn't love their first baby but because they loved spending time with her *so much*, and they also had a business to run. With two, they didn't see how it would work. Now Nell loves being an adoptive mom: "It's just like . . . it's great!" The experience has caused her to think differently about adoption in general than she did when they started out thinking about kids.

> We didn't [go the full adoption route] because it actually seemed harder and more expensive and maybe more challenging for two women to adopt than it was for us to pick a donor and get the job done. You know what I mean, it seemed more possible to take things under our own control somehow. But in looking back, it's like, probably if you found the right adoption agency, it would have been fine. It would have been a wonderful experience and great.

If they had it to do over, they might just skip the biological route altogether.

But there is one element in Allison's biological experience that Nell does value particularly highly—she's ecstatic about the legal aspect of the adoption. She and Allison did have their own version of a marriage ceremony sometime back, but in their state it was not legally recognized. Her adoption of Allison's biological child feels effectively like a legal recognition of their partnership: "First thing in my adult life that was legal!" And it's important to her also as a sign of Allison's commitment:

> It was a big deal. . . . It's an amazing thing when somebody else, the biological mother, is allowing you to do that. . . . You have to have trust and you have to have commitment, but it's like, beyond that, . . . it was recognized by everybody, it wasn't just, "Yeah right, you just went through that little naming ceremony." No. I legally adopted her.

Nell and Allison would have felt a similar pleasure in the public recognition of the family if they had both adopted a child who was not biologically related to either of them, but Nell's sense of pleasure in the sign of commitment from her partner has a different dimension because it was Allison's bio baby. ❖

Where Nell and Louise adopted their partner's children in states with no gay marriage, **Caroline** is a married gay woman living in Massachusetts. She and Bridget married after the birth of their second child, and Bridget adopted both of the children soon after each birth. Had they been married before their kids were born, they still would have adopted to ensure that Bridget was legally the parent (the lack of precedent that the marriage would make her the children's legal guardian made them nervous). Their marriage was spurred by monetary concerns (Bridget's employer would cover her family's insurance if they were married), but it turned out to be romantic and lovely. As with Nell and Allison, the public recognition of their commitment and bond feels important to Caroline and Bridget.

Expanding your family through adoption is not the same as doing it biologically. Both are wonderful, I can say from experience, and the basics of love and family are the same. But adoption, perforce, involves parents in developing a wider—or at least a different—scope of awareness and connection: both in terms of the birth culture that the child comes from, if it's different from that of the adoptive parents, and in terms of the emotional issues adopted children must navigate—issues that parents must work both to help them with and to navigate themselves. The shared learning offers its own special kinds of connections for families.

The changing look of adoption today documents the changing views of what can constitute family in the contemporary world. Part of the changing look is the older faces of the new later adoptive moms and dads, who play a big role in the current adoption scene.

CHAPTER 8

Fifty Is the New Thirty?

Health, Looks, Evolution, and

the New Line of Later Moms

I think I look good for my age. . . . I've always been athletic, but I think I'm even more so—I'm trying to be more so, you know we both are as far as getting physical exercise and eating right—to give her as many years of us as we can.

—JILL, new mom at 46 without fertility tech

I think it would be a shame to be like an old dog mother, I mean I'd be horrified if my girls came home and they were like, "You know, you're just old!" . . . I dress to impress my kids.

—BERYL, adoptive mom at 36 and 40

A few years back when my first child was a babe in arms, I took her grocery shopping. At the register the checker smiled and admired her. "What a cutie," she cooed. I smiled back proudly. And then she asked, "Is that your grandbaby?" "Aah—no," I replied, surprised (nobody had ever called me grandma before!) but still smiling proudly, "actually she's *my* baby." Now the checker looked surprised.

I'm not the only new mom who's heard this or something like it recently. Quite a few women are starting families later and bringing new meaning to the image of the "grey-haired mama"—even if it's only a few strands. Almost all the later moms I know have experienced some version of the grandma question. Sometimes the questions hurt feelings ("the worst!"), and sometimes they just make women laugh (one beautiful greying mom smiles and answers, "No, they're my siblings," and moves on). But gradually the world is getting used to later moms. Another mom (53 and mother of three children between 5 and 7), reports on a recent encounter in an elevator:

> There was a woman—she looked great, she was probably in her late forties or early fifties, but she had these two little kids and [then the three of them] got out. And this woman next to me said, "These days you just don't know if that's the mom or the grandmother!" And I said, "Oh, I agree!"

This evolution in attitudes occurs in part simply because more and more women in their forties and fifties do have young kids. The acceptance that later moms meet these days also seems linked to their appearance—though they may look their age, a lot look pretty good for that age, whatever it is. And it's not just plastic surgery. Most of the changes in the appearance of women in their forties and up springs from fitness and a lifetime of good health—both of which have become increasingly available to humans over the past fifty-plus years. Given all the lectures we get, most people know *how* to stay in shape. And if people are deciding to have kids later in life, they generally have a sense of responsibility to try to stick around long term, which leads to more vigilance about putting fitness knowledge into practice or about maintaining an existing health regime if they are already on one.

The preponderance of the women I talked with were fit and healthy. In that respect they are like new later moms throughout the country. As a group—weirdly but conveniently, given that they're going to be parenting children to a greater age—new later moms are likely to live longer than younger moms. You heard that right.

Longer Life Expectancy

A recent study of the overall health effects on women of the timing of motherhood finds that the optimal age for first birth, in terms of the mother's long-term health, well-being, and longevity is—surprise!—34.[1] While health risks begin to increase again with a birth after 34 (becoming marked after 40), the risk of mortality (that is, death) continues to go down the older you are at first birth, without limit.[2]

Apparently the effects of age are not always what we expect. In this case, the issue isn't just physical—social factors affect health, too. Poor and less educated people tend to live shorter lives and experience more illness than do people better off. Not fair, but a fact in our health-care system. Getting an education and establishing themselves in a good financial situation (both of which often require time) raise the chances that people will have good health care and make informed decisions about their health. At the same time, these factors raise the chances that people will have children later. Early births have a deleterious effect on the body—from both physiological and sociological causes. Mirowsky's study found that the prime ages for childbearing lie between 22 and 40, with 34 being optimal for the mother's long-term health and longevity (mothers in that age band are healthier than childless women of their same age). This is separate from optimal fertility age (quickest time to conception), which is closer to 22. Babies born when the mother is 32 have the lowest mortality rate.

This shift not only means that we can expect longer life spans, it occurs in part because we have them already. Life spans expanded by about two-thirds in the twentieth century, and they may lengthen substantially in the twenty-first as well.[3] Our lengthening life spans ground the "new later" option, since the added years mean we can make new choices about how to spend them and about the sequencing of our life events. In the past, you basically had to have children early because the likelihood was you'd be dead before you were 50. Medical technology's transformation of our expectations about health, quality of life, and life span supports the move toward new later motherhood—providing yet another element in the evolving set of new options for our species.

Without reference to Mirowsky's study, the women I talked to certainly expect to live a while—after all, they have a lot to live for. I heard a lot of "till 90" and "at least into my eighties" when I asked them how long they thought they'd be around. Nobody said 120, but several said 100. Quite a few have parents now in their eighties and nineties, giving them confidence that they could do the same. Others don't have that kind of precedent but think their healthy habits give them a good chance for long life. A few had family histories of early demise, but hoped to be around at least until their kids were grown.

Polly (lawyer and mom at 35, 36, and 40) was a svelte and athletic 42-year-old when we talked. She wants to be around to be a grandma, and the chance that she might not worries her: "Am I going to be around to see all the good stuff?" she wonders. She loves parenting her kids, and she looks forward to the days "when they're adults and on their own and we can really enjoy one another's company." Hoping to be there long term, Polly works to stay fit and healthy. Ditto for **Fiona** (writer and new mom at 35 and 37), a vegetarian who doesn't drink or smoke and who exercises regularly. Fiona also knows there are no guarantees: "I try to live every day like it might be the last, because I've known so many friends who looked like the picture of health and then got cancer or something like that. . . . I guess I'm hoping for 90, but I by no means think that I'll necessarily get there, just because life is so flukey."

Health Issues

The better your health care, the more likely it is that, if you do discover an illness, you'll be able to treat it before it turns lethal.

PROFILE: **Catherine, New Mom at 36 and 37, Cancer at 44, Cancer Free at 45**

Cathy discovered she had breast cancer at 44 and realized later she probably had a hereditary predisposition. She had been getting mammograms since she was 38, and the cancer was detected early. She didn't quite hear that as good news, however:

> They give you an explanation but your head is spinning and you don't even hear them. It's like they are talking in a different language. You're just sitting there thinking you are going to die. Who's going to take care of your children? What about your husband? You start thinking about the worst possible scenario because it is such a shock. So you think, "Oh my god our wills aren't updated! Oh my god my children are going to grow up without a mother!" I mean the horrible things that run through your head. So you have to hear them repeat over and over again, "Your tumor was only 1.2 centimeters. Your cancer has not spread to your lymph nodes." You don't even hear the positive because all you are thinking about is the negative. So it took a while and they had to repeat things.

Her doctors found a small tumor and treated it very aggressively. She had a lumpectomy a month after discovery and started chemo the month after that. One year later, she is cancer free and hopes to stay that way. In the course of learning about her illness, Cathy found that starting your family later is associated with a higher risk of breast cancer—and, it turns out, with a higher survival rate.[4] Looking back she sees her cancer as *"almost* a blessing" because it makes her appreciate what she has all the more. ❖

Jan (scientist and new mom by adoption at 41 and 43) didn't have cancer, but she had her ovaries removed in her thirties because she was showing symptoms predictive of the virulent ovarian cancer that had killed several family members at early ages. Informed preventive measures like these will lengthen many lives in the coming years.

Later pregnancy involves its own health issues. Virtually all potential complications with pregnancy increase for women having their first child over 35 and more so over 40. For instance, rates for preeclampsia rise 60 percent for first-time moms over 40 compared with first-time moms under 30, and rates of gestational diabetes triple for all moms over 40. Fortunately complications tend to be closely supervised by doctors, and overall outcomes are good.[5]

Looking Good

When Gloria Steinem turned 40, a reporter remarked that she didn't look that old. "This is what 40 looks like!" she replied. "We've been lying so long, who would know?" That led her to an ongoing critique of the age prejudice that pushes women to lie about their age. When Steinem turned 60 she reiterated her point—"This is what 60 looks like!" But it's not just prejudice that makes people surprised that Gloria and a lot of other women look good at 60 and now at 70. Something has changed about the way women's bodies age. It still surprises us, however, because we have very different ideas about what "old" looks like—ideas that were current in the very recent past (say fifty years ago or less), and that live on in the cultural memory. In general, we look a lot less worn out than our ancestors would have—if they got this far.

Our sense of what's "old" is in flux. Every few years, we hear that a new decade is the "new 30" or 40, or whatever. Gloria Steinem doesn't look old at 73. Part of the transformation aging women's bodies are undergoing has to do with the fact that we have fewer (and sometimes no) children. Recall that the Hutterite women, with their average eleven kids each, died younger than their husbands. Childbearing involves a lot of wear and tear. Our changed appearance has roots, then, in the combination of better health, better nutrition, more attention to fitness, fewer children, and (sometimes) hair dye and cosmetic surgery.

Nonetheless, aging still involves some wear down. When I asked the women I spoke with about disadvantages they'd encountered with later motherhood, the most common response was "I'm tired!" (This came especially from the moms with babies and toddlers). The follow-up is generally, "and so I'm focusing on staying fit." Even fatigue can have its good effects. Most of them reported that they were more fit than their mothers had been at their age.

Most of the moms I spoke to felt that they looked pretty good. **Caroline** (writer, mom at 38 and 41) feels positive about the way she looks:

> I actually feel sexier now, and more attractive now, than I did in my twenties. I mean I have more self-esteem in that way. And I think that's multifactorial, you know. I'm more sensitive to looking in the mirror and seeing wrinkles, but I don't think of myself as unattractive. And I think of myself still as appealing sexually.

With Diane Keaton (new mom by adoption at 50 and 56) leading the way in *Something's Gotta Give,* smart and sexy older woman characters seem likely to win a big box-office following in the years to come. That's good news for Julianne Moore and Julia Roberts (both new later moms) and the rest of the actress troupe. So far, part of the eroticism (as Diane Keaton's svelte example suggests) lies not in a move toward admiring the physical effects of age, but in limiting those effects. It's the internal effects of age—experience, a sense of perspective, and maybe a willingness to forgive imperfection—that seem to be featured.

I asked the women I spoke with if they had an idea about what they thought the mother of a young child should look like. "Yeah, absolutely," said **Camille** (new mom at 44), "and it doesn't involve a lot of grey hair." Moms varied on that score, some going grey without qualm, but most adding some color because, as **Gretchen** (new mom at 39 and 40) put it, "it's important to me to look young enough that the boys don't get embarrassed." Not that the kids had said any such thing. **Abby**, new mom at 35 and 38, remembers fondly that her son, now nearly 20, bragged to his friends about having the oldest mom. Maybe the issue is entirely one of self-image, at least when kids are young. **Lenore** (former model and mother at 34 and 37, now 61) has always been very health conscious, and though she colors her hair, she's now thinking of giving that up for her health. She's not too worried about it because her overall self-image is positive ("I think I look beautiful!").

Gretchen aims "to try to keep a youthful appearance and a youthful outlook on life," and she thinks her kids will help with that. She would exercise if she had the time, but since she doesn't, she takes the stairs and is finally down to her pre-pregnancy weight. "So now it's time to put it back into all the places that it used to be," she says wryly. Gretchen isn't planning on doing that through surgery, but **Ginger** sees no harm in that route: "I think 50 isn't what it used to be, and if you feel young and energetic, and you go to the gym, and you have saggy boobs and you don't want 'em so saggy anymore, or you want to get rid of a double chin or fix the wrinkles around your eyes, I think you should." **Jeanne**, who doesn't use makeup (it helps if you're stunning to begin with) and can't see herself going in for plastic surgery ("I'm not very sophisticated that way"), *can* imagine having varicose veins removed ("I would do this in an eye-blink"). Different strokes for different folks.

Pushing back the boundaries of life expectancy effectively makes the middle-aged more youthful, and the experience of parenting later in comfortable circumstances adds to that youthful effect.

Sandwiched: Between Elder Care and Kid Care

When you get older, so does the rest of your family. Today's "older generation" is surfing the first big wave of extended longevity, and that means that many of them are getting very old in comparatively good health. Their parents' longevity was the basis for many of the women I spoke with thinking that they had a good chance of living into a long and healthy old age as well. But long-term health isn't in everybody's cards, and even the healthy do die eventually and may need care in that process. Several of the women I spoke with found themselves sandwiched between caring for parents and caring for kids.

❖ PROFILE: **Candice, Lawyer, New Mom at 35 and 41**

Candice met her husband Jack in her early thirties, soon after her dad died. She remains sad that Jack and their kids will never know him. Now ten years later, her mom, Myrna, is 69 and in the late stages of cancer with a two-year life expectancy. Though Myrna and her new husband live in another state, they come to Candice's town for Myrna's treatments. Though Candice views the situation as pretty grim, she describes her mom as making the best of things:

> My mom's pretty spry. A lot of people don't know she has cancer. And my step-father has been a great caretaker. It's been hard. She keeps joking she's my third child, which is not really the case. I mean, the longer her chemotherapy has gone on, the easier it's gotten. They've given her medicines to counteract the side effects, and she's up and about. They'll probably come over for dinner tonight even though she's having chemo today. So she's very positive, she's

convinced she's got her cancer beat, it's all gone. She's going to be in that 10 percent in whom it never returns. She's a pretty easy person to be around.

Nonetheless, caring for her mom as well as her kids shapes Candice's days—she does a lot of driving for Myrna, and she put off returning to full-time work to be available as needed for her mom. Once she did go back to full time, she moved from the corporate world into running her own business from home to achieve the flexibility she needs to accommodate kids and parents. She's in caretaker mode on two fronts. ❖

Colette, new mom at 40, had a similar situation. Her dad had died young, and her mom became very ill just after Colette gave birth. The baby spent a good part of her first weeks with sitters because Colette had to be at the hospital with *her* mother. "I'm happy having my daughter," says Colette. "Life is good, but my mother just died, so I've gone through an incredibly sad period. It's hard to even separate it all out."

One of the drawbacks mentioned by a good number of the new later moms was loss of grandparent access. Some kids will miss it altogether; others will have less of it. Either way, the whole family misses out when they lose contact with the network of older relatives who add another layer of love to the children's lives, share child-rearing wisdom with the parents, and hand on family history. On the logistical level, there's a big loss in the babysitting realm. For instance, Nicole's mom lives out of town, but **Nicole** (broadcaster and new mom at 37 and 41) notes that "even though she has moved away, [my mother] is too old, even if she was living in the same city, to be really helpful with the baby." Though many children already lack access to long-distance grandmas, the later motherhood experience will cut grandma access for even more.

On the other hand, one later mom found her parents, now in their seventies, were more available to visit with her and her kids because they were retired. Another mom, **Daphne**, who adopted at 56, is now 59, and her mom, now 88, loves to spend time with her grandson and is still available for occasional short-term babysitting. She lives close by in a senior assisted-living complex. Daphne describes her son as "very independent, and he's not a rough kid," so his grandma can handle him, though she can't really pick him up.

Sandwiched? The Next Generation

The bulk of new later moms still have young kids and are not ready to retire. As they age, new effects of the later motherhood trend will emerge. One predictable effect will be that, although many later moms will stay healthy long term, some proportion won't. As **Carey** (adoptive mom at 43) points out, "There are going to be a lot of children who are going to be much younger when they lose their parents." As a result, some of *their* children's kids (the grandchildren of the current crop of new later moms) will miss out on grandparent access, especially if today's kids follow their parents' lead and wait till they're in their thirties and forties before they start their families: 35 + 35 = 70, which is perhaps not so frail, but 40 + 40 = 80, which can be getting up there. One more reason to stick to your health club resolution—and a pretty compelling one. Carey thinks these kinds of losses of family connections will lead everyone to innovate around extended family structures—maybe more long-term bonding between unrelated families who grow up together, or more links to distant relatives with kids the same age, or maybe some form of techno family via the Internet.

Along with the losses, some kids will have to deal in their twenties and thirties with the eldercare issues that some later moms are now facing in their forties, fifties, and sixties. When I asked what precautions later parents were taking around this issue, the most common answers concerned money and long-term-care insurance. **Fiona** (new mom at 35 and 37), whose own mother purchased long-term-care insurance, plans to do the same for her kids' sake:

> I hope I'm not a burden on them. I'd love to visit grandkids, and . . . I'd love to live near them and be really involved, if they want me to be. It would be fun to do a lot of babysitting, I think. Get to do it again. I don't know, I think I'd like to be like my mom where I'm not intrusive, but if they'd like me to be around, I'd love it!

Though her mom lives in another town, she comes regularly to visit and is very involved with her grandchildren's lives via email. She's "done a good job of not being at all pushy," her daughter reports. Fiona feels her mom (now 66, and 22 when Fiona was born) handled potential burdens (financial and personal) well. She hopes to do the same. Financial planning might feel harder if you're paying for college at the same time that you're thinking about retiring, but it's an unavoidable part of the later motherhood mix. At least, given their bigger earning potential, new later moms have a good chance of covering those bases and ensuring that kids won't get stuck holding the bag monetarily.

The moms I spoke with had several basic responses to the question about when they hoped their kids would have kids. While most moms said "whenever they're ready," some hoped their kids would be a little younger than they had been. **Rosalind** (new mom at 40) feels experience is important:

> [Because I waited], I knew my foibles, my pitfalls, and all those kinds of things so much better. And it gave me the tools to have a much better relationship. And I would also want her to have the opportunity to explore her freedom and her independence before she got into a relationship and a family.

Even with that in mind, Rosie still hopes her kids will feel ready in their late twenties or early thirties, because she wants to be around to spend time with her grandkids ("purely selfish!"). Rosie works at keeping fit and figures that running around after her daughter will help her in that realm. Fiona expects that her daughters will probably be moms in their mid-thirties, too, because she imagines they'll want careers first: "They both dream of different jobs that they'd like to do. . . . I don't want them to rush into it, but I don't want them to wait so long that their bodies couldn't do it." Of course the employment scene and the fertility scene may look rather different twenty or thirty years from now, so it's hard to predict what ages will make most sense for career women who want kids.

Menopause

If you have your child at 35, by the time you hit 50 that child is 15 and you've got a house full of hormones. The combination of teenagers and menopausal mamas might strike fear into a few hearts. But symptoms vary widely, as does their ETA (52 average, but I spoke to women who'd seen the start as early as 40, and as late as 60). It's hard to predict how it will play out in any individual house.

Most of the women I interviewed had not yet arrived at menopause. Several had been through the special short tour of menopause induced by fertility technology; often, before their ovaries are stimulated to produce the extra eggs needed for IVF, women go through a preliminary chemical menopause. Generally this lasts ten to fourteen days. For **Yvonne** (editor and new mom at 39), who felt very unhappy with her doctor and the clinic, it lasted a bit longer:

> The idea is they put you into menopause and then they control your ovulation. Well, they couldn't pull me out to ovulate. So I went through a month of menopause. They said, "Oooo, you're going to have a bad change of life." I'm like, "Thanks. That's what I really needed to know right now."

The fertility side trip into menopause is unlike the full version not only in being brief (usually), but in its abruptness—several of the moms I talked with spoke of being "thrown into menopause." For most women, menopause creeps in gradually, though once it's fully ensconced, apparently, you're not in doubt. Because the menopause experience varies widely, some women suffer what I've heard described as "massive emotional lurches and sudden plummets into inexplicably intense weepy depression," while other people notice nothing. Most people fall somewhere in between. Massive emotional lurches don't sound like they'd ever be much fun, but with young kids around they would be particularly bad.

Though menopausal symptoms vary, hot flashes, mood swings, and sleeplessness are among the major ones. Then there's osteoporosis, vaginal dryness, and diminished desire—symptoms that have led many women, especially in the Viagra-plumped universe, to choose estrogen in spite of its potential dangers.

Andrea, now 48 and the adoptive mother of a 4-year-old, has been menopausal since her early forties. She takes hormones, in ever-decreasing doses, toward a goal of eventually being weaned from them altogether. She's not ready to go off them yet, because she remembers an incident from when her baby was very young:

> I'd gotten really busy, really busy, really busy, and had forgotten to get my prescription refilled for my hormones. . . . So finally I said, "I'm cured! It's a miracle, I don't have menopausal symptoms anymore." And then one morning, I went in the garage, I put him in his car seat, shut the door and got ready to walk around the car to the driver's side and had this heat attack that was so severe and intense that it caused me to have anxiety. I was paralyzed, sweat was pouring off my face, and I was holding onto the car, and I thought I was going to pass out. . . . [I] thought that I would pass out in my garage with my baby strapped in a car seat and the door to the garage was shut. He couldn't have gotten out of the car seat on his own.

. . . I worked my way over to the driver's side, I opened the door, and I just pushed the button to open the garage door, and I left my door open and just kind of sat on the side of my car, cause I figured . . . at least if I pass out . . . someone will see me and at least come and get my baby out of the car. And it was the most frightening feeling. And I went, as soon as I calmed myself down and got myself cooled off and got myself together, I drove right to Walgreen's, got my hormone pills, and never missed another one.

Daphne, new mom at 56, had already finished with menopause by the time she became a mom, but a few years earlier she had what she called "severe symptoms," including huge mood swings and sleeplessness. The sweats didn't bother her. She used hormone cream for two years and then weaned herself on her own. She advises that someone going through menopause with symptoms like hers should get some hormonal help if they have a baby.

Melanie, dentist and new mother at 35 and 38 of a daughter and a son who are now young adults, describes herself as "well into menopause" at 54. She "can't imagine doing this without hormone replacement." By "this" she means her busy life, which includes a full practice and a full house. She uses bio-identical hormones to avoid overdoses of estrogen that might lead to problems down the line. "My goal," she explains, "is to live to be 100 and to have enough money to live on and to be reasonably healthy." She can't imagine doing without the hormones altogether—without them she wouldn't sleep, and she'd lose the energy to keep up with her office and family.

But where Andrea, Daphne, and Melanie found some use of hormones essential, **Marina** (new mom at 46) never felt the need for them. In fact, her symptoms were so mild she didn't notice when she went into early menopause around 40—just as she was starting to think about a family. So it took her a while to discover she would need to go the egg-donor route.

Renata, a new later mom and businesswoman now in her early fifties, has a daughter wending her way through the teenage years. Renata entered menopause several years back, and as she describes it, her menopausal mood swings made things rough for her family for a while: "I now don't believe that PMS is in people's minds. I think it does change how you address things, how you handle issues, just your general mood. . . . I think my daughter would stay upstairs cause she didn't want to come downstairs, for fear of what she might do wrong."

That special degree of late-afternoon craziness that kids can display only exacerbated the ferocity of Renata's bad moods when she was tired. Even her forgiving husband called her mean. Renata compares her experience of menopause and child-rearing to her mom's:

> My mother was a grandmother when she was my age. And so she'd come get [my sister's] kids on her good days and take 'em home, and not see 'em on her bad days. Whereas [with me] my kids saw the good and the bad—that was one thing I really did not like. I did not like myself during that period.

For eight months Renata took hormones, but then weaned herself off them because she didn't like taking them. Some of the moodiness is gone now, but the tendency still asserts itself at intervals (for some people menopausal symptoms seem to last for a limited period, but for others it can be part of life for quite a while). Renata now controls her moods through sheer force of will ("I'm more conscious of it, so I work harder not to act crazy, not to let those small things bother me"). She found that going back to work after a several-year hiatus helped too: "Because it didn't allow me to sit and think about feeling bad. . . . Cause it *forced* me . . . even if I'm in a bad mood, I've still got to go deal with that client." Mood swings often involve depression, and menopausal symptoms may get treated with antidepressants. For Renata, work in itself was an antidepressant, so she avoided that medication, and now at her house everyone's life has improved.

Hormone replacement therapy (HRT) has been widely used for years. Doctors saw it as a treatment for menopausal symptoms and also as a ward against heart disease and Alzheimer's. Recent evidence, however, from the National Institutes of Health shows that use of estrogen and progestin relates directly to an increase in cancer risk, a rise in heart-disease risk, and a small rise in risk of Alzheimer's. When that evidence came out in 2002, many women went off HRT—and in 2003 U.S. breast cancer rates dropped a huge 7.2 percent.[6] At the moment, some doctors recommend HRT for severe symptoms, for as brief a period as possible.[7] Sometimes those are supplemented with antidepressants as needed. Other doctors and patients prefer herbal or bio-identical remedies. As new studies refine the understanding of what treatments cause what effects, either good or bad, each woman has to do her own research and consult her doctor to figure out the treatment best suited to her version of the change of life. Clearly menopause management will be a critical area of research in the coming years as millions of baby-boomer women move into that time zone. Many are there already.

Evolution Now: Grand/Mothering

Later moms might be said to combine the roles of mother and grandmother—at least in some respects.[8] While the new later moms differ in child-rearing experience from their peers who are grandmothers, they share other life experience and the element of worldly wisdom.

Grandmothers have always been important to the welfare of their families—both in terms of providing extra funds and babysitting and in handing on family traditions. Anthropologists (led by Kristen Hawkes) attribute to grandmothers an essential role in the development of the human brain.[9] Humans are among the very few animals who experience menopause. The Grandmother Hypothesis postulates that, because prehistoric grandmothers who were past menopause were not bearing children of their own, they could help carry and gather berries for their daughters' toddlers while the mothers nursed the newborns. Because human toddlers didn't have to forage for themselves at an early age, their brains could develop further. Grandmas contributed the added value that gave humanity its evolutionary advantage.

The new later motherhood may mean a decrease in access to actual grandmothers (though if health and longevity continue to increase, that will be less and less the case). On the other hand, new later mothers today are continuing in a new way the essential work of midlife women before them by providing younger folk with added value. This time the added value comes in the form of additional funds from higher salaries, of increased information and ability to solve problems from their expanded education and experience, and of higher status based in achievement. Only this time, they're the mothers, not the grandmothers. Women of what used to be largely a grandmotherly age (late thirties and early forties on up) are now helping transition us all into the contemporary world's new life patterns of extended longevity.

Epilogue

Readiness Matters

When I embarked on this investigation into the effects of the new later motherhood trend, I had no idea how far and in how many directions it would take me—into the realms of economics, sociology, anthropology, biology, adoption, international relations, human resource management, demographics, and health. And into the groundbreaking life stories of many amazing women. This book only begins the process of tracking the nexus of factors contributing to, and the many ramifications rippling from, this big change in human behavior.

As with all human experience, the new later motherhood involves many and sometimes conflicting dimensions. It emerges as part of a new stage of human evolution—one in which we can both live longer in good health than ever before and reliably control our fertility. These two enormous changes together make the new later motherhood possible. Fertility control puts us in a position to counter the dangers posed by rising world population levels that threaten our planet's resources. Equally significantly, it allows us to develop new resources by moving us toward a world in which women, as Crystal Eastman put it, "[can] exercise their infinitely varied gifts in infinitely varied ways" for the first time. The women I spoke with had found ways to satisfyingly combine family with outside work—either simultaneously or in sequence, and they are major contributors to the functioning of their communities. This combination made the women I spoke with very happy. They were pleased with who they had become.

That's excellent for the moms and their communities, but what about their kids? What does it mean that increasing numbers of children are being raised by educated mothers with good salaries and a say in the business of the nation? The effects of these changes are positive and multiple: kids and families have more effective advocates, moms and dads can provide well for them, and these parents stress the value of education and innovation. Of course, it's not just moms who started at 35 and over who fit this description. The 35-year-old cutoff is a statistical convenience, and the trend to starting later than *their* moms did affects moms all along the age continuum, with linked effects. The new later moms in concert with educated women with work experience who start their families at all ages are changing the landscape of family together.

But as we've seen, there are some particular effects for new later moms, and in the years to come we'll see how these will shape the lives of their children long term. There's bound to be data available in a few years that tell us how a woman's age at first birth affects her children's college grades or their professional status. The *Freakonomics* writers already inform us that having a mother who was 30 or older when her first child arrived correlates positively with high school test scores.

It will be harder to gauge the emotional development or personal skills of new later moms' kids from databases, but there's a book waiting to be written based on interviews. How does having a new later mom affect a child's overall abilities or sense of well-being? Or does it make no difference? Will the new later children be exceptionally innovative, given all the time and resources invested in them? Will they fall apart under the weight of too much attention and expectation? How will their often smaller families play out over the long term? How will they deal with the earlier loss of some parents? Since most of the kids are still fairly young, it will be a while before we find out, and it seems likely that responses will vary.

But there are a few around already who can tell us that it will have at least some quite positive effects. One 20-something whose parents were 32 and 36 at her birth—her mother was not quite "later" by my definition but was part of the general trend among women to wait for family until they're professionally established—reports that she used to feel "vaguely pissed off about this, because I felt like they sort of cheated me out of a good five years of time with them." But on reflection, she realizes that the timing was "really quite perfect." Both of her parents were tenured and had the ability to flex their time to be with her, and they'd "dug themselves out of their post-grad financial hole, so I could have things like a She-Ra dress-up kit and really excellent schooling." The nicest thing about this remark lies in its testimony to her parents' success in that job, since their daughter wants all the time with them she can have. Though data on the long-term effects is sparse as yet, all the women I spoke to with children of college age or older reported that their kids are doing just fine.

The moms I spoke with felt that their parenting skills had improved over what they would have been earlier as a result of their having lived longer and matured. Most felt they were more patient than they would have been earlier and able to put things in perspective. **Amy**, lawyer and later mother of two, thinks,

> I'm more focused on them—because I have a career, because I know who I am. And so I'm not going through that sort of soul-searching— "What path will I take?" "What will I be like as a person?"—which people go through in their twenties. So I think it gives me more time to focus on them and what they're like.

Even **Sharon**, stay-at-home new later mother of four including triplets, when she compares her current child-rearing methods with what she believes they would have been earlier in her life, can say:

I think that I would never have been able to give them the room to grow, and I would never have allowed them the individuation that I give them now. I think I would have been worried—"what will people think, they're wearing shoes that don't match." . . . Cause it was too important to me that it be okay . . . as opposed to now, I'm more like, "Well that's a good mistake to make now, cause maybe you won't later make the really stupid mistake."

Andrea, another lawyer and a single adoptive mom at 44, boils down her experience:

You've gotten to travel, you've gotten to do stuff that's just for you, you've gotten to have the outrageous car, the outrageous handbag that cost too much money, take the most wonderful trips, not have to worry about getting a sitter. And so for me, at this point in time in my life, it's all good. . . . I'm happy, and I think that their happiness depends largely on your happiness. And if you aren't capable of taking care of yourself, and you aren't having a satisfying life, they are not having a satisfying life. And I think that in my twenties, I would have felt like I was missing something.

When a woman wants to be there for kids and feels that she's in a good position to do a good job of raising them, she's ready.

As the fruit of a diverse set of intersecting causes, the new later motherhood trend is dynamic—a lot had to change to bring the trend about, and as changes continue on many fronts in modern life, the trend may shift, or it may become more marked.

When the trickle up of women into the upper levels of business management reaches the critical point, the trickle down of benefits to women and men in the rank and file may finally become a river. At that point, it may become easier for career-minded women to start their families sooner, if they feel ready in other ways. The business case for family friendliness has already been made—flexibility and a wider range of viable career-track options attract a better pool of workers, who become very loyal when they're treated well. In a world where good workers are in high demand, it's largely obstinacy and failure of imagination that still ties some industries to the old full-time career model (pumped up far beyond the old model's forty-hour workweek). But that can change.

Emerging possibilities for preempting infertility—like egg or ovarian tissue freezing—may mean that, for the next generation of women, fertility anxiety becomes a thing of the past. But in the present, that anxiety remains a reality in the lives of many women hoping to have kids someday (but not quite yet). It's an especially painful reality for women having infertility trouble in the here and now. Real information about the slope of the rise in infertility rates with age, about how to address infertility most effectively if it occurs, and about when and how to move on to alternative routes to family—all of this can help women frame and address their concerns. The women's stories offered here give readers an informed basis for thinking about their own life trajectories and options for family. Though there are no guarantees, many women can and do have babies with their own genetic material in their late thirties and very early forties, and if fertility wanes, many people find other roads to family happiness, or to happiness without kids.

Insurance could help. I second Debora Spar's call for a national dialogue on all aspects of what she calls the baby business—a dialogue I'd expand to include not just the fertility-technology and adoption dynamics that she explores but the basics of how we as a nation value families and the citizens they produce. A fundamental question is whether we are prepared to expand the availability of infertility insurance and adoption benefits so that it's not just the well-off who can have babies via fertility tech and adoption.

Modern women's lives differ markedly from those of all previous women. Given the shortness of the time since these changes have occurred, adjustments remain to be made before the new patterns gel. Taking the "it was your choice, you suffer the consequences" approach to infertility management ignores the ways in which the modern world has changed for women who want to participate in and make contributions to the nation's business. The nation needs their know-how and that of their kids to come.

For the women I spoke with, and for their families, the new later motherhood experience has had overwhelmingly positive effects: their kids are deeply wanted; the moms have satisfying work, whether in business or at home; parents are in better positions to support their children well; and moms have the confidence, education, and experience to be articulate advocates for their children and to operate as equal companions within their marriages. If they are single, they have good wages and strong support networks.

These are reasonable goals for parents, and they have positive effects for their kids, but the wider community (including the business world) has not provided women with the means to reach those goals. Instead, women have had to create their own shadow benefits system to provide well for their families and themselves on all levels—and a fundamental part of that system, for many, is starting families later. By waiting until they feel ready, at whatever age, women are working to reform the system that too frequently links motherhood with poverty in old age. The benefits flow to all. Readiness matters.

ACKNOWLEDGMENTS

First of all, my deepest thanks to the women who participated in the interviews that are the basis of this study and whose voices you hear throughout. An inspiring and articulate bunch, they made no bones about their views and shared their experience openly and thoughtfully. In exchange for that openness, they receive confidentiality—their names are changed here, and in the cases where their situations might identify them, some details are altered. I am grateful as well to the other observers of the new later trend who shared their thoughts but requested anonymity.

I would like to thank the colleagues, friends, and acquaintances who assisted my thinking about this new phenomenon and who helped me function in many disciplines outside my own. My profound appreciation to Aliaksandr Amialchuk now of the University of Toledo, who helped me frame my economics questions and selflessly and tirelessly ran huge amounts of data. I cannot thank you enough. My gratitude as well to my colleague in economics Chinhui Juhn, who listened carefully and advised well.

In the realms of sociology, anthropology, and family studies, thanks to Steve Mintz, Tracy Karner, and the late Janet Chafetz at the University of Houston, John Mirowsky at the University of Texas, and Jenifer Bratter at Rice University, as well as to Ellen Galinsky at the Families and Work Institute, Sarah Blaffer Hrdy at University of California–Davis, and Adam Pertman at the Donaldson Adoption Institute, for encouragement and helpful advice. On the historical front, thanks to Page Hedden Wilson for sharing her memories of her esteemed mother, Worth Tuttle Hedden.

In the world of fertility, thanks to Drs. Paula Amato, Donna Baird, David Dunson, Shirley Fong, Lisa Otey, and Joseph Stanford for thoughtful input and clarifications. At the CDC, thanks to Anjani Chandra, PhD, and Sharon Kirmeyer, PhD, and especially to Thomas J. Mathews, MS, for emailing with me at considerable length about a wide variety of natality data. Thanks to Joyce Zeitz and Marty Beaird at the American Society for Reproductive Medicine for answering my questions.

It turns out that many people have thoughts on the new later motherhood phenomenon. I thank all those who shared their insights with me, including my good friends Dina Alsowayel, Victoria Jones, Kim Howard, Olga Malea, Suzanne Raitt, Melanie Springer, Jeff Tollett, and especially Polly Koch, who read and commented on many drafts, always to helpful effect.

Unending gratitude to Sally Russ, MaryScott Hagle, and Zita Giraldo and to all my Friends of Women's Studies cohort who have been wonderful supporters of my work and great personal friends as well. And especially to Carey Shuart, a stalwart friend and a woman who acts on her convictions.

My office life is idyllic due to my stellar team, which in the past few years has included the following wonder women: Oakley Allred, Marteba Beck, Lynn Dale, Margaret Garza, Elisa Garza-Leal, Erin Graham, Kasi Jackson, Ann Kennedy, Lauran Kerr, Kim McGill, Beverly McPhail, Amy O'Neal, Karina Puente, Pat Sayles, Jeanne Scheper, Andrea Short, Luziris Pineda Turi, Carol Williams, and Tiphanie Yanique Galiber. Thanks, too, to our dean, John Antel, and to the University of Houston English Department for ongoing support.

Thanks to my student assistants, Carol Park, Shawn Halbert, Elaine Rusin, Nikki Monmouth, Heena Momin, Dominique Melissanos, Kacey Cawyer, and Brandi Anderson for their good work.

Looking northward, my heartfelt gratitude to my truly super agent Mary Ann Naples who believed in the project from the start and stuck by it through thick and thin. And thanks to her great team, including Debra Goldstein, Elizabeth Little, and Laura Nolan. Deep appreciation as well to my first editor Amy Scheibe, who acquired the project for Basic Books with gusto and who made the first phase of this publishing experience terrific. Many thanks also to my second editor, Amanda Moon, who guided the book to publication with grace and zeal. Thanks to their top team, including Tim Brazier, Maris Kreizman, Michele Jacob, Julie McCarroll, Jane McGraw, Susan Ranis, Carol Smith, and Brent Wilcox.

Special thanks to my family in Massachusetts—Jack, Jackie, Mindy, Mark, Geneva, Hannah, and Jeanne—and to those family members scattered in other regions—including Glen, Annabelle, Mike, and Perry—for their total support from the start. And most of all to my darlings in Texas—Patrick, Anna, and Sophie, who raised the questions in the first place.

APPENDIX A: WHO'S IN THE STUDY

Over two and a half years, I interviewed 113 new later moms (NLMs). They came to me through the "snowball method": I put out calls in schools, doctors' offices, and listservs and invited some individuals in distinctive circumstances. Respondents were interviewed, individually or in small groups, and they referred others, and so forth. Four answered questionnaires. Four spoke on a public panel, with some individual follow-up. Though not a weighted nationally representative study, the method provided a variety of respondents as well as assisted in locating them. I followed up where possible in national databases on respondents' indications about the issues linked to the new later motherhood trend. I also interviewed a few non-NLMs on background issues.

The racial breakdown of the group was eight African Americans (7 percent), six Hispanics (5.3 percent), one Arab (0.9 percent), and ninety-eight whites (86.7 percent). This maps against a national landscape in 2006, in which 8.6 percent of NLMs were African American, 12 percent Hispanic, 10.8 percent Asian, and 67.6 percent white. Efforts to interview Asian NLMs were unsuccessful (see Preface for more on Asian data).

By 2007, fifty-three of those in the study had one child, forty-nine had two, ten had three, and one had five. Overall, 101 children were born to mothers ages 34 to 39 (six 34-year-olds insisted on inclusion); fifty-two children were born to mothers 40 to 46; two children were adopted by mothers 36 to 39; and twenty-eight were adopted by mothers 40 to 56.

Most interviewees had kids under age 12; twenty-one had grown or teenaged children. By study's end, they had 183 kids total, with some considering more. Thirty children had been adopted by twenty-three moms. Nine women were gay and partnered (in two cases, both members of a couple were interviewed). Ten were single moms at the time their child arrived, though four had since married. The rest (ninety-four) were straight and married when they became parents. Three were divorced from the father of their children when interviewed (two of those had since remarried), and three divorced during the study.

The group was highly educated: All but six had bachelor's degrees (those six had an associate's or RN degree or were just short of a bachelor's); eighty-six had at least one graduate degree. Twenty were staying at home at the time of the interview, seventy-one worked full time, eighteen worked part time, two were students, one was looking for work, and one had retired. They were comparatively high earners: All but two were living in households with incomes over $60,000; most fell in the $100,000 to $200,000 household-income range, and some in higher. Seventy-eight lived in or near Houston; one lived abroad; and the rest were in cities across the United States (including Boston; New York; Washington, D.C.; Chicago; Dallas; San Francisco; and Los Angeles).

Though most got pregnant without aid (I heard "it happened much faster than we expected" a lot), thirteen employed some fertility technology successfully for some or all of their children. Five employed fertility technology unsuccessfully and then adopted (sometimes a first child, sometimes a second), and one employed fertility technology unsuccessfully and then had a child the low-tech way.

Of the adoptive parents, eleven adopted domestically and twelve internationally. Most adopted newborns or children under 2. Four were lesbians who adopted their partners' biological or adopted children. One mother attempted to adopt without success. Several others had considered adoption but had not acted. Three were in the process of adopting further when the study ended. All but one of the international adoptions were interracial. Of the domestic adoptions, three involved black parents adopting black children, two involved white parents adopting white kids, two involved white parents adopting black children, and one white woman with a Hispanic husband adopted a Hispanic child.

APPENDIX B: WORK STATUS DATA[1]

Both the 1990 and 2000 Census data indicate that, while they have young children, new later moms tend to stay in the workplace in higher proportion than moms who start their families earlier. Table B.1 compares the work status of new later mothers (NLM) in 1990—full time (FT), part time (PT), total working full time and part time (F&P), or not working (NW)—to the work status of moms who started their families earlier (EM), according to the age of their youngest child at home. (See Table B.1.)

New later mothers with a youngest child 6 or younger stayed at full-time jobs in substantially larger proportions than earlier moms with a youngest child of the same age. Earlier mothers moved back into the workplace in increasing proportions as their youngest children grew older, and by the time those children were 7 to 18, they were back in the workplace in larger proportion than the new later moms. See Chapter 4 for discussion.

The number of children she has at home affects the likelihood that a mom (new later or earlier) will decide to leave work for some period, as is indicated in Table B.2. An important factor in the overall rates of difference in behavior around work between new later and earlier moms is that new later mothers were twice as likely to have only children as earlier moms, in 1990. It was not the only factor, however, since new later moms with two children were still more likely to be working full time than earlier moms with two children with youngest children in the same age category. The size of the likelihood that new later moms will have onlies may be changing over time, as more women who might have stopped at one in prior years now decide to go for two. Preliminary data suggests that was the case in 2000. (See Table B.2.)

The data for 2000 is not as complete, but it shows a similar pattern to that presented in Table B.1, and is presented in Table B.3. Table B. 4 presents parallel data from 1990 for direct comparison with Table B.3. (See Table B.3.)

To test the possibility that the 35-to–40-year-old group might be behaving in a way not representative of the whole group of later moms, here follows the same kind of comparison with 35-to–40-year-olds from the 1990 Census (Table B.4). Both censi indicate that 35-to–40-year-olds tend to work full time slightly more when they have young children than the rest of their group as a whole, in both the earlier mom and the new later mom sets. Balanced with the tendency toward understatement described

---

1. Data in all of these tables are the author's calculations, based on the 1990 and 2000 Censi.

in the note above, that might put these numbers right on target. The point here is not to insist on particular numbers for 2000, since those are not fully available. The general pattern does seem noteworthy, however. Though there are other points of interest in these tables individually and in the changes over time they document, for our purposes it seems that the relative work-status patterns of new later and earlier moms remained similar in 1990 and 2000. (See Table B.4.)

TABLE B.1² 1990 Census work-status data for all moms (16 to 53) with kids 18 and under, distinguished by the age at which they started their families, and divided according to the age of their youngest child

	New Later Moms				Earlier Moms				NLM/EM percent difference*		
	FT	PT	F&P	NW	FT	PT	F&P	NW	FT	PT	NW
Kids <=1	51.8	25.2	77.0	23.0	37.1	28.1	65.2	34.8	+14.7	-2.9	-11.8
Kids <=3	53.4	21.8	75.2	24.8	40.4	25.5	65.9	34.1	+13.0	-3.7	-9.3
Kids <=6	54.4	20.3	74.7	25.3	43.6	24.2	67.8	32.2	+10.8	-3.9	-6.9
Kids 7-18	55.4	17.4	72.8	27.2	60.5	18.4	78.9	21.1	-5.1	-1.0	+6.1

*Percent difference compares new-later-moms data to earlier-moms data. For example, NLMs with kids one year or younger were 14.7 percent more likely to work full time than EMs, in 1990, 2.9 percent less likely to work part time, and 11.8 percent more likely to work overall. The difference between the NW figures will be the same as that between the F&P figures, with positive or negative value reversed.

2. The 1990 Census identifies new later moms ages 35 to 53, while the 2000 allows us to reliably identify only new later moms 35 to 40 years old at the time of the Census (see footnote to Figures 3.1 and 3.2 for discussion). This limits us to looking at data about mothers of children 5 and younger in the 2000 tables.

Table B.2 1990 Census work-status data for moms 16 to 53 with kids 18 and under, distinguished by the age at which they started their families and the number of children in the household, organized according to the age of their youngest child at home

	New Later Moms 35–53				Earlier Moms 16–53				NLM/EM percent difference		
	FT	PT	F&P	NW	FT	PT	F&P	NW	FT	PT	NW
Kids<=1 All	51.8	25.2	77.0	23.0	37.1	28.1	65.2	34.8	+14.7	-2.9	-11.8
-1	55.5	25.96	81.46	18.53	43.21	32.28	75.49	24.50	+12.29	-6.32	-5.97
-2	43.66	24.23	67.89	32.11	37.75	26.90	64.65	35.34	+5.91	-2.67	-3.23
-3	32.69	17.95	50.64	49.35	27.64	23.88	51.52	48.47	+5.05	-5.93	+0.88
Kids<=3 All	53.4	21.8	75.2	24.8	40.4	25.5	65.9	34.1	+13.0	-3.7	-9.3
-1	57.35	22.14	79.49	20.50	46.73	28.37	75.10	24.90	+10.62	-6.23	-4.4
-2	45.42	21.14	66.56	33.43	41.24	24.63	65.87	34.12	+4.18	-3.39	-0.69
-3	31.77	18.81	50.58	49.41	30.78	22.96	53.74	46.25	+0.99	-4.15	+3.16
Kids<=5 All	54.2	20.5	74.7	25.3	42.7	24.4	67.1	32.9	+11.5	-3.9	-7.6
-1	57.91	20.81	78.72	21.26	49.04	26.73	75.77	24.21	+8.87	-5.92	-2.95
-2	46.92	20.07	67.99	33.00	43.80	23.63	67.43	32.56	+3.12	-3.56	+0.44
-3	32.94	18.33	51.27	48.73	33.38	22.76	56.14	43.84	-0.44	-4.43	+4.89
Kids<=6 All	54.4	20.3	74.7	25.3	43.6	24.2	67.8	32.2	+10.8	-3.9	-6.9
-1	58.17	20.55	78.72	21.26	49.91	26.17	76.08	23.91	+8.26	-5.62	-2.65
-2	47.00	20.02	67.02	32.97	44.85	23.42	68.27	31.72	+2.15	-3.4	+1.25
-3	33.12	19.05	52.17	47.83	34.46	22.87	57.33	42.66	-1.34	-3.82	+5.17
Kids 7–18 All	55.4	17.4	72.8	27.2	60.5	18.4	78.9	21.1	-5.1	-1.0	+6.1
-1	56.95	17.01	73.96	26.04	64.74	16.81	81.55	18.45	-7.79	+0.2	+7.59
-2	52.68	18.50	71.18	28.82	60.94	18.87	79.81	20.19	-8.26	-0.37	+8.63
-3	41.76	17.78	59.54	40.45	53.05	20.13	73.18	26.81	-11.29	-2.35	+13.64

TABLE B.3   2000 Census work-status data for both new later and earlier moms who were 35 to 40 at the census and for all earlier moms (16 to 53 at the census)

	New Later Moms 35–40				Earlier Moms 35–40				NLM/EM percent difference		
	FT	PT	F&P	NW	FT	PT	F&P	NW	FT	PT	NW
Kids <=1	57.2	20.0	77.2	22.7	46.1	18.2	64.3	35.6	+11.1	+1.8	-12.9
Kids <=3	58.4	17.8	76.2	23.7	49.4	16.1	65.5	34.4	+ 9.0	+1.7	-10.7
Kids <=5	58.9	17.3	76.2	23.7	52.1	15.7	67.8	32.1	+6.8	+1.6	- 8.4

(<=5 since the children of NLMs could be no more than 5 when the cutoff is 40)

	New Later Moms 35–40				Earlier Moms 35–40				NLM/EM percent difference		
	FT	PT	F&P	NW	FT	PT	F&P	NW	FT	PT	NW
Kids <=6	N/A	N/A			53.4	15.7	69.1	30.8	N/A		
Kids 7–18	N/A	N/A			66.8	15.1	81.9	18.0	N/A		

	Earlier Moms-2 16–53				NLM/EM-2 percent difference		
	FT	PT	F&P	NW	FT	PT	F&P
Kids <=1	43.3	24.3	67.6	32.3	+13.9	-4.3	-9.6
Kids <=3	46.8	21.9	68.7	31.3	+11.6	-4.1	-7.6
Kids <=5	49.2	20.7	69.9	30.1	+ 9.7	-3.4	-6.4
Kids <=6	50.3	20.4	70.7	29.3	N/A		
Kids 7–10	63.1	16.6	79.7	20.3	N/A		
Kids 7–18	66.3	15.0	81.3	18.7	N/A		

TABLE B.4 · 1990 Census work-status data for both new later and earlier moms who were 35 to 40 at the census (for direct comparison with 2000 data)

	New Later Moms				Earlier Moms*				NLM/EM percent difference		
	FT	PT	F&P	NW	FT	PT	F&P	NW	FT	PT	NW
Kids <=1	52.7	25.6	78.3	21.6	40.7	22.3	63.0	36.9	+12.0	+ 3.3	-15.3
Kids <=3	54.6	22.5	77.1	22.8	43.7	20.3	64.0	35.9	+10.9	+ 2.2	-13.1
Kids <=5	55.16	21.9	77.06	22.94	47.6	20.0	67.6	32.4	+7.56	+1.9	-9.46
Kids 7–18	N/A				62.7	18.3	81.0	18.8	N/A		

*The earlier moms in this chart were 35 to 40 at the time of the census and have kids of the ages indicated. Those with a youngest child 1 and under may have only one child (in which case they started at 34) or they may have several kids, and the moms may have started their families recently, long before, or anywhere in between.

FOR FURTHER READING

Bookstores teem with motherhood and parenting texts. I've listed here several that I found helpful on a range of topics related to the new later motherhood trend.

Harlyn Aizley, *Buying Dad: One Woman's Search for the Perfect Sperm Donor* (Los Angeles: Alyson Books, 2003).

Harlyn Aizley, ed., *Confessions of the Other Mother: Non-Biological Lesbian Moms Tell All* (Boston: Beacon Press, 2006).

Joan Blades and Kristin Rowe-Finkbeiner, *The Motherhood Manifesto: What America's Moms Want—and What to Do about It* (New York: Nation Books, 2006).

Stephanie Coontz, *Marriage, a History: From Obedience to Intimacy, or How Love Conquered Marriage* (New York: Viking, 2005).

Ann Crittenden, *The Price of Motherhood: Why the Most Important Job in the World Is Still the Least Valued* (New York: Henry Holt, 2001).

Susan J. Douglas and Meredith W. Michaels, *The Mommy Myth: The Idealization of Motherhood and How It Has Undermined Women* (New York: Free Press, 2004).

Crystal Eastman, "Now We Can Begin," in *Crystal Eastman: On Women and Revolution*, ed. Blanche Wiesen Cook (New York: Oxford University Press, 1978). (Originally published in 1919.)

Katherine Ellison, *The Mommy Brain: How Motherhood Makes Us Smarter* (New York: Basic Books, 2005).

Carol Evans, *This Is How We Do It: The Working Mothers' Manifesto* (New York: Hudson Street Press, 2006).

Karin Evans, *The Lost Daughters of China: Abandoned Girls, Their Journey to America, and the Search for a Missing Past* (New York: Tarcher/Penguin, 2000).

Ellen Galinsky, *Ask the Children: The Breakthrough Study That Reveals How to Succeed at Work and Parenting* (New York: Quill/HarperCollins, 1999).

Linda Gordon, *The Moral Property of Women: A History of Birth Control Politics in America* (Urbana: University of Illinois Press, 2002).

Julia E. Hanigsberg and Sara Ruddick, eds., *Mother Troubles: Rethinking Contemporary Maternal Dilemmas* (Boston: Beacon Press, 1999).

Janet Hanson, *More Than 85 Broads: Women Making Career Choices, Taking Risks and Defining Success on Their Own Terms* (Chicago: McGraw Hill, 2006).

Heidi Hartmann, "The Family as the Locus of Gender, Class, and Political Struggle: The Example of Housework," *Signs: A Journal of Women in Culture and Society* 6, no. 3 (1981): 366–394. Also collected in *Feminism and Methodology,* ed. Sandra Harding (Bloomington: Indiana University Press, 1987).

Sally Haslanger and Charlotte Witt, eds., *Adoption Matters: Philosophical and Feminist Essays* (Ithaca, NY: Cornell University Press, 2005).

Sharon Hays, *The Cultural Contradictions of Motherhood* (New Haven, CT: Yale University Press, 1996).

Virginia Held, *The Ethics of Care: Personal, Political, and Global* (New York: Oxford University Press, 2006).

Sarah Blaffer Hrdy, *Mother Nature: Maternal Instincts and How They Shape the Human Species* (New York: Ballantine Books, 1999).

Ann Hulbert, *Raising America: Experts, Parents, and a Century of Advice about Children* (New York: Knopf, 2003).

Jerry A. Jacobs and Kathleen Gerson, *The Time Divide: Work, Family, and Gender Inequality* (Cambridge, MA: Harvard University Press, 2004).

Anne Lamott, *Operating Instructions: A Journal of My Son's First Year* (New York: Fawcett Columbine, 1993).

Bill McKibben, *Maybe One: A Case for Smaller Families* (New York: Plume/Penguin, 1999).

Angus McLaren, *A History of Birth Control: From Antiquity to the Present Day* (Cambridge, MA: Blackwell, 1990).

Helena Michie and Naomi R. Cahn, *Confinements: Fertility and Infertility in Contemporary Culture* (New Brunswick, NJ: Rutgers University Press, 1997).

Steven Mintz, *Huck's Raft: A History of American Childhood* (Cambridge, MA: Harvard University Press, 2004).

Peggy Orenstein, *Flux: Women on Sex, Work, Love, Kids, & Life in a Half-Changed World* (New York: Anchor Books, 2000).

Peggy Orenstein, *Waiting for Daisy: A Tale of Two Continents, Three Religions, Five Infertility Doctors, an Oscar, an Atomic Bomb, a Romantic Night, and One Woman's Quest to Become a Mother* (New York: Bloomsbury Books, 2007).

Pamela Paul, *The Starter Marriage and the Future of Matrimony* (New York: Villard/Random House, 2002).

Adam Pertman, *Adoption Nation: How the Adoption Revolution Is Transforming America* (New York: Basic Books, 2000).

Miriam Peskowitz, *The Truth behind the Mommy Wars: Who Decides What Makes a Good Mother* (Emeryville, CA: Seal Press, 2005).

Helena Ragoné and France Winddance Twine, eds., *Ideologies and Technologies of Motherhood: Race, Class, Sexuality, Nationalism* (New York: Routledge, 2000).

John M. Riddle, *Eve's Herbs: A History of Contraception and Abortion in the West* (Cambridge, MA: Harvard University Press, 1997).

Sara Ruddick, *Maternal Thinking: Toward a Politics of Peace* (Boston: Beacon Press, 1989).

Pepper Schwartz, *Peer Marriage: How Love between Equals Really Works* (New York: Free Press, 1994).

Deborah Siegel and Daphne Uviller, *Only Child: Writers on the Singular Joys and Solitary Sorrows of Growing Up Solo* (New York: Harmony/Random House, 2007).

Rita J. Simon and Rhonda M. Roorda, *In Their Own Voices: Transracial Adoptees Tell Their Stories* (New York: Columbia University Press, 2000).

Debora L. Spar, *The Baby Business: How Money, Science, and Politics Drive the Commerce of Conception* (Cambridge, MA: Harvard Business School Press, 2006).

Judith Stacey, *In the Name of the Father: Rethinking Family Values in the Postmodern Age* (Boston: Beacon Press, 1996).

Gloria Steinem, *Doing Sixty and Seventy* (San Francisco, CA: Elders Academy Press, 2006).

Jane Jeong Trenka, Julia Chinyere Oparah, and Sun Yung Shin, eds., *Outsiders Within: Writing on Transracial Adoption* (Boston: South End Press, 2006).

Eckart Voland, Athanasios Chasiotis, and Wulf Schiefenhövel, eds., *Grandmotherhood: The Evolutionary Significance of the Second Half of Female Life* (New Brunswick, NJ: Rutgers University Press, 2005).

Toni Wechsler, *Taking Charge of Your Fertility: The Definitive Guide to Natural Birth Control, Pregnancy Achievement, and Reproductive Health* (New York: Collins, 2006).

Joan Williams, *Unbending Gender: Why Family and Work Conflict and What to Do about It* (New York: Oxford University Press, 2000).

Adoption Resources

There is no one source of reliable data on adoptions, but if you're exploring you might start with the following Web sites:

Evan Donaldson Adoption Institute, www.adoptioninstitute.org

U.S. Department of Health and Human Services, Children's Bureau, Administration for Children and Families, www.childwelfare.gov

The Adoption History Project, www.darkwing.uoregon.edu/~adoption/index.html

NOTES

Preface

1. These cuts stem from lowered expectations among employers about the reliability of mothers, with attendant lower raises for women as a group, and actual reduction of hours worked in order to care for kids, often due to lack of adequate childcare (itself due to the lower salary—a vicious circle). AAUW, *Behind the Pay Gap* (2007).

2. From 2007 to 2010, the overall birth rates plunged among U.S. women ages 15–19 and 20–24. The declines shrink with each step up the age ladder: –9 percent among those 25–29,-4 percent among 30–34-year-olds, and –2.4 percent among women 35–39. The rate for women ages 40–44 *rose* 8 percent in the same period. Rates for first births were similar, except among 30–34-year-olds, whose rate rose 1 percent in 2010. (All data from CDC Birth Data Reports for the years in question.) Census data for the first half of 2011 indicate that the overall decline continued; William Frey, "2011 Puts Brakes on U.S. Population Growth," Brookings Institution (December 28, 2011).

3. In 2007, 68.3 percent of 2006 female high school graduates were in college, as were 66.1 percent of male graduates. In 2010, 74 percent of 2009 female high school grads and 62.8 percent of male grads were in college. Bureau of Labor Statistics, *College Enrollment and Work Activity Reports for 2007 High School Graduates*, and *College Enrollment and Work Activity Reports for 2010 High School Graduates*.

4. In 2010, one in 12.43 first births were to later moms, whereas in 2007, it was one in 12.59. Overall in 2010, moms 35 or older had one in 6.9 of total births, whereas they had one in 7.05 in 2007.

5. Improved contraceptive information and access also played a role in the decline among teens, as abstinence-only programs were phased out in many states after 2007.

6. The 40–44-year-old rate had jumped 7 percent in the three years prior (2005–2007), and more than 70 percent since 1990. CDC, Final Birth Data for 2006, NVSR 57, no. 7 (January 7, 2009). The rate among women ages 35–39 increased 50 percent between 1978 and 2007, though it has since fallen slightly with the recession. CDC, Final Birth Data for 2007, NVSR 58, no. 24 (August 2010).

7. "The Effects of Motherhood Timing on Career Path," *Journal of Population Economics* 24, no. 3 (July 2011): 1071–1100. The overall wage gain to all women averages out to 3 percent per year of delay, but the gain is realized only by college grads, at 5 percent. The figures given in this discussion extrapolate from the study's conclusions and were confirmed in email correspondence between Miller and the author.

8. Amalia Miller, "Motherhood Delay and the Human Capital of the Next Generation," *American Economic Review: Papers and Proceedings* 99, no. 2 (2009): 154–58.

9. Mikko Myrskylä and Rachel Margolis, "Happiness: Before and After the Kids," Max Planck Institute for Demographic Research Working Papers, cited by permission.

10. Peter McDonald, "Low Fertility and the State: The Efficacy of Policy," *Population and Development Review* 32, no. 3 (September 2006): 485–510.

11. Increased labor force participation is not the only factor, however. Policy decisions around the way government service roles and elections are structured also affect women's participation. Torben Iversen and Frances Rosenbluth, "Work and Power: The Connection between Female Labor Force Participation and Female Political Representation," *Annual Review of Political Science* 11 (2008): 479–95.

12. Frances Rosenbluth, Matthew Light, and Claudia Schrag, "The Politics of Gender Equality," *Women & Politics* 26, no. 2 (2004): 1–25. See also Torben Iversen and Frances Rosenbluth, *Women, Work and Politics: The Comparative Political Economy of Gender Inequality* (New Haven: Yale University Press, 2010).

13. Families and Work Institute, "Generation and Gender in the Workplace" (New York: American Business Collaboration, 2006).

14. "Census Bureau Reports 'Delayer Boom' as More Educated Women Have Children Later," www.census.gov/newsroom/releases/archives/fertility/cb11–83.html (released May 9, 2011; accessed March 25, 2012).

15. Gretchen Livingston and D'Vera Cohn, "More Women Without Children," Pew Research Center Publications (June 25, 2010). This report sets the number of women who have not borne children between ages 40–44 in 2008 at 18 percent overall, including 24 percent of those with bachelor's degrees, 25 percent of those with master's degrees, and 23 percent of those with PhDs. This report also does not account for women who have adopted, most of whom would not call themselves "childless."

16. Anjani Chandra et al., *Fertility, Family Planning, and Reproductive Health of U.S. Women: Data from the 2002 National Survey of Family Growth*, National Center for Health Statistics, Vital Health Stat 23(25), 2005, Table 67: 106.

17. Pamela Tsigdinos, *Silent Sorority: A Barren Woman Gets Busy, Angry, Lost and Found* (BookSurge, 2009).

18. Derived from Brady E. Hamilton et al., "Births: Preliminary Data for 2010," NVSR 60, no. 2 (November 2011), Table 3: 24.

19. The CDC final birth data report for 2010 is due out in late 2012. The preliminary report indicates that the average age at first birth should rise.

20. Across age blocks, that breaks down to 65 percent of 30–34 year olds; 65 percent/35–39; 63/40–44; and 69/45–49. The 65 percent overall includes 70 percent of white women, 49 percent of black women, 76 percent of Asians and 39 percent of Hispanics (CDC birth data for 2009, National Bureau of Economic Research, http:/www.nber.org/data/vital-statistics-natality-data.html [accessed February 2012]). Data on advanced degrees comes from the 28 states employing the revised birth certificate in 2009 (66 percent of 2009 births), and thus may not fully reflect proportions for the U.S. overall. Data on BAs is complete.

21. The proportion of PhDs among women having a first birth in each age group within the revised certificate states is: 30–34/6.7 percent; 35–39/7.96 percent; 40–44/8.3 percent; 45–49/10.8 percent.

22. Kathryn Edin and Maria Kefalas, *Promises I Can Keep: Why Poor Women Put Motherhood before Marriage* (Berkeley: University of California Press, 2005).

23. "Births: Preliminary Data for 2010," Table 4: 25.

24. Emily Greenman, "Asian American–White Differences in the Effect of Motherhood on Career Outcomes," *Work and Occupations* 38, no. 1 (February 2011): 37–67.

Introduction

1. Earlier books on aspects of later motherhood include Jann Blackstone-Ford, *Midlife Motherhood: A Woman-to-Woman Guide to Pregnancy and Parenting* (New York: St. Martin's Griffin, 2002); Madelyn Cain, *First Time Mothers, Last Chance Babies: Parenting at 35+* (Far Hills, NJ: New Horizon Press, 1994); Pamela Daniels and Kathy Weingarten, *Sooner or Later: The Timing of Parenthood in Adult Lives* (New York: W. W. Norton, 1982); Maggie Jones, *Motherhood After 35: Choices, Decisions, Options* (Tucson, AZ: Fisher Books, 1996); Ellen Rose Lavin, PhD, with Samuel H. Wood, MD, *The Essential Over 35 Pregnancy Guide: Everything You Need to Know About Becoming a Mother Later in Life* (New York: Avon, 1998); Nancy London, *Hot Flashes, Warm Bottles: First-Time Mothers Over Forty* (Berkeley, CA: Celestial Arts, 2001); Lois Nachamie, *So Glad We Waited! A Hand-Holding Guide for Over-35 Parents* (New York: Three Rivers Press, 2000); Doreen Nagle, *But I Don't Feel Too Old to Be a Mommy: The Complete Sourcebook for Starting (and Restarting) Motherhhod Beyond 35 and After 40* (Deerfield Beach, FL: Health Communications Inc., 2002). As this book went to press, I discovered an excellent book by Julia Berryman, Karen Thorpe, and Kate Windridge that confirms some of the dynamics of the later motherhood experience that my study uncovered (like younger husbands), from an earlier point in the trend: *Older Mothers: Conception, Pregnancy and Birth After 35* (London: HarperCollins/Pandora, 1995).

2. Author's calculations, based on Centers for Disease Control and Prevention (CDC) natality statistics, available at www.cdc.gov.

3. More precisely, it's 594,591 (data from Table 6 in Brady E. Hamilton, Joyce A. Martin, and Stephanie J. Ventura, CDC, National Center for Health Statistics, "Births: Preliminary Data for 2005," at http://www.cdc.gov/nchs/data/hestat/prelimbirths05_tables.pdf#6). In 2004, the final data report number was 585,407 births to later moms. National Vital Statistics Report, 55, no. 1 (September 2006), 36. Fewer than 5 percent of these mothers conceived using in vitro fertization—author's calculation based on data published by the CDC and the Society for Assisted Reproduction, http://www.cdc.gov/ART/ART2004.pdf; and https://www.sartcorsonline.com/rptCSR_Public MultYear.aspx?ClinicPKID=0 (all accessed June 14, 2007).

4. John Mirowsky, "Age at First Birth, Health and Mortality," *Journal of Health and Social Behavior* 46, no. 1 (March 2005): 32–50.

Chapter 1

1. Worth Tuttle, "Autobiography of an Ex-Feminist: I. Before Marriage," *The Atlantic Monthly,* December 1933, pp. 641–49; and "II. A Feminist Marries," *The Atlantic Monthly*, January 1934, pp. 73–81. Compare with Caitlin Flanagan, "How Serfdom Saved the Women's Movement: Dispatches from the Nanny Wars," *The Atlantic Monthly,*

March 2004, pp. 109–28. See also Flanagan's "To Hell with All That: One Woman's Decision to Go Back to Work," *New Yorker*, July 5, 2004, pp. 38–42, which backs off from its condemnation of moms who work and shares much with Tuttle's second installment.

2. Tuttle, "A Feminist Marries," p. 81.

3. Patricia Mellencamp, "Situation Comedy, Feminism and Freud: Discourses of Gracie and Lucy," in *Studies in Entertainment*, ed. Tania Modleski (Bloomington: Indiana University Press, 1986), 80–95.

4. Tuttle, "A Feminist Marries," p. 78.

5. Her novels include *Wives of High Pasture* (1944), *The Other Room* (1947), and *Love Is a Wound* (1952). Her family memoir, *Two and Three Make One: The Story of a Family* (1956), appeared under the pseudonym Winifred Woodley.

6. See "Lucy's $50,000,000 Baby: Little Desi's Arrival Launched a Whole New Industry," *TV Guide*, April 3–9, 1951, cover and pp. 5–7.

7. The biblical Onan (Genesis 38:7) famously practiced withdrawal (a.k.a., coitus interruptus), and though his use of this form of birth control was firmly condemned (the Lord slew him), his primary error lay not in employing this method per se, but in his unwillingness to impregnate his brother's widow on command. Only later did "Onanism" come to be associated with masturbation and interpreted as sinful because seed was "wasted."

8. Jon Knowles et al., "A History of Birth Control Methods," http://www.plannedparenthood.org/files/PPFA/fact-bc-history.pdf (accessed June 4, 2007).

9. John M. Riddle, *Eve's Herbs: A History of Contraception and Abortion in the West* (Cambridge, MA: Harvard University Press, 1997), p. 126.

10. You can find it at http://womenshistory.about.com/library/etext/bl_eastman_crystal_1920.htm (accessed June 14, 2007).

11. To the extent that the experience of the degreed and the non-degreed differs (and the salary data indicates that in this respect the experience does differ), there remains more to explore about the new later motherhood demographic.

12. Author's calculations, based on education data in the CDC 2003 natality database. Currently available data hints that new later moms have a higher proportion of graduate degrees, but the full data won't be available for a few years.

13. Ann Crittenden, *The Price of Motherhood: Why the Most Important Job in the World Is Still the Least Valued* (New York: Henry Holt, 2001), pp. 50–51.

14. Elaina Rose, "Education and Hypergamy in Marriage Markets," working paper, University of Washington, March 2004, p. 9.

Chapter 3

1. Economists debate the exact relation of a woman's delay of motherhood to wages. I find that the census provides a rough but interesting measure—a snapshot of the effect of delay for a large population that allows me to break the wages down by the kind of degree a mother holds. Because it is not a "panel study," I don't get to compare one woman's wages across her career and directly see the correlation of her age at first birth with her wage, but the census does demonstrate that there is a notable overall correla-

tion. The effect of delay within each decade of women's lives may change over time as business adjusts to the presence of women in management and as family-friendly policies are more widely adopted and employed by both women and men. The 2000 Census presents some difficulties for determining at what age women started their families, although that can be figured out with a reasonably small degree of error for women 35 to 39 (less than 5 percent of the women identified as new later mothers in this group are not) and with a somewhat larger degree of error (less than 14.5 percent) for moms 40 to 45. To verify the trend in the 2000 data, I have also run the same calculations for the 1990 Census, which does not have the same identification problem, and found a similar upward trend in wages among full-time working women with BAs or higher degrees. Because the more recent data is of the most interest, I present the numbers for the 2000 group here, divided into moms 35 to 39 at the time of the census and moms 40 to 45 at the time of the census. Given that delay of children associates with raised salary, to the extent that the pool of women documented here includes some women who are not really new later moms (because, though their oldest children at home were born after they were 35, they have other children born when they were younger), the pattern given here should understate the gain in wages rather than distorting it to seem bigger than it actually is. Tracking this kind of data would be made much easier and more precise if more of the relevant questions were asked in the census and in smaller national studies. This data would provide important bases for understanding and responding to changes in citizens' behavior in the business and social policy worlds.

2. Kasey Buckles, "Explaining the Returns to Delayed Childbearing for Working Women," working paper, May 2007. This paper looks at women in the National Longitudinal Survey of Youth (1979 to 2004) who had a first birth between 16 and 36 years of age. Cited with permission. http://www.nd.edu/~kbuckles/research.html.

3. The higher salaries shown in the census documents only pertain to women with degrees; a much higher proportion of women who start their families at or after 35 have degrees than the general population.

4. Not all management women with kids are later moms, though many are. The presence of moms of all stripes in the workplace works cumulatively to change the scene, either through activism by the women themselves or by their male employers trying to hold on to valuable women workers.

5. U.S. Department of Labor, Bureau of Labor Statistics, *Women in the Labor Force: A Databook*, Report 973 (Washington, DC, 2004), p. 25, http://www.bls.gov/cps/wlf-databook.pdf (accessed June 14, 2007).

6. Catalyst, "2005 Catalyst Census of Women Board Directors of the Fortune 500 Shows 10-Year Trend of Slow Progress and Persistent Challenges," http://www.catalystwomen.org/pressroom/press_releases/3_29_06%20-%20WBD%20release.pdf (accessed June 14, 2007).

7. Betsy Morris, "Trophy Husbands Arm Candy?" *Fortune Magazine*, October 14, 2002.

8. James T. Bond et al., *Highlights of the National Study of the Changing Workforce* (New York: Families and Work Institute, 2002), 43; and Joanne Cleaver, citing *2006 Society for Human Resource Management Job Satisfaction Report*, in "Moms Take Control of Fast-Forward Lives," *Houston Chronicle*, August 7, 2006, p. D–1.

9. Bureau of Labor Statistics, *Women in the Labor Force: A Databook*, Report 996 (Washington, DC, 2006), pp. 8, 19, and 59.

10. Louise Story, "Many Women at Elite Colleges Set Career Path to Motherhood," *New York Times*, September 20, 2005, p. A1; see also, Jack Shafer, "Weasel Words Rip My Flesh! Spotting a Bogus Trend on Page One of Today's *New York Times*," *Slate*, September 20, 2005, http://www.slate.com/id/2126636 (accessed June 12, 2007); and Louise Story's response, "Background: Reporting on the Aspirations for Young Women," *New York Times*, September 23, 2005, web edition only, www.nytimes.com (accessed June 16, 2007).

11. United States Central Intelligence Agency, *World Factbook*, https://www.cia .gov/library/publications/the-world-factbook/index.html (accessed June 16, 2007).

12. Deborah Rhode, ed., *The Difference "Difference" Makes: Women and Leadership* (Stanford, CA: Stanford University Press, 2003).

13. Lisa Belkin, "The Opt-Out Revolution," *New York Times Magazine*, October 26, 2003.

14. Jenny Anderson, "The Fork in the Road," *New York Times*, August 6, 2006.

15. In 2005, 76.9 percent of women with their youngest child between 6 and 17, 62.6 percent of women with children under 6, 59 percent of women with children under 3, and 53.5 percent of women with infants (1 and under) were in the labor force. U.S. Department of Labor, Bureau of Labor Statistics, *Women in the Labor Force* (Washington, DC, 2006), p. 13; Sharon R. Cohany and Emy Sok, Bureau of Labor Statistics, "Trends in Labor Participation of Married Women with Infants," *Monthly Labor Review*, February 2007, http://www.bls.gov/opub/mlr/2007/02/art2full.pdf (accessed June 17, 2007). These numbers have gone up and down by several percentages in the past ten years, and the reasons behind that are endlessly debated without a clear resolution to date.

Chapter 4

1. Miriam Peskowitz, *The Truth behind the Mommy Wars: Who Decides What Makes a Good Mother?* (Emeryville, CA: Seal Press, 2005).

2. David Popenoe, National Marriage Project, on *The O'Reilly Factor*, Fox News (February 14, 2005). Cited at http://www.billoreilly.com/show;jsessionid=DF269774 D262DA202969C34B8A0D52C3?action=viewTVShow&showID=136#3.

3. Sara McLanahan and Karen Booth, "Mother-Only Families: Problems, Prospects and Politics," *Journal of Marriage and the Family* 51 (1989): 557–80; Ann Crittenden, *The Price of Motherhood: Why the Most Important Job in the World Is Still the Least Valued* (New York: Henry Holt, 2001), 147.

4. Stephen J. Rose and Heidi I. Hartmann, *Still a Man's Labor Market: The Long-Term Earnings Gap* (Washington, DC: Institute for Women's Policy Research, 2004), 9–11. This data pools part-time and full-time workers; a look at full-time workers only might yield a larger percentage loss, given the larger benefits packages that generally come with full-time jobs.

5. Daphne de Marneffe, *Maternal Desire: On Children, Love and the Inner Life* (New York: Little, Brown, 2004).

6. Crittenden, *The Price of Motherhood*, p. 12.

7. See, for instance, Bonnie Thornton Dill, "The Dialectics of Black Womanhood," *Signs: A Journal of Women in Culture and Society* 4, no. 3 (1979): 543–55.

8. Linda Hirshman, *Get to Work: A Manifesto for Women of the World* (New York: Viking Press, 2006).

9. Leslie Bennetts, *The Feminine Mistake: Are We Giving Up Too Much?* (New York: Voice/Hyperion, 2007).

Chapter 5

1. Robert Schoen, "California Divorce Rates by Age at First Marriage and Duration of First Marriage," *Journal of Marriage and Family* 37 (1975): 548–55; Matthew D. Bramlett and William D. Mosher, "Cohabitation, Marriage, Divorce and Remarriage in the United States," *Vital and Health Statistics*, series 23, no. 22 (Washington, DC: CDC, National Center for Health Statistics, 2002), 18ff.

2. Paul R. Amato, Alan Booth, David R. Johnson, and Stacy J. Rogers, *Alone Together: How Marriage in America Is Changing* (Cambridge, MA: Harvard University Press, 2007).

3. Pamela Paul, *The Starter Marriage and the Future of Matrimony* (New York: Villard, 2002).

4. Pepper Schwartz, *Peer Marriage: How Love between Equals Really Works* (New York: Free Press, 1994), 4.

5. Schwartz, *Peer Marriage*, 6–7.

6. Schwartz, *Peer Marriage*, 13.

7. Schwartz, *Peer Marriage*, 11.

8. Schwartz, *Peer Marriage*, 196.

9. CDC, "Table 27. Life expectancy at birth, at 65 years of age, and at 75 years of age, according to race and sex: United States, selected years 1900–2004," in *Health, United States, 2006* (updated February 2007), p. 193, http://www.cdc.gov/nchs/data/hus/hus06.pdf#027.

10. David Dunson, Donna Baird, and Bernardo Colombo, "Increased Infertility with Age in Men and Women," *Obstetrics and Gynecology* 103 (2004): 57–62.

11. Fathers in their thirties have 1.5 times more risk of autistic children than do fathers in their teens and twenties, fathers in their forties have five times the risk, and fathers in their fifties have nine times the risk. Abraham Reichenberg et al., "Advancing Paternal Age and Autism," *Archives of General Psychiatry* 63 (2006): 1026–32; see also Shankar Vedantam, "Autism Risk Rises with Age of Father," *Washington Post*, September 5, 2006, p. A1; Roni Rabin, "It Seems the Fertility Clock Ticks for Men Too," *New York Times*, February 17, 2007.

12. If female sperm becomes a real option (see the end of Chapter 6), it will change this dynamic entirely for families formed by that means.

13. See the research of Toni Falbo at http://utopia.utexas.edu/articles/opa/only_children.html?sec=parents&sub=preschooland; also, Denise F. Polit and Toni Falbo, "The Intellectual Achievement of Only Children," *Journal of Biosociological Science* 20 (1988): 275–85; for other discussion of the situation of onlies, see Deborah

Siegel and Daphne Uviller, eds., *Only Child: Writers on the Singular Joys and Solitary Sorrows of Growing Up Solo* (New York: Harmony Books, 2007).

Chapter 6

1. *Creating a Life: Professional Women and the Quest for Children* (New York: Talk Miramax Books, 2002). While it's certainly true that women over 42 have a low chance of pregnancy with their own eggs, Hewlett exaggerates the situation of women 35 to 40. For instance (pp. 216–17), she quotes data from "the Mayo Clinic," without any further documentation, claiming that "fertility drops 20 percent after age 30, 50 percent after age 35, and 95 percent after age 40. While 72 percent of 28-year-old women get pregnant after trying for a year, only 24 percent of 38-year-olds do." These numbers are much too low (see the section called What Are My Odds? later in this chapter).

2. Bernardo Colombo and Guido Masarotto, "Daily Fecundability: First Results from a New Data Base," *Demographic Research* 3 (2000): article 5; David Dunson, Bernardo Colombo, and Donna Baird, "Changes with Age in the Level and Duration of Fertility in the Menstrual Cycle," *Human Reproduction* 17 (2002): 1399–1403; David Dunson, Donna Baird, and Bernardo Colombo, "Increased Infertility with Age in Men and Women," *Obstetrics and Gynecology* 103 (2004): 57–62; Bruno Scarpa, David Dunson, and Bernardo Colombo, "Cervical Mucus Secretions on the Day of Intercourse: An Accurate Marker of Highly Fertile Days," *European Journal of Obstetrics Gynecology and Reproductive Biology* 125 (2006): 72–78. The European Fecundability Study documents a group of people using natural family-planning methods (which work for both achieving pregnancy and avoiding it). Because they raise the likelihood each month that the sperm and the egg will meet, these techniques offer a much better gauge of human capacity for fertility than studies in which intercourse is not keyed to fertile times. The study excluded couples known at the time the study began to be permanently infertile or to have illnesses that might cause subfertility, such as endocrine disorders. The researchers did not test couples' fertility, however, so the group did include any individuals who had fertility problems without knowing or who chose not to report it.

3. This study estimates infertility (the diagnosis if a couple has been trying consistently to conceive for a year without success) at 8 percent for women aged 19 to 26, 13 to 14 percent for women aged 27 to 34, and 18 percent for women aged 35 to 39. (The study didn't look at women over 40.)

4. This has been demonstrated in the Fédération CECOS study and in the European Fecundability Study. The Fédération CECOS study looked at women with sterile husbands, women who were getting artificially inseminated with donor sperm on the day they ovulated. Though the circumstances mean that the situation was more controlled than fecundity studies that rely on the reporting by individuals about activities conducted in private, they also involve an unusual medical situation and only one fertilization attempt per month, which would negatively affect the likelihood of impregnation, so the study's findings on infertility rates were disputed. The study did make clear, however, that there was a decline in speed to impregnation over time. Fédération CECOS et al., "Female Fecundity as a Function of Age: Results of Artificial Insemina-

tion of 2193 Nulliparous Women with Azoospermic Husbands," *New England Journal of Medicine* 306 (1982): 404–6; see also J. Bongaarts, "Infertility after Age 30: A False Alarm," *Family Planning Perspectives* (May 1982): 75–78; Dunson, Colombo, and Baird, "Changes with Age."

5. One recent study raised questions about this, but has not been duplicated so far. Joshua Johnson, Jacqueline Canning, Tomoko Kaneko, James K. Prue, and Jonathan L. Tilly, "Germline Stem Cells and Follicular Renewal in the Postnatal Mammalian Ovary," *Nature* (March 11, 2004): 145–50.

6. That means, given that 82 percent of women 35 to 39 became pregnant in one year in the study, an additional 9 percent became pregnant in the second year; so, overall, 90 percent of those in their study became pregnant within two years. Of those women at the lower end of the 35- to 39-age range who didn't get pregnant in the first year, 63 percent got pregnant in the second year, as did 43 percent of the women at the upper end of that range.

7. Dunson, Colombo, and Baird, "Changes with Age."

8. The basics of natural family-planning techniques are taught, with variations, as Toni Wechsler's fertility awareness method (outlined in *Taking Charge of Your Fertility: The Definitive Guide to Natural Birth Control, Pregnancy Achievement, and Reproductive Health*, rev. ed. [New York: Collins, 2001]) and as the Creighton Model Fertility Care System (http://www.creightonmodel.com), which has a standardized system of instruction that is based on meeting with a knowledgeable teacher for several sessions over a few months (and which is endorsed by the Catholic Church). These techniques are all about timing: having sex at the right time of month (when the cervical mucous is viscous and flowing) will get a woman pregnant much more quickly than the hit or miss, "whenever we're in the mood" method, assuming the eggs and sperm involved are viable. Mucous signals ovulation more reliably than any other indicator, and tracking temperature upon waking each day (part of the Wechsler method but not Creighton) increases accuracy even further. Wechsler provides no teachers.

9. A recent (math-laden) paper offers a theoretical model for accurately timing intercourse in order to promote conception or, if conception doesn't happen, to diagnose infertility within six or even three months, instead of waiting the standard year. Bruno Scarpa, David Dunson, and Elena Giacchi, "Bayesian Selection of Optimal Rules for Timing Intercourse to Conceive Using Calendar and Mucus," *Fertility & Sterility* 87 (2007).

10. Dunson, Colombo, and Baird, "Changes with Age."

11. Christopher Tietze, "Reproductive Span and Rate of Reproduction among Hutterite Women," *Fertility and Sterility* 8 (1957): 89–97.

12. Joseph W. Eaton and Albert J. Mayer, "The Social Biology of Very High Fertility among the Hutterites: The Demography of a Unique Population," *Human Biology* 25 (1953): 206–64.

13. One IVF study (done in Israel, where unlimited IVFs are government funded for women up to age 45, and for two children) found that women 40 or younger continued to improve their chances of a delivery with each IVF cycle—up to a total of fourteen cycles, at which point 88 percent of patients had delivered a live child

(remember, these are people who were having difficulty to begin with, so it doesn't represent the average woman's situation). After fourteen cycles, there was no further increase. Among women 41 to 45, chances of a live birth increased with each IVF cycle up to a total of nine cycles, at which point 49 percent of patients had delivered. Shai E. Elizur, Liat Lerner-Geva, Jacob Levron, Adrian Shulman, David Bider, and Jehoshua Dor, "Cumulative Live Birth Rate Following In Vitro Fertilization: Study of 5,310 Cycles," *Gynecological Endocrinology* 22, no. 1 (January 2006): 25–30. In most U.S. states, nine cycles would mean a payout of more than $100,000, as well as a great many hormone injections, for a 50 percent chance of success.

14. Author's calculation based on the CDC's 2004 ART report, p. 81, available at http://www.cdc.gov/ART/ART2004/ (accessed June 19, 2007). The report does state that 95 percent of egg donations involved women 35 and older in 2004 (p. 51), but does not link its reporting of success rates to age.

15. In 2005, the number of later babies was 594,591 (CDC preliminary count). The number of moms involved is not yet available for 2005, but 577,500 is a reasonable estimate, given the 2004 data. The number of mothers is lower than the number of babies because some were multiple births. In 2004, 585,407 babies were born to about 568,940 moms. CDC National Vital Statistics Reports for 2004 (final, NVSR 55, no. 1) and 2005 (preliminary) and 2004 database. All such statistics are accessible at http://www.cdc.gov.

16. In 2003, 2.3 percent (1,020 births) of the 43,464 births to 41- and 42-year-olds combined involved IVF with their own eggs, as did 1.3 percent (196 births) of the 14,940 births to 43- and 44-year-olds in that year. (Based on birth data from the CDC National Vital Statistics Report for 2003 [final, NVSR 52, no. 1], CDC, *2003 Assisted Reproductive Technology Success Rate: National Summary and Fertility Clinic Reports,* December 2005, p. 75, http://www.cdc.gov/ART/ART2003/index.htm [accessed June 19, 2007], and the IVF statistics on 43- and 44-year-olds reported in the SART 2003 Clinic Summary Report.) The numbers for 2004 appear to be similar. An additional percentage of these births occurred via egg donation. The number of births to women of all ages via egg donation in 2003 was 5,769 (CDC 2003 ART report, p. 75). The number increased to 6,042 in 2004 (CDC 2004 ART report, p. 81).

17. Author's calculation based on CDC and SART data. Of the 4.4 percent, 3.0 percent involved IVF and 1.4 percent involved egg donation.

18. Overall in 2004 about 74,806 cycles were undertaken by women 35 and over, of which about 18,979 were successful. The overall number does not tell us how many women attempted IVF, however, as some women did more than one cycle in a year.

19. CDC, "Fertility, Family Planning, and Reproductive Health of U.S. Women: Data from the 2002 National Survey of Family Growth," *Vital and Health Statistics,* series 23, no. 25, December 2005, pp. 108 and 109.

20. CDC, "Pelvic Inflammatory Disease," Fact Sheet, http://www.cdc.gov/std/PID/STDFact-PID.htm#common.

21. CDC, "Fertility, Family Planning, and Reproductive Health, 2002" (Table 97), http://www.cdc.gov/nchs/data/series/sr_23/sr23_025.pdf.

22. A study based on the CDC's 2002 National Study of Family Growth finds that, at least among married women, reports of infertility have declined. Elizabeth Stephen and Anjani Chandra, "Declining Estimates of Infertility in the United States: 1982–2002," *Fertility and Sterility* 86, no. 3 (September 2006): 516–23. Those who object point to problems with the group analyzed. David S. Guzick and Shanna Swan, "The Decline of Infertility: Apparent or Real?" *Fertility and Sterility* 86, no. 3 (September 2006): 524–26.

23. Based on William D. Mosher and William F. Pratt, "Fecundity and Infertility in the United States: Incidence and Trends," *Fertility and Sterility* 56, no. 2 (August 1991): 192–93.

24. Debora L. Spar, *The Baby Business: How Money, Science, and Politics Drive the Commerce of Conception* (Boston: Harvard Business School Press, 2006), 53.

25. This particular table gets around: a doctor flashed it on the screen at a fertility lecture I attended a few years back, using it for the same obfuscatory purpose, and I've seen it circulated online as proof of an increase in modern infertility. Though this table is attributed in its footnote to a 1991 article by George B. Maroulis, a well-known fertility researcher, it is actually a reorganization of data from a chart in Maroulis's essay ("Effect of Aging on Fertility and Pregnancy," *Seminars in Reproductive Endocrinology* 9, no. 3 [August 1991]: 165–75). That chart did not conflate data from several different centuries and cities in Europe but assigned each population its own line. Maroulis's title and his discussion in the article, which distinguish between the "natural" fertility of the earlier populations and the controlled fertility of the twentieth-century U.S. line, are omitted in the table.

26. A recent article about the experience of a couple with an IVF twin pregnancy describes their decision process: "[The woman] had just turned 31. There was no reason to panic. Until, that is, getting pregnant just wouldn't happen. . . . What would Oprah do? She'd probably be more patient, let it ride for another six months, and relax, take a vacation. But we were beyond the point of being able to enjoy a margarita and a suntan. We needed to reassert control over our lives, and we couldn't wait." So they spent more than twenty thousand dollars, had IVF, and became pregnant with twins. The article then explores the difficulties of twin pregnancy for mama and babies and ends on a positive note as the two babies are about to come home from the hospital several weeks after their birth. The anxiety that leads the parents to take the IVF road so early on would seem to have been fed by the current emergency mood around fertility. Sarah Bernard and Hugo Lindgren, "Gangs of New York: The High Cost of Multiple Births," *New York*, June 12, 2006.

27. Clinicians report that as many as 50 percent of very early pregnancies abort spontaneously—that's among women of all ages, and most of these losses occur before a woman knows she's pregnant. Once a pregnancy is established, about 15 percent miscarry overall. Whereas the rate of miscarriage among 20- to 29-year-olds with established pregnancies was 10.1 percent in one study, among women over age 40, it was 30 percent. Laura A. Schieve, Lilith Tatham, Herbert B. Peterson, James Toner, and Gary Jeng, "Spontaneous Abortion among Pregnancies Conceived Using Assisted

Reproductive Technology in the United States," *Obstetrics and Gynecology* 101, no. 5 (May 2003): 959–67.

28. Tarun Jain, Stacey A. Missmer, and Mark D. Hornstein, "Trends in Embryo-Transfer Practice and in Outcomes of the Use of Assisted Reproductive Technology in the United States," *New England Journal of Medicine* 350, no.16 (April 15, 2004): 1639–45.

29. March of Dimes website, http://www.marchofdimes.com, search "Down syndrome" (accessed June 11, 2007).

30. J. A. Collins, "An Estimate of the Cost of In Vitro Fertilization Services in the United States in 1995," *Fertility & Sterility* 64 (1995): 538–45.

31. Tarun Jain, Bernard L. Harlow, and Mark D. Hornstein, "Insurance Coverage and Outcomes of In Vitro Fertilization," *New England Journal of Medicine* 347, no. 16 (August 29, 2002): 661–66.

32. For an in-depth discussion of the insurance issue, see Spar, *The Baby Business*.

33. Given the limited testing of the technique to date, egg freezing is not recommended generally, except for women with cancer who want to freeze their eggs before undergoing chemotherapy. Allison Aubrey, "Fertility Procedure Freezes Eggs for Later Use," on *Morning Edition*, National Public Radio, August 22, 2005, http://www.npr.org/templates/story/story.php?storyId=4809662.

34. Natalie Angier, "Study of Mice Reproduction Discovers Egg Regeneration," *New York Times*, March 11, 2004, Science section.

35. Steve Connor, "The Prospect of All-Female Conception," *The Independent*, April 13, 2007, http://news.independent.co.uk/sci_tech/article2444462.ece (accessed June 21, 2007).

Chapter 7

1. See Table 2 in Marianne Berry, Richard P. Barth, and Barbara Needell, "Preparation, Support, and Satisfaction of Adoptive Families in Agency and Independent Adoptions," *Child and Adolescent Social Work Journal* 13, no. 2 (April 1996): 166.

2. See Jane Jeong Trenka, Julia Chinyere Oparah, and Sun Yung Shin, ed., *Outsiders Within: Writing on Transracial Adoption* (Boston: South End Press, 2006). For another perspective, see Rita J. Simon and Rhonda M. Roorda, *In Their Own Voices: Transracial Adoptees Tell Their Stories* (New York: Columbia University Press, 2000).

3. U.S. Department of Health and Human Services, *How Many Children Were Adopted in 2000 and 2001?* (Washington, DC: National Adoption Information Clearinghouse, 2004), 1, http://www.childwelfare.gov/pubs/s_adoptedhighlights.pdf (accessed January 10, 2007).

4. Fifty-eight percent of people know someone who has been adopted, has adopted a child, or has relinquished a child for adoption. Adam Pertman, *Adoption Nation: How the Adoption Revolution Is Transforming America* (New York: Basic Books, 2000); Evan B. Donaldson Adoption Institute 1997 Public Opinion Benchmark survey.

5. There are many books available on attachment disorders as well as online discussion groups.

6. U.S. Department of Health and Human Services, *How Many Children Were Adopted in 2000 and 2001?* For international statistics, see U.S. Census Bureau, "Facts for Features: National Adoption Month," Press Release, Washington, DC, September 20, 2004, http://www.census.gov/Press-Release/www/releases/archives/facts_for_features_special_editions/002683.html (accessed January 10, 2007).

7. Child Welfare Information Gateway, *Foster Care: Numbers and Trends*, U.S. Department of Health and Human Services, 2005, http://childwelfare.gov/pubs/factsheets/foster.cfm.

8. See Evan B. Donaldson Adoption Institute, "Foster Care Facts," http://www.adoptioninstitute.org/FactOverview/foster.html (accessed June 12, 2007).

9. Al Hunt, "Blocking Gay Adoptions Hurts Kids," *Wall Street Journal,* March 21, 2002. For a list of studies, go to www.hrc.org, and search under Parenting (accessed June 12, 2007).

10. American Civil Liberties Union, "Howard v. Arkansas—Case Profile," http://www.aclu.org/lgbt/parenting/12137res20050301.html (accessed June 12, 2007).

11. Lynette Clemetson and Ron Nixon, "Breaking through Adoption's Racial Barriers," *New York Times,* August 17, 2006, p. 1.

12. ABC News, "Foreigners Vie to Adopt Black U.S. Babies: Whether from Lack of Knowledge, Stigmas or Racism, Americans Seem Hesitant to Adopt across Racial Lines," March 5, 2005, http://abcnews.go.com/WNT/print?id=547647 (accessed June 12, 2007).

13. For details on the Convention, see the U.S. State Department website, at http://travel.state.gov/family/adoption/convention/convention_2300.html (accessed June 12, 2007).

14. Internationally, fifty-six boys are adopted for every one hundred girls. John Gravois, "Bringing Up Babes: Why Do Adoptive Parents Prefer Girls?" *Slate,* updated January 16, 2004.

15. Lisa Bennett and Gary J. Gates, *The Cost of Marriage Inequality to Children and Their Same-Sex Parents,* A Human Rights Campaign Foundation Report, April 13, 2004, http://www.hrc.org/Content/ContentGroups/Publications1/kids_doc_final.pdf (accessed June 12, 2007).

Chapter 8

1. John Mirowsky, "Age at First Birth, Health and Mortality," *Journal of Health and Social Behavior* 46, no. 1 (March 2005): 32–50. A first birth before 20 in contemporary culture predicts both a physical predisposition to certain illnesses related to physical immaturity and a greater likelihood of poverty or other social disadvantage (lack of education, unstable family situations, stress), which can cause additional illness. A study of centenarians led by Thomas Perls found that women who gave birth after 40 were four times more likely to live to be 100 or more than women in the general population; Mary Duenwald, "Scientist at Work: Thomas Perls; Discovering What It Takes to Live to 100," *New York Times,* December 25, 2001. Because the women involved were giving later birth in the 1940s, and circumstances have since changed for

overall health, this data may not be directly predictive about women who give birth at or after 40 in the twenty-first century.

2. The interviews for this study come from 1986, with follow-up to track deaths, and they measure the optimal age for the entire population of adult women in the United States. Thus the results do not account for recent changes—including the facts that many more people are having children later (which might shift the optimal age higher for the group of new moms) and that the use of fertility technology (which might have long-term health effects, either positive or negative, that have not yet been documented) has increased in that interval. This is the first study to measure the relation of a woman's age at first birth to her longevity, so further studies may shed more light on these dynamics.

3. The average life span in the United States in 2004 is 80 for women and 75 for men (overall 78), and many people live well into their eighties and nineties. The overall average was 47 in the United States in 1900.

4. N. Kroman, J. Wohlfahrt, K. W. Andersen, H. T. Mouridsen, T. Westergaard, and M. Melbye, "Parity, Age at First Birth and the Prognosis of Primary Breast Cancer," *British Journal of Cancer* 78, no. 11 (1998): 1529–33.

5. For instance, there was no increase in infant death between first-time moms over 40 and first-time moms under 30 and only a .05 percent increase in neonatal death. W. M. Gilbert, T. S. Nesbitt, and B. Danielsen, "Childbearing beyond Age 40: Pregnancy Outcomes in 24,032 Cases," *Obstetrics and Gynecology* 93, no.1 (1999): 9–14. See also Marilynn Marchione, "High-Risk Pregnancies on the Rise, But So Are Successes: Results Overturn Decades of Gloomy Dogma about Who Is Medically Fit to Have a Child," *Houston Chronicle* (Associated Press), February 12, 2007, p. A3.

6. http://www.msnbc.msn.com/id/16206352/ and http://www.nhlbi.nih.gov/whi/whi_faq.htm (accessed July 20, 2007).

7. Gina Kolata, "Hormones and Cancer: Assessing the Risks," *New York Times*, December 26, 2006. See also Gina Kolata, "Health Risk to Older Women Is Seen in Hormone Therapy," *New York Times*, April 4, 2007.

8. Their bodies can differ from those of actual grandmothers who rear their children's kids because they haven't experienced the same wear and tear that comes from years of childcare, often in stressful circumstances. Grandmothers who rear their grandchildren generally have a hard time of it. Often they have limited financial resources and a range of health issues.

9. Kristen Hawkes, J. F. O'Connell, N. G. Blurton-Jones, H. Alvarez, and E. L. Charnov, "Grandmothering, Menopause and the Evolution of Human Life Histories," *Proceedings of the National Academy of Sciences of the United States of America* 95 (1998): 1336–39.

INDEX

14990